TOGETHER AS ONE:

INTERFAITH RELATIONSHIPS BETWEEN AFRICAN TRADITIONAL RELIGION, ISLAM, AND CHRISTIANITY IN NIGERIA.

HYACINTH KALU

INTERFAITH SERIES, VOL. II

TOGETHER AS ONE:
Interfaith Relationships between African Traditional Religion, Islam, and Christianity in Nigeria.

TOGETHER AS ONE:
Interfaith Relationships between African Traditional Religion, Islam, and Christianity in Nigeria.

(Interfaith Series, Vol. II)

Hyacinth Kalu

iUniverse, Inc.
Bloomington

Together as One: Interfaith Relationships between African Traditional Religion, Islam, and Christianity in Nigeria. (Interfaith Series, Vol. II)

iUniverse books may be ordered through booksellers or by contacting:

iUniverse
1663 Liberty Drive
Bloomington, IN 47403
www.iuniverse.com
1-800-Authors (1-800-288-4677)

Because of the dynamic nature of the Internet, any web addresses or links contained in this book may have changed since publication and may no longer be valid. The views expressed in this work are solely those of the author and do not necessarily reflect the views of the publisher, and the publisher hereby disclaims any responsibility for them.

Any people depicted in stock imagery provided by Thinkstock are models, and such images are being used for illustrative purposes only.
Certain stock imagery © Thinkstock.

ISBN: 978-1-4620-2735-4 (pbk)
ISBN: 978-1-4620-2946-4 (ebk)

Library of Congress Control Number: 2011909656

Printed in the United States of America

iUniverse rev. date: 06/13/2011

CONTENTS

To my lovely parents:
Maurice Kalu Arunsi and Felicia Ogonnaya Kalu

LIST OF ABBREVIATIONS

ACRA	Advisory Council on Religious Affairs
ACYDF	African Christian Youths Development Forum
AD	Anno Domini
AH	Anno Hegirae or After Hegira
AIDS	Acquired Immune Deficiency Syndrome
AIFF	Argungu International Fishing Festival
ATR	African Traditional Religion
BBC	British Broadcasting Corporation
BCE	Before the Common Era
CAN	Christian Association of Nigeria
CBO	Catholic Boys' Organization
CCC	Catechism of the Catholic Church
CCN	Christian Council of Nigeria
CE	Common Era
CGO	Catholic Girls Organization
CMO	Catholic Men's Organization
CSN	Catholic Secretariat of Nigeria
CWO	Catholic Women's Organization
CWR	Council for World Religions
FESTAC	Festival of Arts and Culture
HIV	Human Immunodeficiency Virus
JNI	Jama'atu Nasril Islam
LGA	Local Government Area
NAN	News Agency of Nigeria
NCC	National Communications Commission

NGO	Non-Governmental Organization
NIFAA	Nigerian Inter-Faith Action Association
NIPPS	National Institute for Policy and Strategic Studies
NIREC	Nigeria Inter-religious Council
NIYF	Nigerian Interfaith Youth Forum
NPO	Non Profit Organization
NSCIA	Nigeria Supreme Council for Islamic Affairs
NT	New Testament
NYSC	National Youth Service Corp.
OAIC	Organization of African Instituted Churches
OIC	Organization of Islamic Conference (or Countries)
OT	Old Testament
OTRA	Organization of Traditional Religions of Africa pbuh peace be upon him.
SABM	Southern American Baptist Mission
SAC	Société Africaine de Culture
SCIA	Supreme Council of Islamic Affairs
SSS	State Security Service
St.	Saint
UK	United Kingdom
US	United States
USA	United States of America
Vatican II	Second Vatican Council
VS	VERSUS
WCC	World Council of Churches

INTRODUCTION

In Nigeria, a religious divide separates followers of African Traditional Religion, Muslims, and Christians. This separation and division has led to series of riots, violence, aggressions, and conflicts. In fact, more than 30,000 Nigerians have lost their live to religious violence between 1980 and 2002, while the greater proportion of the population live in abject poverty. On a daily basis, we hear and witness cases of religious rascality, assassinations, callous murders, and savage terrorist acts.[1] Human rights group estimates that about 10,000 people have died in religious motivated violence between 2002 and 2005.[2] Sad to note that between 2005 and today (2011), hardly does a year, if not a month, pass by without a report of religious violence of different proportions in the Nigerian dailies. To use the words of Dele Omotunde:

> Religious riots have become a routine event in Nigeria. Burning houses, destroying property, maiming and killing innocent people have become a 'normal' way of religious life. The question is no longer 'if' but

---

[1] Jan H. Boer, *Nigeria's Decade of Blood: 1980-2002*. (Ontario, Canada: Essence Pub., 2003), 93-97.

[2] Greg Benzow, "Interfaith Dialogue in Nigeria: The need for reconciliation" *Qantara New*. December 8, 2005.

'when'. Religious violence has now become Allah's or God's unwritten commandment that must be obeyed, at least in Nigeria.[3]

The religious communities in Nigeria have failed largely to live up to their religious values and message of peace, unity and love; they have employed religion as instrument of violence and conflict. Looking back to history, Nigeria has been in the news in last fifty-one years of her independence (1960-2011) as a major theater of religious violence and aggression. This is traceable back to the first military coup led by Major Chukwuma Nzeogwu (a Christian), that saw the removal and death of Sir Abubakar Tafawa Balewa (a Muslim) from office and the enthronement of a Christian, General Aguiyi Ironsi, as Head of State in 1966, and the subsequent Nigeria-Biafra civil war of 1967-1970, which was overtly seen as a war of religion between the Christian South and the Muslim North.

This ugly situation raises a big question: How can Nigeria remain a secular state, and still maintain its plurality of religion and at same time survive disintegration because of religious violence, conflict and intolerance? Often, attention to this problem is wrongly focused. Attention is given mostly to the immediate cause of the problem and nothing, so to say, has been done to study the history of the problem, to identify not just the immediate causes but also the remote causes.[4]

---

[3]   Dele Omotunde, "Tyranny of the Fanatical", *Tell Magazine*, October 28, 1991, p.3.

[4]   Attention is indeed wrongly focused because oftentimes in Nigeria religious problems are treated as if they are political and committees with political undertones are set up to study and offer solutions on something they know nothing about. Religious problem should start primary with a religious approach with those who know about the religious history of Nigeria as members of the committee.

Another problem is that the presence of some religions is ignored in some parts of the country. Generally, the presence of traditional religions and their contribution to growth of peace, as well as violence, in Nigeria is ignored in the discussion of the place and role of religion in Nigeria. Attention is mainly focused on Islam and Christianity, or in most cases, particularly in the South-East, on African Traditional Religion and Christianity. Many studies done on the issues and problems of religious peace and conflicts in Nigeria have unfortunately followed this line of choosing two religions against one. It is this type of deficiency that this work hopes to address by being all-inclusive, not leaving out any of the three major religions in Nigeria. This all-inclusive approach informed the choice of the title of this second volume of interfaith series: *Together as one: Interfaith Relationships between Christianity, Islam and African Traditional Religion in Nigerian*,

Primarily, this title underscores the fact that, though tribe and tongue may differ, though religious differences exist, Nigeria is still one sovereign nation. The opening phrase: *Together as One* resonates with the opening statement of the Constitution of the Federal Republic of Nigeria that states:

> We the people of the Federal Republic of Nigeria, having firmly and solemnly resolved, to live in unity and harmony as one indivisible and indissoluble sovereign nation under God, dedicated to the promotion of inter-African solidarity, world peace, international co-operation and understanding, and to

provide for a Constitution for the purpose of promoting the good government and welfare of all persons in our country, on the principles of freedom, equality and justice, and for the purpose of consolidating the unity of our people, do hereby make, enact and give to ourselves the following Constitution.[5]

That this *unity and harmony as one indivisible and indissoluble sovereign nation under God* is being threatened is a truism in Nigeria today. Worst of all, this threat is carried out in the name of the same God under whom this unity and harmony is pledged. In other words, religion that should be an instrument of unity and harmony in Nigerian has become the very instrument that is posing the greatest threat to the survival of Nigeria as a united sovereign nation. For religion to avert this threat, the religions in Nigeria must commit to nothing other than **Interfaith Relationships** among the religious bodies in Nigeria, namely **Christianity, Islam, and African Traditional Religion**. If anyone of these three is left out, as has been the case, stability and harmony will not be attainable in Nigeria. Hence, this work is advocating a trialogical model of interfaith relationships in Nigeria rather than being content with the usual dialogical model, which over the years has not yielded many dividends in the religious peace process of the nation.

This second volume of our work particularly explores the areas of conflicts and harmony among the three religions in Nigeria. This exploration is done both from the dialogical and trialogical perspective, in view of highlighting the beauty of a trialogical interfaith relationships over and

---

[5]   Opening Statement of 1999 Constitution of the Federal Republic of Nigeria. http://www.nigeria-law.org/ConstitutionOfTheFederalRepublicOfNigeria.htm (accessed November 1, 2008)

above the dialogical approach. For a better handling, this volume is divided is into five chapters.

Chapter one defines and contextualizes interfaith relationships. It departs from a global perspective and narrows down to what could be understood as interfaith relationships within the Nigerian religious context. It tells what interfaith is and what it is not, as well as the objectives of such relationships.

Chapter two examines the basic tenets of the three religions in Nigeria—African Traditional Religion, Islam, and Christianity. This chapter highlights the belief systems of these religions with the intention of guiding us to see the areas of collaboration, agreement, disagreement, and conflict between them.

Chapter three examines interfaith activities and relationships among the three religions in Nigeria, but on the negative side. This chapter looks into the ugly but factual history of religious violence, riots, and conflicts in Nigeria. It will also look into other areas of divergence among these religions. The aim of this chapter is not to re-open old wounds, but to study the past to reveal the causes of those terrible and sad incidents as a means of identifying ways of preventing their future occurrences.

Chapter four examines the positive side of interfaith relationships among the three religions from a dialogical perspective; placing side by side two religions. It looks into areas of convergence among them, actions for common good in Nigeria, and day-to-day life of communion among people of the same community but different religious persuasions. It emphasizes what unites them rather than what divides them.

Chapter five does the same as chapter four, but from a trialogical perspective. Instead of two religions at a time, which has been the *modus operandi* of religious and interfaith scholarship in Nigeria, this chapter studies the three religions simultaneously.

Finally, comes the evaluation and conclusion, which ends this second volume of the work on interfaith series as well as signals the beginning of the third and last volume in this series.

CHAPTER ONE

DEFINING AND CONTEXTUALIZING INTERFAITH RELATIONSHIPS

1.1 UNDERSTANDING INTERFAITH RELATIONSHIPS.

The key phrase in this work is **interfaith relationships**. This section is aimed at providing a working understanding of what this phrase and this concept is all about, especially at it applies to Nigeria.

Interfaith relationships as encounters and or activities between people of different religious traditions have been happening ever since people began to identify themselves with a particular type of religious belief and practice. As a contemporary or modern movement, interfaith relationships are understood to have begun with the First Parliament of the World's Religions in Chicago in 1893. Recalling the moving interfaith event of this Parliament, Braybrooke writes:

> When the parliament opened on 11 September 1893, more than four thousand people crowded into the hall of Columbus. At ten o'clock, representatives of a dozen faiths marched down the aisle, arm in arm.

On the platform the central position was taken by Cardinal Gibbons, 'clad in scarlet robes' . . . Henry Barrows describes those seated next to the Cardinal. 'On either side of him were grouped the Oriental delegates, whose many colored raiment vied with his own in brilliancy. Conspicuous among these followers of Brahma and Buddha and Mohammed was the eloquent monk Vivekananda of Bombay, clad in gorgeous red apparel, his bronze face surmounted with a huge turban of yellow. Beside him, in orange and white, sat B.B. Nagarkar of the Brahmo-Samaj and Dharmapala from Ceylon.' One can sense the organizers' excitement . . . that, after all the time and correspondence, people from around the world had assembled in Chicago. Names on papers had begun to become friends. As Barrows said in his opening address, 'When, a few days ago, I met for the first time the delegates who have come to us from Japan, and shortly after the delegates who have come to us from India, I felt that the arms of human brotherhood had reached almost around the globe.[6]

Looking at the above quotation of what could be called the origin of interfaith relationships in our age; we can define interfaith relationships as a process of bringing better understanding between religious people and communities. It is an exchange to determine what is shared and is different about religions. In other words, interfaith relationships are

---

[6]   Marcus Braybrooke, *Pilgrim of Hope: One Hundred Years of Global Interfaith.* (New York: SCM, 1992), 26.

"the interaction of mutual presence, speaking and listening, witnessing the commitments, the values, and the rituals of others.[7]

Interfaith relationships, within our context, refer to activities involving African Traditional Religionists, Muslims, and Christians. It entails activities for mutual understanding held among these differing religious bodies. These activities begin with some initial assumptions; assumptions that Leonard Swidler in his *The Dialogue Decalogue* calls the ten "commandments" for engaging in constructive interreligious dialogue. These commandments are (to paraphrase):

1. The purpose of dialogue is to increase understanding.
2. Participants should engage in both interfaith and intra-religious dialogue.[8]
3. Participants should be honest and sincere.
4. Participants should assume that other participants are equally honest and sincere.
5. ach participant should be allowed self-definition.
6. There should be no preconceptions as to areas of disagreement.
7. Dialogue can only occur between equals.
8. Dialogue can only occur where there is mutual trust.
9. Participants must be self-critical of their religious traditions.

---

[7]   Paul F. Knitter, *Jesus and the Other Names.* (Maryknoll, NY: Orbis, 1996), 14.

[8]   Interfaith here refers to interactions and relationships between different religions (ATR, Christians and Muslims), while Intra-religious dialogue refers to interactions and relationships among members of the same religion. For example, the Catholics, Anglicans, Lutherans, and Methodists interacting and relating to one another as a people who share the same Christian religious faith is intra-religious dialogue.

10. Participants must attempt to experience how the traditions of others affect them holistically.[9]

Interfaith relationships are, therefore, built upon three fundamental things: respect for all religions, tolerance for all cultures, and love for all life.

The concern for global peace has made interfaith relationships among various religions of the world, not just Nigeria, imperative. A recent national survey of U.S. faith communities by Hartford Seminary found that interfaith activity among faith communities has more than tripled since 2000. The survey, sponsored by the Cooperative Congregational Studies Partnership, found that slightly more than 2 in 10 congregations (22.3 percent) reported participating in an interfaith worship service in the past year. Nearly 4 in 10 congregations (37.5 percent) reported joining in interfaith community service activities.[10]

Nevertheless, there are so many concepts that are confused with interfaith encounter, relationships, and activities. It is necessary at this stage of this work to point out what interfaith is not. Interfaith relationships are not a process of proselytism, that is, attempts at encouraging people to convert from one religion or belief to another. It is not apologetics, that is, an intellectual defense of ones faith. This means that interfaith activities in Nigeria is not aimed at converting Christians to Islam, or Muslims to Christianity, neither does it imply converting followers of African Traditional Religion to any of the other religion, and vice versa. However, it should be mentioned that interfaith relationships do enrich evangelism and apologetics. Affirming this view, Jason Barker, using Christianity

---

9   Leonard Swidler, "The Dialogue Decalogue: Ground Rules for Interreligious Dialogue," *Journal of Ecumenical Studies* 20.1 (1983): 1 - 4.

10   Jennifer Riley, The Christian Post, "*Survey: Interfaith activities increase significantly*". Fri, May. 12 2006

as a case point, observed that interreligious activities would increase the efficacy of evangelism. By clearly understanding the beliefs and practices of other religious communities, evangelists can more effectively identify the ways in which the gospel can be presented. Apologetics will also improve, as Christians understand more clearly the objections that other religions have to Christianity.[11]

Again, interfaith relationships are not a forum for debate and hostile argumentation. Their purpose "is neither to attack nor to defend—there will be no winner at the end of it."[12] This does not mean that there will not, or should not, be open disagreement during interfaith dialogue or trialogue. Because differences that are at the core of peoples' belief systems are the issue here, there will be frequent disagreement. In a dialogue or trialogue, we should be concerned in some way with questions, which arise because of serious differences in doctrines between adherents of different religions or religious faiths. The ensuing debate or discussion could take the form of an argument conducted from points of view that are distinctly doctrinal. This often leads to disagreement. If two doctrines are or are taken to be in head-on collision with each other by those who accept these doctrines, the holder of one doctrine would argue with the holder of the other doctrine with the object of showing that he is partly or wholly in error. However, open disagreement should primarily occur only when a participant believes that another participant (or participants) has made or promoted a misconception of the first's beliefs or practices. For example, in the hypothetical case of dialogue between a Christian and a Traditional Religionist, it would be inappropriate for

---

[11]   Jason Barker, *The Watchman Expositor: The Key to effective religious dialogue.* 1998,Vol. 15, No 4.

[12]   Stephen E. Robinson, *How Wide the Divide?* (Downers Grove, Ill: InterVarsity, 1997), 21

the Christian to tell the Traditionalist that the he or she is a heathen and an idol worshipper. Again, it would be inappropriate for a Christian to describe Islam as a bloodthirsty religion. These and other such examples will necessarily bring about differences and disagreement in interfaith relationships. However, interfaith relationships are not the forum for attempting to prove the superiority of one belief system over another.

As there are many different reasons for interfaith activity, so there are many different types of interfaith engagement. John Hick, recently interviewed by the International Interfaith Centre as part of its Faith and Interfaith video series, identified three main types of interfaith activity:

> I myself have been involved in three kinds of interfaith dialogue. One is highly intellectual . . . And this was between intellectuals of the different faiths and it was a matter of trying to understand one another's belief systems and discussing them—not trying to persuade each other that the other was wrong but in actual fact learning from the others. Then in California I was involved in a totally different kind of thing, much more ground level, in which quite ordinary people, not religious leaders, not the rabbis and ministers and so on, but ordinary people, got together in one another's houses—Christians, Jews, Muslims this was—and they were interested to find out about daily life, what you do in family life, how you deal with children's problems, what you eat and what you don't eat and all that sort of thing, and this was enormously creative of interfaith friendships, genuine friendships. The third thing was the one I

mentioned in Handsworth (Birmingham, U.K) where people of different faiths were getting together to cope with specific local concrete problems.[13]

In other words, Hick identifies interfaith activities of intellectuals, interfaith activities of daily life by 'ordinary people', and interfaith activities for social action.

Diana Eck identifies six types of interfaith of activities, namely: 1) Parliamentary style of dialogue that occurs at the level of international faith organization in the manner of 1893 World's Parliament of Religion in Chicago. 2) Institutional dialogue such as the regular meetings between representatives of the Vatican and The International Jewish Committee for Interreligious Consultation. 3) Theological dialogue that takes seriously the questions and challenges posed by people of other faiths. 4) Dialogue in community or the dialogue of life, which is the search for good relationships in ordinary life. 5) Spiritual dialogue that attempts to learn from other traditions of prayer and meditation. 6) Inner dialogue, which is that conversation that goes on within ourselves in any other form of dialogue.[14]

For our use and purpose, looking at the six types of interfaith relationships identified by Eck, our study will centered more on community interfaith relationships or interfaith relationships of life that occurs at the daily interactions of the followers of these religions in Nigeria, and spiritual and inner forms of interfaith activities, as well as the institutional form of interfaith relationships that will bring together leaders and representatives of the various

---

[13] John Hick, "Interfaith Studies: John Hick's descriptions of types of interfaith activities." http://www.interfaithstudies. org/interfaith/hicktypes.html (assessed: March 16, 2009)
[14] Diana Eck, *Inter-religious dialogue as a Christian Ecumenical Concern.* (New York: Columbia University Press, 1998), 13.

religions in Nigeria. These forms of interfaith activities will work better in Nigeria than would parliamentary and theological forms of interfaith relationships. This is because the religious problems in Nigeria occur on a regular basis at the community level, as such addressing the problems through interfaith activities at the same community level that will include spiritual activities of prayer and meditation, daily interactions and programs for the community's well-being, will facilitate and promote inner conversion and a change of attitude towards one another. Instead of seeing one another as rivals, members of the same community will see and understand themselves as brothers, sisters, and friends. The religious leaders will now harmonize the activities at the community level collectively and individually in their various religious groups, while educating their members on the need for peace, tolerance and respect.

1.2 THE NECESSITY OF INTERFAITH RELATIONSHIPS IN NIGERIA

Many reasons and factors make interfaith relationships in Nigeria today as urgent as never before in the entire history of Nigeria. Dominant among these are the following:

i) The ugly reality of religious violence, conflict and poverty in Nigeria.
ii) The obvious consequences of religious violence in Nigeria.
iii) The need for peace and harmony.
iv) The brotherhood and sisterhood that binds us together as one Nigeria.
v) Globalization and increasing bonds of friendship.
vi) Global, national and communal responsibility.
We shall briefly discuss each of these headings.

I.) The ugly reality of religious violence and conflict in Nigeria.

Religious violence has become an almost a daily occurrence in Nigeria. There is virtually no area in all the six geopolitical zones in Nigeria that has not witnessed one or more such crises. The thousands of lives lost across the country over the years in the course of religious crises has become an issue of great concern to all well-meaning citizens of Nigeria. Consequently, Nigerians across all religions and lifestyles are calling for more pragmatic steps towards building a culture and climate of religious harmony, tolerance and freedom in the society. The best way to achieve this result is none other than the promotion and practice of interfaith relationships in Nigeria. For, unless we come together and closer to each other, we may not appreciate and accommodate the religious views of one another. I share the view of Jacob Olupona, a renowned professor of religion, as reported by Mcphilips Nwachukwu, that any meaningful resolution of conflict in Nigeria that hopes to bring lasting peace must anchor on interfaith dialogue. [15]

Obviously, if we are serious about addressing the ugly reality of religious violence in Nigeria, then interfaith relationships understood as a unique way to foster peace, cooperation, interactions, and better relationships among different religious faith communities, are not an option but a *conditio sine qua non.*

---

[15] Mcphilips Nwachukwu, "At CBAAC, Olupona Canvasses Inter-Faith Dialogue as Panacea to Religious Crises." *Vanguard News*, April 3, 2008.

II.) The obvious consequences of religious violence in Nigeria.

Another basis for an urgent need for interfaith relationships in Nigeria is the obvious consequences of religious violence. As a pluralistic society with multi-religious faith and ethnic groupings, it is obvious that prolonged religious discrimination and violence would and do have many negative consequences. Hence, religious violence and its attending consequences must be avoided at all cost through interfaith relationships among the religions in Nigeria because once set in motion, it is very difficult to cure discriminations and quell conflicts based on religious inflexibility and intransigence. Interfaith relationships are an antidote to such intransigence, fanaticism and discrimination.

III.) The need for peace and harmony.

If peace is the precondition for progress, then justice is the precondition for peace. There can be no peace and meaningful progress in Nigeria unless there is at least relative peace and harmony among the religions. For there to be peace in Nigeria today and tomorrow, Nigerians must face the issue of justice; there must be some confession of guilt and some form of reparation. Religions have contributed to the peace of Nigeria, but they have also led to division, hatred, and war. Religious people have too often betrayed the high ideals they themselves have preached. We feel obliged to call for sincere acts of repentance and mutual forgiveness, both personally and collectively, to one another, to humanity in general, and to the Earth and all living beings. This can only happen within the context of interfaith relationships. As expressed by Hans Küng, "No peace among nations without peace among the religions.

No peace among the religions without dialogue between the religions."[16]

On December 22, 2003, *All Africa Global Media* reported that President Olusegun Obasanjo had expressed the need for inter-religious harmony and peace among the various religious believers in the country. According to the President, under no circumstances should there be religious acrimony among adherents, adding that if various religious believers cannot live together in peace, there was no basis for them to lay claim to be worshipping God. He said, "Religion is for us to know God and if we want to know God, we must know those created by God. If we cannot live together why do we claim to be worshipping God?"[17]

In order to achieve the desired peace and harmony required among the religions in Nigeria and the nations, interfaith relationships that recognize pluralism, respect diversity, and strive for the harmony, which is at the very core of peace, are a necessity.

IV.) The brotherhood and sisterhood that binds us together as one Nigeria.

Another basis for interfaith relationships is the brotherhood and sisterhood that binds us together as one nation. Whether we are Igbo, Hausa, Yoruba, Igala, Tiv, Ibibio, Urhobo, Ijaw, or Efik, Christians, Muslims, or ATR, there is something that still binds us together in the midst of these diversities, namely we are all brothers and sisters. It is in the spirit of interfaith relationships that we can truly see, appreciate and celebrate the brotherhood

---

[16]   Hans Küng, *Islam: Past, Present & Future*. (Oxford: One World Books, 2007), xxiii.

[17]   "President Obasanjo Speaks Need for Interreligious Harmony and peace in Nigeria" *All Africa Global Media*. Dec 22, 2003.

and sisterhood we share; a relationship that has been distorted by religious indifference, intolerance, suspicion and violence.

V.) Globalization and increasing bond of friendship.

The world has become a global village where isolation from one community, state, and nation is no longer possible. As a matter of fact, every geopolitical zone in Nigeria has become so cosmopolitan that you have people across the nations living everywhere, working together for the well-being of all side by side with people from other tribes and religions, unlike many years back when the East was only for easterners and for Christians, and the south was southerners and ATR only, and the north for northerners and Muslims only. We live in a time of unprecedented mobility of peoples and intermingling of cultures. We are interdependent and share an inescapable responsibility for the well-being of the entire world. The effect of this global community is seen in increasing bonds of friendship between people who otherwise were seen as strangers.

The increasing trend of globalization and the bond of friendship requires among other things: a) Commitment to a culture of non-violence, tolerance and respect for life, and b) Commitment to a culture of equal rights and partnership between men and women of all religions. These commitments can truly be made only within the context of interfaith relationships. In the spirit of such relationships, that strengthens global unity and peace, Christians, Muslims, and ATR should be "ever aware of their duties to foster unity and charity among individual, and among nations, and reflect at the outset on what people have in common and what tends to brings them together."[18]

VI.) Global, national and communal responsibility.

One of the obvious bases for interfaith relationships in Nigeria is the collective responsibility that we all have as religious people and Nigerians for the well being of the earth, our country, state, and community. As Paul Knitter would say,

> Global responsibility is the raw material for the common ground of dialogue ... A global responsibility for *soteria*—for the well-being of the threatened earth and all its threatened tenants—can provide the framework, content, motivation, fiber, and directives for a dialogue among religions ... If people today are looking for something that will ground their trust in the possibility of authentic dialogue and that will direct their efforts to make this responsibility a reality, I think they can find it here: a global responsibility for human and ecological well-being. Because such a concern for *soteria* naturally and automatically creates *solidarity*, it will provide motivation and commitment for the task of interreligious conversions ... Persons from all religious traditions can see, feel, and respond to the crises facing our earth (nation and communities); such recognition can lead to the conclusion that the religions must respond to these crises. A sense of

---

[18]   *Nostra Aetate,* 1

solidarity is an invitation to interaction and conversation.[19]

All three religions and their followers in Nigeria are concerned with making positive changes towards a better society. They all, in some way, desire to make better or heal or avoid what is not right or working well in the nation and in the local communities. As expressed by Gordon Kaufman,

> Every religious tradition promises salvation in some form or the other, i.e., promises true human fulfillment, or at least rescue from the pit into which we humans have fallen. Every religious tradition thus implicitly invokes a human or humane criterion to justify its existence and its claims.[20]

There are no way the religious aspirations of making the world and society better can be achieved in the midst of wanton destructions of life and property occasioned by religious violence. These aspirations can only be achieved in an atmosphere of interreligious harmony, activities, interactions and collaboration. No one religion can do it all alone. We all need one another to make Nigeria better; hence the necessity of interfaith relationships in Nigeria.

---

[19]   Paul F. Knitter, *One Earth Many Religions: Multifaith Dialogue & Global Responsibility*. (New York: Orbis Books, 1995), 79.

[20]   Gordon Kaufman, *The Theological Imagination: Constructing the Concept of God*. (Philadelphia: Westminster Press, 1981), 198-199.

CHAPTER TWO

THE BASIC TENETS OF AFRICAN TRADITION RELIGION, ISLAM, AND CHRISTIANITY.

This chapter examines the basic tenets of the three religions in Nigeria—African Traditional Religion, Islam, and Christianity. The importance of this study is to understand what these religions believe in as it will help us to see the areas of collaboration, agreement, disagreement, and conflict between them.

2.1 BASIC BELIEFS AND DOCTRINES OF AFRICAN TRADITIONAL RELIGION (ATR).

African Traditional Religion is a religion with different versions and expressions among the various African, Nigerian and Igbo communities. Yet, in the midst of this diversity of expressions, there exists basic tenets and doctrines that are common (with some variations based on local cultures) to all followers of ATR. These basic tenets and doctrines are:
   a) Belief in God
   b) Belief in divinities

c) Belief in spirits
d) Belief in ancestors
e) Belief in worship: sacrifice and prayer
f) Belief in the sacredness of life and morality
g) Belief in peace and harmonious relationship in the community
h) Belief in life after death

We shall treat each of these tenets in detail.

2.1.1. Belief in God.

Belief in God, who is called the Supreme Being, is at the center of African Traditional Religion. Observing this fact, Pere Noel Baudin, a French Roman Catholic, wrote, "In these religious systems [ATR] the idea of God is fundamental; they believe in the existence of a supreme, primordial being, the lord of the universe which is his work. Although deeply imbued with polytheism, the blacks have not lost the idea of the true God."[21] The traditional concept of God is strongly colored and influenced by the historical, geographical, social and cultural background or environment of each people. Expressing the depth of belief in God among followers of traditional African religion, and how this belief underlies their basic existence, John Mbiti writes,

> In African traditional religion, knowledge of God is expressed in proverbs, short statements, songs, prayers, names, myths, stories and religious ceremonies. All these are easy to remember and pass on to other people, since there are no sacred writings

---

[21] Pere Noel Baudin, *Fetishism and Fetish Worshippers* (Paris: L'Harmattan, 1885), 9

in traditional societies. God is no stranger to African people, and in traditional life there are no atheists. This is summarized in an Ashanti proverb that 'No one shows a child the Supreme Being'. That means that everybody knows of God's existence almost by instinct, and even children know him.[22]

God in ATR is generally called the Supreme Being with various indigenous names among various communities. For example, in Nigeria, the Igbos call him *Chukwu*, the Yorubas called him *Olodumare,* the Hausas call him *Allah*, the Efiks call him *Abasi*, and the Binis call him *Osanobua*.

In ATR the Supreme Being is not an impersonal absolute principle, he is personal, having will, emotions and intelligence. Among his divine attributes are: creator, supreme and absolute, self-existent, omnipotent, omnipresent, omniscient, unique, and transcendent. Emphasizing the omnipotent attribute of the Supreme Being, Cosmas Obiego writes,

For the traditional people, *Chukwu* (Supreme Being) is the omnipotent God. This concept is the fruit of existential experience, not so much of abstract speculation. It is articulated in the traditional names, proverbs, and sayings; and in their understanding of *Chukwu's* exercise of power over nature.[23]

---

[22] John Mbiti, *African Religions and Philosophy*, 2nd Ed. (Ibadan: Heinemann Educational Books, Ltd, 1990), 29.

[23] Cosmas Obiego, *African Image of the Ultimate Reality Analysis of Igbo Idea of Life and Death in Relation to Chukwu.* (Berlin: Peter lang, 1984), 97.

On the omnipresent, and omniscient attributes of the Supreme Being in ATR, Chibueze Udeani, writes,

> Among the Igbos, just as in other African societies, the Supreme Being is simultaneously everywhere and he knows everything. The Igbo saying *'Onwero ihe gbalu Chukwu ghari'* (Nothing puzzles God) expresses their belief in God's omnipresence and omniscience. His omniscience is absolute, unlimited and an intrinsic part of his nature and being. God is the discerner of heart, no matter how much a person may try to conceal his deed, hence such names like Chukwuma (God Knows), Chima-Obi (God knows the hearts) etc.[24]

ATR believes that the Supreme Being has not only divine attributes; he equally possesses moral attributes, which include holiness, goodness, mercy, spirituality, purity, and justice.[25]

In ATR, the Supreme Being is generally not involved in the day-to-day affairs of his creatures. He is the withdrawn God *(dues otiosus)* who "after the work of creation retired to a distant place, having little contact with the world and daily operation. He may be appealed to at times of great crisis."[26] Affirming this traditional notion of the Supreme Being in ATR, Benjamin Ray writes,

---

[24]   Chibueze Udeani, *Inculturation as Dialogue: Igbo Culture and the Message of Christ.* (Amsterdam: Rodopi, 2007), 51.

[25]   John Mbiti, *Introduction to African Religion*, 2nd ed. (Ibadan: Heinemann, 1991), 55-66.

[26]   Lewis M. Hopfe and Mark R. Woodward, *Religions of the World,* 8th ed. (New Jersey: Prentice Hall, 2001), 51.

Having formed the immutable structures
of the sky and earth and the orderly human
cycle of birth, life and death, the Supreme
Creator God remains in the background like
a distant ruler or patriarch, occasionally
intervening but generally leaving the
fortunes and misfortunes of everyday life to
lesser agents, the gods and spirits.[27]

In ATR the One Creator, the Supreme Being, and the
divinities, the lesser gods and spirits are essential to the
full range of traditional religious experience.

2.1.2. Belief in Divinities.

Connected to the belief in the Supreme Being is the belief
in divinities, also called deities or lesser gods. The lesser
gods or divinities "represent a hierarchy of messengers
or links between the spiritual and material world. Each
divinity governs a sphere of life or human activity and may
be connected to a natural object or place."[28] The divinities
are functionaries in the theocratic, existential and daily
governance of the universe and the people in it. They are
the sons and or deputies of the Supreme Being. Explaining
this, Bolaji Idowu writes,

Orisha-nla, (archdivinity among the Yoruba)
is a derivation partaking of the very nature
and metaphysical attributes of Olodumare

---

[27] Benjamin C. Ray, *African Religions: Symbol, Ritual, and
Community*, 2nd ed. (New Jersey: Prentice Hall, 2000), 45
[28] Azim Nanji, "African Religions" in *The Religious World:
Communities of Faith*. Robert F. Weir, Ed. (New York:
Macmillan Publishing Co. Inc., 1982), 37

(the Supreme Being). Hence, he is often known as a deity, son and deputy, vested with the power and authority of royal sonship ... *Olokun* (Benin) is known as the son of Osanobwa—the son vested with power and majesty of his Father. All Akan divinities are called sons of *Onyame*. It is in consequence of the derivative relationship [with the Supreme Being] that these divine beings are entitled to be divinities or deities.[29]

In ATR these deities or divinities are not created but are said to be brought into being or that they came into being in the nature of things with regard to the divine ordering of the universe. That is to say, they are not the handiwork of any god or human, neither do they owe their existence to any superior maker or creator. Each divinity has its own local name in the local language which is descriptive either of his/her allotted function or the natural phenomenon which is believed to be a manifestation or emblem of his/her being. Among the Yoruba, the divinity who is believed to be the divine representative of Wrath is called *Jakuta*, (one who hurls or fights with stone); in Nupe he is called *Soko egba* (God's axe). Among the Igbo, the archdivinity is called *Ala* (Earth or ground). She is the Earth-goddess and is the archdivinity for fertility.

These divinities are directly involved in the day-to-to life of the community more than the Supreme Being is. In most cases sacrifice are offered directly to them and through them to the Supreme Being.

---

[29]   E. Bolaji Idowu, *African Traditional Religion: A Definition.* (New York: Maryknoll, 1975),169.

2.1.3. Belief in spirits.

Below the deities in the hierarchy of beings are the spirits. The spirits in general belong to the ontological mode of existence between God and man. Spirits according to African belief are ubiquitous; there is no area of the earth, and there is no object or creature, which has not a spirit of its own or which cannot be inhabited by a spirit. However, there are still localized spirits that are identified with certain objects or particular places. Reporting on this, Mbiti writes, "The majority of the people hold that the spirits dwell in the wood, bush, forest, rivers, and mountains or just around the village. Thus, the spirits are in the same geographical region as men."[30]

There are good and bad spirits. The good spirits have a positive influence on the people while the bad have a negative influence; and the safest thing to do is to keep away from the latter. One way the spirits exercise influence on people in ATR is through possession. Reporting on this, Mbiti writes,

> Spirit possession occurs in one form or another in practically every African society . . . The spirit speaks through the possessed person, so that he now plays the role of a medium, and the messages he relays are received with expectations by those to whom they are addressed. But on the whole, spirit possessions, especially unsolicited ones, result in bad effects. They may cause severe torment on the possessed person . . . During the heights of spirit possession; the individual in effect loses his own personality

---

[30] Mbiti, *African Religions and Philosophy*, 79.

and acts in the context of the 'personality' of the spirit possessing him.[31]

In ATR, many communities have temples and shrines dedicated to different spirits. Belief in the spirits is not limited to the natural spirits of the sky: the sun, moon, star, rainbows, rain, storms, winds, thunder and lightening or the earth spirits; there are also human spirits. The human spirits are those who were once ordinary men, women or children, and the living dead—the Ancestors. The living dead are the spirits that normally matter most on the family level in ATR.[32]

2.1.4. Belief in Ancestors.

Associated with the belief in God, divinities and spirits, is the belief in and veneration of ancestors. The ancestors are held in a very high esteem in ATR.

They are far closer to the people than the gods are. In ATR, not every body can become an ancestor. An ancestor is a person who died a good death after having faithfully practiced and transmitted to his descendants the laws left to him by his fore-bearers. He is a person who contributed to the continuation of the linage by leaving many descendants. Also, must have been a peacemaker, a link that fostered communion between the living and the dead, through sacrifices and prayers. In most cases, but not all cases, he is the first-born in the family. The first-born is a candidate 'par excellence' for becoming an ancestor because he is able to maintain the chain of the generation in a long genealogy.

---

[31]   Ibid, 80-81.

[32]   Mbiti, *Introduction to African Religion*, 70-79

The ancestors are believed to be the guardians of family affairs, customs and traditions and ethical norms. Offence in these matters is ultimately an offence against the ancestors who in that capacity, like the gods, act as invisible police of the families and communities.[33] Emphasizing this fact, Oliver Onwubiko writes,

> Beliefs concerning ancestors are an important element in African religions and are forces to reckon with in the formation of the African religious life and mentality, because they are situated in the family life and spring out of the family structure . . . The ancestors, as spirits, are believed to be present in the family in a number of ways, at times, as physically reincarnated members. The Yoruba express this aspect of African religion when they say: *Babajide*, which means, 'Father is awake and is here.'[34]

Although physically dead, the ancestors are spiritually alive. According to Mbiti:

> The ancestors are the living-dead. They are the closest links that men have with the spirit world . . . [They] are bilingual: they speak the language of men, with whom they lived until 'recently'; and they speak languages (*sic*) of the spirits and of God, to whom they are drawing nearer ontologically. These are the 'spirits' with which African peoples are most

---

[33] Emefie Ikenga-Metuh, *Comparative Studies of African Traditional Religion.* (Onitsha: Imico, 1987), 149.

[34] Oliver Onwubiko, *African Thought, Religion and Culture.* (Enugu: Snaap Press, 1991), 61.

concerned: it is through the living-dead that the spirit world becomes personal to men. They are still part of the human families, and people have personal memories of them.[35]

The belief in the ancestors emphasizes communion and communication between those who are alive on earth and those who are 'alive' in the spirit world. The latter have the power to influence, help, or molest the former, while the former through libations and sacrifices relate and appease the latter. It must be noted that the "ancestors are not considered as gods, and are therefore not worshipped in that sense, nor is the ancestor cult[36] the same as cults of the dead."[37]

2.1.5. Belief in worship: Sacrifice and prayer.

Belief in the place and efficacy of worship is very basic in ATR. Relationships and communion with the Supreme Being, the divinities, spirits and ancestors are realized and maintained through worship, which can be through the ritual[38] of sacrifice and or simple prayer. However,

---

[35] Mbiti, *African Religions and Philosophy*, 82.
[36] Ancestor cult refers to a recurring set of devotional rituals in African Traditional Religions by which the ancestors are venerated. On the other hand, the cult of the dead refers to necromancy—the practice of communicating with the spirit of the dead to get certain answers or to predict the future.
[37] James R. Lewis, *Encyclopedia of Death and the Afterlife.* (Detroit: Visible Ink Press, 1995), 4.
[38] A ritual or rite is a set form of carrying out a religious action or ceremony. It is a means of communicating something of significance, through word, symbol and action. A ritual word is powerful since it is spoken in seriousness and solemnity,

in the strictest sense, only God and the divinities are worshipped and this is done through sacrifices, offerings, prayers, invocations, praises, music and dance. In many localities in Africa, there is no direct cult of the Supreme Being, yet God is the ultimate object of worship that the people approach through intermediaries: religious functionaries, the ancestors and the divinities. ATR has an abundance of temples, shrines, groves and altars used for public and private worship. Some special trees, rivers, forests, mountains, considered manifestations of the sacred, often serve as places of worship. This has led some scholars to imagine that it is these natural objects that are being worshipped—to the amusement of the traditional religionists. The good spirits and all the ancestors are venerated and constantly implored to intervene on behalf of humans.

Discussing the concept of sacrifice in relation to worship in ATR, Onwubiko writes:

> Sacrifices are important element (*sic*) in African religion. Three kinds of sacrifices are prominent in most communities and these are: (i) Expiatory (ii) Petitive and (iii) Thanksgiving sacrifices.
> Expiatory sacrifices are offered to ward off evil spirits and to placate and an enraged deity or an ancestor.
> Petitive sacrifices are to ask for a favor or a blessing from God, the ancestors, spirits or deities.
> Thanksgiving sacrifices feature when blessing or favors have been received.

---

and it is repeated every time that ritual is done. In ATR, there is ritual for everything.

For sacrifices to be efficacious and to achieve their purpose, the African believes that they must be offered at particular spots, by particular persons and at a particular time of the day, week, or year, as the case may be.[39]

On prayer, Onwubiko continues,

Prayer is a constant element in African life and religion. It is a means of contact and communion with the Supreme Being, the gods, and the ancestors. Prayers are, at times, spontaneous and determined by occasions and circumstances. Libation is often a feature of African prayer. It is the outpouring of wine to a deity or to an ancestor, as a sign of goodwill and communion with it.[40]

In practical terms, however, sacrifice and prayer go hand in hand during worship in African traditional religion.

2.1.6. Belief in the sacredness of life and morality.

The practical aspect of belief in ATR is not only worship but also emphasis on human dignity and conduct. Belief in God and in the other spiritual beings implies a certain type of conduct, conduct that respects the order established by God and watched over by the divinities and the ancestors. At the centre of traditional African morality is human life. Africans have a sacred reverence for life, for it is believed to be the greatest of God's gifts to humans. To protect and nurture their lives, all human beings are inserted within

---

[39]   Onwubiko, *African Thought, Religion and Culture*, 62.
[40]   Ibid, 63

a given community and it is within this community that one works out one's destiny and every aspect of individual life. The promotion of life is therefore the determinant principle of African traditional morality and this promotion is guaranteed only in the community.

There are norms and taboos that try to address the need of the individual human person for security of life and property. For example, most traditional African groups have stiff penalties for willful murder of a person, including bringing about the death of a fetus. That is to say, while murder, strictly defined as intentionally taking another person's life, is a taboo in ATR, an exception that allows for murder is made to that rule if the killing occurs within the context of war. Any one guilty of murder would be required to repair the crime usually by providing another human being to the family of the person killed, a person relatively close in age to the deceased. The offender would then be bound to take his/her own life through public hanging.[41]

In this light, Onwubiko emphasized,

> The unborn are protected, and abortion is tabooed. Sources of life are sacred. The sacredness associated with life goes to explain the rigidity with which sexual intercourse and sexual organs are treated in African traditional religion. Again, the sacredness of life makes it an abomination for anyone, under any circumstances to take his own life. Suicide is never permitted.[42]

---

[41] Francis A. Arinze, *Sacrifice in Igbo Religion*. (Ibadan: university Press, 1970), 38.

[42] Onwubiko, *African Thought, Religion and Culture*, 23-23

The sacredness of life in ATR is expressed among the Igbos in names like: *Nduka* (Life is supreme), and Nduka-aku (Life is more important than wealth).

2.1.7. Belief in peace and harmonious relationships in the community.

In ATR the basis of religion is peace and harmonious relationships between the members of the community and with the gods and ancestor. In traditional African societies, peace is not an abstract poetic concept, but rather a down-to-earth and practical concept. In ATR, peace is conceived not in relation to conflict and war, but in relation to order, harmony and equilibrium. It is a religious value in the sense that the order, harmony and equilibrium in the universe and society is believed to be divinely established and the obligation to maintain them is religious. It is also a moral value since good conduct is required of human beings if order, harmony and equilibrium are to be maintained. In ATR, the concept of peace includes good human relationships, prosperity, personal well-being and good health, and the absence of war and conflict.[43] Peace is the totality of well-being, the fullness of life here and hereafter (what the Yorubas call *Alafia*), the sum total of all that man may desire. It is an undisturbed harmonious life.[44]

Harmonious living is clearly a pivotal value. African Traditional Religion, which has been rightly referred to as the womb of the people's culture, plays a key role

---

43 Robert Rweyemamu, "Religion and Peace: An Experience in with African Traditions," in *Studia Missionalia*. Vol., 5, no. 38, 1989, p.381

44 Joseph Awolanu, "The Yoruba Philosophy of Life," in *Presence Africaine*, Vol.3, no. 2, 1970, p. 21.

in the realization of this all-important value among every traditional African group. Religion is central in inculcating the promotion and realization of harmonious inter-relationships among individuals and the community.[45] Harmony is thus a fundamental category in traditional African religion and thought. In the community, harmony entails smooth relationships between persons and other beings. Explaining the seriousness of this belief in ATR, Theophilus Okere writes,

> The goal of interaction of beings in African world-views is the maintenance of the integration and balance of the beings in it [the world]. Harmonious interaction of beings leads to the mutual strengthening of the beings involved, and enhances the growth of life. A pernicious influence from one being weakens other beings and threatens the harmony and integration of the whole.[46]

The harmony that is to be maintained for humans to experience peace is not only social but also spiritual and cosmic. In many communities, there are specific periods of the year marked out for the promotion of peace. During this period, which may last for a week or a month, litigations are suspended while quarrels and all forms of violent and

---

[45]   Emefie Ikenga-Metuh, *God and man in African Religion.* (London: Geoffrey Chapman, 1981), 48.

[46]   Theophilus Okere, "The Kite may perch, the Eagle may perch: *Egbe bere Ugo bere*: An African Concept of Peace and Justice." *In International Philosophers of Peace.* (New York: Boston University, 1998), 9

unjust acts are avoided for fear of incurring the wrath of God, the deities and the ancestors.[47]

If a person breaks either the spiritual or the cosmic harmony, the lack of peace that ensues affects the entire community. Sometimes individual reparations in terms of sacrifices are not enough to restore the harmony and all the members of the community are called upon to right the wrong.

In ATR peace and harmony are believed to be gifts from God. Since human beings are aware of their limitations in attaining and maintaining peace in their persons and within their societies, and are aware of the fact that God is the source of universal order and harmony, they regularly turn to him to ask for peace. While recognizing their co-responsibility in this regard, traditional Africans equally believe that true peace is a gift of God.[48]

2.1.8. Belief in life after death.

An important feature of ATR is the belief in life after death. Death is not the end of life. It opens the way to another life that may be better or worst depending on one's state in the present life. According to John Mbiti,

> Death is conceived of as a departure and not a complete annihilation of a person. He moves on to join the company of the departed, and the only major change is the decay of the physical body, but the spirit moves on to another state of existence. Some

---

[47]   Chinua Achebe, *Things Fall Apart*. (New York: Anchor Books, 1994), 29-32.
[48]   Peter Sarpong, "African Traditional Religion and Peace," in *Studia Missionalia*. Vol., 5, no. 38, 1989, p.365

of the words describing death imply that a person goes 'home' which means that this life is like a pilgrimage: the real 'home' is in the hereafter, since one does not depart from there.[49]

Among the Yoruba, the structure of the afterlife depends on the level of goodness of a person's life. If *Olorun* believes that a person has led a good life, he may grant reincarnation; if not, he may send the soul to a place of punishment.[50] One's life continues after death as an ancestor or in the manner of reincarnation.

The belief in an afterlife is a fundamental reason for the elaborate rites during funerals in ATR, especially among the Igbo. According to Onwubiko,

> Funeral ceremonies in Igboland are elaborate and highly expensive and are celebrated according to the status of the deceased. A common characteristic of all funeral ceremonies is that they are believed to determine the place the decease would enjoy in the spirit world, and they also condition reincarnation. The dead who have not received these ceremonies are believed not to be able to enter the spirit land and as such they do not belong to the "village" of the dead or to that of the living.[51]

In many communities during funerals, the deceased are buried with and accompanied by their professional or occupational identities. The kings are even accompanied

---

[49] Mbiti, *African Religions and Philosophy*, 52-53.
[50] Lewis, *Encyclopedia of Death and the Afterlife*, 9.
[51] Onwubiko, *African Thought, Religion and Culture*, 90-91

by slaves. The belief is that they continue their normal life and social status in the afterlife. Reporting on this, James Lewis writes,

> Some societies bury the dead with weapons, personal belongings, food, money, and other items to assist in the journey from this world to the next. Often the corpse is ritually treated with a view toward starting its new life. The body is treated carefully, so as not to bruise it or change its appearance . . . Through these rites the spirit of the deceased is carried to its new position in the life beyond and the balance of the surviving society is restored.[52]

2.2 BASIC BELIEFS AND DOCTRINES OF ISLAM.

The Islamic belief system and doctrines can be classified under two major aspects: the six articles of faith and the five (or six) pillars of faith (or acts of worship), which are expressed in the Qur'an and in the hadith (the sayings and customs of the Prophet—Muhammad). As noted by Salman Hakim,

> The teachings of the Qur'an and the Hadith (sayings of Prophet Mohammad) revolve around two Arabic words namely, īmān (Faith) and āmāl (Acts). Īmān is like the roots of a tree and āmāl are the stems, leaves or other parts of it. Just as without the roots, the tree cannot survive, similarly, without faith, the acts are useless; without acts

---

[52] Lewis, *Encyclopedia of Death and the Afterlife*, 6.

faith is useless. The teachings of the Quran emphasize mostly on the beliefs and give an overview of the acts, whereas the Hadith explains both beliefs and acts in details.[53]

The six articles of faith which are the core beliefs in Islam are:
a) Belief in One God.
b) Belief in Angels.
c) Belief in Scriptures.
d) Belief in Prophets.
e) Belief in Resurrection/Last Judgment.
f) Belief in Predestination/Free will.

The five (or six) pillars of faith, which Muslims perform to express their faith and belief, are:
a) Testimony of faith: *Shahadah.*
b) Prayer: *Salat.*
c) Almsgiving: *Zakat.*
d) Fasting: *Sawm.*
e) Pilgrimage: Hajj.
f) Jihad.[54]

These beliefs and acts are almost universal among Muslims of all faith communities, including those in Nigeria. Expressing this fact, John Esposito writes,

Despite the rich diversity of practice and rituals according to culture and sects or

---

[53] Salman Hakim, *Basic Beliefs of Islam.* (Nashville: Thomas Nelson Publishers, 2008), 2.

[54] Some Islamic scholars include Jihad as the sixth pillar of faith or act of worship. Cf. Frederick Mathewson Denny, *An Introduction to Islam*, 3rd ed. (New Jersey: Prentice Hall, 2006), 126.

faith communities, the six articles of faith and the five [or six] pillars of faith in Islam remain the core and common denominator, the essential and obligatory practices all Muslims accept and follow.[55]

We shall explain each of these beliefs in brief detail, beginning with the articles of faith.

2.2.1 The six articles of faith:

These, as mentioned above, are six in number; and righteousness for Muslims consist in believing in these articles as recorded in the Qur'an: Surah 2:177, "It is not righteousness that you turn your faces towards east or west [in prayer]; but it is righteousness—to believe in Allah and the last Day, and the Angels, and Book, and the Messengers."

2.2.1.1. Belief in one God.

The first fundamental belief in Islam is the belief in the "absolute unity of God."[56] There is only one Supreme, Eternal, Infinite and Unparallel entity, Allah. He alone is the creator of the entire universe. The Qur'an declares, "That is God, your Lord. There is no god but Him, the Creator of everything. So worship Him. He is responsible for everything" (6:102). The oneness of God in Islam is understood in term of a strict monotheism, which in Arabic

---

[55] John L. Esposito: *Islam: The Straight Path,* 3rd ed. (Oxford: Oxford University Press, 2005), 88.

[56] Frederick Mathewson Denny, *An Introduction to Islam,* 3rd ed. (New Jersey: Prentice Hall, 2006), 97.

is *tawhid*. Commenting in this, Hans Küng writes, "Belief in one God (tawhid), from the verb 'declare to be one' (wahhada) derived from the noun 'one only' (wahid), is the basic dogma of Islam, and is meant quite practically."[57]

The oneness of God forbids associating or equating God with anything divine or human. This "uniqueness of God is the basic morality of the Qur'an. To give allegiance or put trust in anything other than Allah is idolatry, the greatest sin of Islam."[58] This belief in expressed in the Qur'an—*the Purity Surah 112*, thus: "Say: He is Allah, the One and Only; Allah, the Eternal, Absolute; He begets not, nor is He begotten; and there is none to be compared with him."

In Islamic tradition, Allah has one hundred most beautiful names, but only ninety-nine are known to humanity. Among these ninety-nine, the most commonly used names that appear at the beginning of almost all the *surahs* are: the Most Gracious and the Most Merciful. Commenting on this Küng writes,

> God is not only the All-Mighty, creator, the Just Judge, but also the All-Merciful. Most *surahs* are proclaimed 'In the name of God, the Most Gracious, the Most Merciful.' *Ar-rahman*, 'the one, who has mercy' or 'the merciful,' became almost a kind of proper name for God.[59]

Küng's assertion is verified in Surah 17:110 that says, "Call upon Allah, or call upon Rahman: by whatever name you

---

[57] Hans Küng, *Islam: Past, Present and Future*. (Oxford: One World, 2007), 77-78.

[58] Karen Armstrong, *A History of God: The 4,000-Year Quest of Judaism, Christianity and Islam*. (New York: Ballantine Books, 1993), 149.

[59] Küng, *Islam: Past, Present and Future*, 84.

call upon him, it is well: for to Him alone belong the Most Beautiful Names."

2.2.1.2. Belief in Angels.

The second doctrine of belief in Islam is the belief in Angels who are genderless and are made of light. The angels are messengers and helpers of God. There are good and bad angels. The head of the evil or bad angels is Satan (*Iblīs*) who was cast out of heaven after he refused God's command to bow down to Adam (Surah 7:11-18). *Iblīs* has a great host of evil followers of angelic origin.[60] The good angels are more numerous, and they have different missions. Angel Gabriel brought the divine message to Mohammad. Two angels (*Kiraaman* and *Katibeen*) are assigned to record the actions of human beings; the angel of death (Azrael) takes the soul out of the body upon death. Angels *Munkir* and *Nakir* question each person on the Day of Judgment.[61]

As part of the unseen spiritual world, which interacts intimately with humanity, belief in Angels is essential in Islam. The Qur'an makes "at least eighty-one references to angels to show how very importance they are."[62] Some of the references to Angels in Qur'an are *Surahs* 35:1; 2:177; 2:285; 4:136; 22:75.

---

[60] Denny, *An Introduction to Islam*, 98
[61] Hakim, *Basic Beliefs of Islam*,3
[62] Suzanne Haneef, *Islam: The Path of God*. (Chicago: Kazi Publications, Inc., 1996), 25.

2.2.1.3. Belief in Scriptures.

Muslims are required to believe in four books; the Torah, given through Moses; the Psalms, given through David; the Gospel, given through Jesus; and the Qur'an, given through Mohammad. The first three books, according to Islam, have been altered in time by their followers, leaving the Qur'an as the purest and only unaltered book. Muslims believe that the Qur'an is the only book that can never be distorted as God has himself taken the responsibility of its protection, "We have, without doubt, sent down the Message; and we will assuredly guard it (from corruption)." (15:9)

Writing on this belief, Denny says:

> All scriptures are entirely God's, but peoples before Islam—the Jews and Christians—had corrupted their original message to suit their inclinations. The Qur'an, then, is the purest extant scripture on earth, because it has been preserved from tampering. God sent it as a mercy to humankind, so that they might be brought back to the original true faith of Abraham. Moses was given the Tawrāt (Torah), David the Zabūr (Psalms), and Jesus the Injīl (Gospel).[63]

Though Muslims accept the Bible as scripture, they do not regard its present form as authentic and reliable.[64] The only authentic and reliable scripture is the Qur'an.

---

[63]   Denny, *An Introduction to Islam*, 98
[64]   Haneef, *Islam: The Path of God*, 27

2.2.1.4. Belief in Prophets.

Islam believes that God had sent prophets to every nation and culture at one time or the other. These prophets spoke to their people in their native tongues. Allah, as recorded in the Qur'an, revealed to the Prophet Muhammad thus, "To every people was sent a messenger . . . We did not send a messenger except to teach in the language of his own people, in order to make things clear to them."[65]

There have been hundreds of prophets, according to Islamic tradition, throughout various ages, and nations before the visible manifestation of the Prophet Muhammad. As expressed by Seyyed Nasr, "there are one hundred and twenty-four thousand prophets whom God sent before Muhammad."[66] It is the general belief in Islam that there is a link between all these prophets and Muhammad. The idea of prophecy in Islam is that Prophethood is indivisible, and the Qur'an requires recognition of all prophets as such without discrimination. Yet not all the prophets are of equal dignity and mission; some of them are particularly outstanding in qualities of steadfastness and patience under trials. Abraham, Noah, Moses, and Jesus were such great prophets.[67]

In Islam, the prophets are categorized into three groups: those who only received the message from God; those who, in addition to receiving the message, have a divine mandate to propagate the message they received; and those who, in addition to the two groups, established new religions based on the message and mandate they received from God. In the words of Nasr:

---

[65] Surah 10:47; 14:4
[66] Seyyed Hosseein Nasr, *Ideals and Realities of Islam*. (Pakistan: Suhail Academy, 1993), 86.
[67] Fazlur Rahman, *Prophecy in Islam: Philosophy and Orthodoxy*. (Chicago: University of Chicago Press, 1979), 13

Although all prophecy implies a meeting of the Divine and human planes, there are degrees of prophecy dependent upon the type of message revealed and the function of the messenger in propagating that message . . . There is first of all the *nabi*, a man who brings news of God's message, a man whom God has chosen to speak to . . . But the message which he receives is not necessarily universal. He may receive a message which is to remain within him and not be divulged openly or is meant to be imparted to only a few in the cadre of an already existing religion . . . There are those who belong to another category of prophets, or a new level of prophecy, namely those who not only receive a message from heaven but are also chosen to propagate that message for the segment of humanity providentially destined for it. The prophet with such a function is called the *rasul*. He is also a *nabi* . . . Above the *rasul* stands the prophet who is to bring a major new religion to the world, the 'possessor of firmness and determination' *(ulu'l-'azm)* . . There are then all together three grades of prophecy, that of the *nabi,* the *rasul* and the *ulu'l-'azm* . . .The Prophet (Muhammad) was at once a *nabi*, a *rasul* and *ulu'l-'azm.*[68]

Although God has spoken in the past through prophets, in Islam Muhammad is believed to be the last and the greatest of all the prophets. This Islamic idea of Muhammad as the last and greatest of all the prophets is succinctly captured in the following words:

---

[68]   Nasr, *Ideals and Realities of Islam,* 85-87

The particularity of the Prophet, which distinguished him from those, that came before him is that he is the last of the prophets, the seal of prophecy who, coming at the end of the prophetic cycle, integrates in himself the function of prophecy as such ... and brought the cycle of prophecy to a close. After him there will be no new *sharia* or Divine Law brought into world until the end of time. There will be no revelation after him, for he marks the termination of the prophetic cycle.[69]

Islam frowns at anyone within the religion who claims to be a prophet or to have received a new revelation from Allah after the Prophet Muhammad. For instance, one of the reasons, among other things, which led to the Baha'i group breaking away from Islam to becoming an autonomous religion is their claim and belief that prophecy did not end with the Prophet Muhammad, and that Husayn Ali, who assumed the name *Bahaullah* (the glory of God) is the promised messiah after Muhammad.[70] In the words of Hopfe and Woodward, Baha'is believe that,

Divine revelation is a continuous and progressive process and that the mission of messengers of God represents successive stages in the spiritual growth of humanity. Baha'is believed that Bahaullah is the most recent messenger of God, with God's message for humankind today.[71]

---

[69] Ibid, 84-85
[70] Hopfe and Woodward, *Religions of the World*, 369.
[71] Ibid.

In Islam, this is unacceptable.

2.2.1.5. Belief in Resurrection/Last Judgment.

Muslims believe that after the end of the world every human will be resurrected from the grave. They will be held accountable for whatever they have done in their lives. The day is known as the Day of Judgment. On this day, justice will be done to every individual soul. The innocent ones will stay in Heaven, whereas the corrupted ones will go to hell. This day is unknown to anyone on earth and it will be catastrophic. According to Mary Fisher, "At that unknown time of the final judgment, the world will end cataclysmically: 'The earth will shake and the mountains crumble into heaps of shifting sand,' (Surah 73:14); then comes the terrible confrontation with one's own life."[72]

Describing the belief in the resurrection and the last day, Denny writes,

> The last Judgment is set forth in many Qur'anic passages as the denouement of the historical process. It is known by such names as "the Day of Doom" (*yaum al-din*), "the Last Day" (*al-yaum al-akhir*), "the Day of Resurrection" (*yaum al-qiyama*), "the Hour", "the Day of Distinguishing" (the saved from the damned), and others. The final judgment period descends swiftly, heralded by a peal of thunder, a shout, or a trumpet blast.[73]

---

[72] Mary Pat Fisher, *Living Religions*, 6th ed. (New Jersey: Prentice Hall, 2005), 377.

[73] Denny, *An Introduction to Islam*, 100.

2.2.1.6. Belief in Predestination/Free will.

This is one of the main aspects of Islam. It is also called Divine Decree. Muslims believe that unlike living beings, God is not limited by anything; even time. Everything that has happened, is happening, or will happen is evident to Him. Living beings are given a free choice to do whatever they want, but God knows what choices they will make. However, God's knowing does not restrict anyone from making a free choice.

This doctrine, says Denny, has been one of the most frequently and passionately discussed of all Islamic tenets.[74] Explaining this belief of Divine Decree, Haneef writes,

> While this is the last of Islam's articles of faith, it is of greatest importance for our lives. It can be summed up in one brief, comprehensive sentence: All things, both good and evil, proceed from God Most High. But what does this actually mean? In summary, this statement tells us that all things proceed from a single unified Will and Command—God's. Nothing is outside it . . . Good is part of His plan and so is evil—or what seems evil to our limited perspective. Consequently, whatever happens has been permitted and decreed by God; conversely, if something does not happen, it is because He did not permit or decree it.[75]

On this belief, the Qur'an states: "Nothing can happen to us except what Allah has decreed for us: He is our protector, and on Allah let believers put their trust." (9:51)

---

74 Ibid, 102.
75 Haneef, *Islam: The Path of God*, 58

2.2.2 The five (six) pillars of faith

The edifice of Islamic religious belief and social practice rests on the five (or six) pillars of faith, underlined by the Prophet Muhammad in his last address at Arafat and through which the message of God is understood.[76] Writing on the pillars of faith, Andrew Rippin says,

> For classical Islam, the notion of the "five pillars" represents the epitome of the revealed law as enacted through ritual activity. The five actions—witness of faith (shahadah), prayer (salat), almsgiving (zakat), fasting (sawn), and pilgrimage (hajj)—are duties for which an individual is responsible, separate from general ethics and rules for interpersonal relationships. They are an integral part of the belief system of Islam, being a part of the explication of the theological statements of belief from at least the tenth century onwards, as illustrated by the work of al-Baghdadi (d. 1037).[77]

We shall proceed to explain each of these pillars.

2.2.2.1. Testimony of Faith: *Shahadah.*

The *Shahadah* is a simple statement declaring belief, bearing witness in one God, and accepting Muhammad as the messenger. It goes this way:

---

[76] Akbar S. Ahmed, *Islam Today: A Short Introduction to the Muslim World.* (New York: I. B. Tauris, 1999), 32.

[77] Andrew Rippin, *Muslims: Their Religious Beliefs and Practices*, 3rd ed. (New York: Routedge, 2005), 103.

*La illaha illa Allah. Muhammadu al rasul
Allah*
No god but God. Muhammad is his
messenger.[78]

The testimony of faith is not simply an affirmation of the
existence of God, but an acknowledgement and belief that
Allah is the only true God, true reality and perfection,
and that Muhammad is the last and most authoritative
messenger of God to humankind. This testimony is the
gateway into the religion and the essence of Islamic belief
and life. According to Denny,

> This "testimony," known in Arabic as *shahada*,
> is the closest thing to a creed in Islam. It is
> sufficient to simply utter it once in one's life,
> freely and as a believer, to become a Muslim.
> Then all of the other elements of belief and
> the prescribed duties become immediately
> incumbent on the one who has testified by
> means of the shahada.[79]

This testimony is given repeatedly throughout the day when
the *muezzin* calls the faithful to prayer. It "affirms Islam's
absolute monotheism, an unshakable and uncompromising
faith in the oneness or unity of God, as well as trust and
faith in His messenger, Muhammad"[80]

---

[78]   Denny, *An Introduction to Islam*, 97
[79]   Ibid.
[80]   Esposito: *Islam: The Straight Path*, 88.

2.2.2.2. Prayer: Salāt.

Salāt (prayer or worship) is the foundation of Islamic devotion. Salāt is "an intense, highly regulated, formal observance that features cycles of bodily postures climaxing in complete prostration in an orientation facing the qibla toward the Kaaba in Mecca."[81] It is obligatory for Muslims to pray five times a day and each prayer takes about five to ten minutes. The prayer times are "early morning (*salāt al-fajr*), noon (*salāt al-duhr*), mid-afternoon (*salāt al-'asr*), sunset (*salāt al-maghrib*), and evening or night (*salāt al-'ishā')*."[82] In addition to these prayer times is the mandatory (in some Islamic nations) Friday midday (congregational) prayer (*salāt al-juma*) that features a sermon.[83]

Every prayer time starts with a "call to prayer by a *muezzin*, who climbs up a tower in the local mosque and calls out a chant to remind Muslims to pray."[84] In most places today, the call to prayer is done electronically. More importantly, every prayer begins with a ritual washing or purification known as ablution. Hence, the premise or the key for prayer is purification from any form of ritual impurity. This is not primarily a hygienic regulation but a symbolic purification of the person who comes before God in worship. The ritual washing of hands, mouth, nose, and face, arms to the elbow, head and feet, achieves this purification or ablution. Expressing the essence of ablution before prayer, Denny writes, "Purification according to Muhammad is half the faith. In another place, the Prophet said, the key to paradise is prayer (*salāt*) and the key to

---

[81] Denny, *An Introduction to Islam*, 109.
[82] Ibid, 110
[83] Ibid.
[84] Mary Pope Osborne, *One World Many Religions: The Ways We Worship*. (New York: Alfred A. Knopf, 1996), 33.

prayer is purification. Unless you are pure you may not perform the *salāt*."[85] Accordingly, the Qur'an expresses:

> O you who believe! When you prepare for prayer, wash you faces and hands (and arms) to the elbow; rub your heads (with water); and wash your feet to the ankles. If you are in state of ceremonial impurity, bathe your whole body. (5:6)[86]

With the ritual washing, the worshipper enters the mosque or place of prayer for the *salāt*. According to Nanji,

> The pattern of *salāt* may be divided into seven steps: The first step consists of facing the *qiblah* (Mecca), raising one's hands to the ears, and pronouncing the *takbir*, or recitation of praise: "God is Great" (*Allahu Akbar*). The worshipper remains silent, readying his attention for the performance of the prayer. During the second step, known as the "standing," the chapter *al-Fatiha* is recited together with additional verses from the Qur'an. With the recitation of another *takbir*, the worshipper bows, with his hands on his knees, and in his bent position, praises God. After assuming the standing position, the worshipper prostrates himself, with his head touching the ground, as a sign of humility and submission. The fifth step

---

[85] Denny, *An Introduction to Islam*, 103-104

[86] The following acts constitute ceremonial impurities in Islam: Emission of semen, menstrual flow, sexual acts before prayer, vomiting, touching a corpse, and in some tradition using the restroom shortly before prayer.

involves raising oneself from prostration while reciting another *takbir* and remaining in a sitting position, praying. There follows another act of prostration, when the praises of God are repeated. The final step involves the sitting position and silent recitation of prayer, after which the individual worshippers turn their faces to the right and left to greet their neighbors. This greeting, or *Salam*, concludes the prayer proper.[87]

As explained by Akbar Ahmed, "the daily prayers help Muslims to remember God and prevent them from incorrect or wicked acts. By bowing their heads to the ground Muslims accept the omnipotence of God. It also encourages humility and the notion of equality. The prayer helps them transcend the mundane and the everyday."[88] Stressing more on the essence of prayer in Islam, Küng writes,

> If the typical symbol for Jews must still be the pious Jew with the Torah scroll and for Christians the Eucharist, for Islam it is the shared ritual prayer of Muslims as they prostrate themselves before God with their forehead touching the ground. This is a tangible expression of the central concern for Islam: not a new social system nor a political ideology, not an anthropology nor even a theology, but rather the quite practical surrender to God which is expressed in prayer, in the attitude of faith and in particular rites and obligations.[89]

---

[87] Nanji, *Islam*, 320-321.

[88] Ahmed, *Islam Today*, 33

[89] Küng, *Islam: Past, Present and Future*, 78.

In prayer, God and only God is praised and worshiped, and there is no mediator. While *salāt* is obligatory for all Muslims, *du'a* (voluntary prayer) and *dhikr* (remembrance of God), though types of prayer, are not obligatory but are encouraged of all Muslims as a way of drawing closer to God.

2.2.2.3. Almsgiving: *Zakat.*

The word *Zakat* means "to grow" or "to purify." It literally means to gain Allah's blessings and purify the wealth by helping the needy.[90] Muslims believe that everything belongs to God, whether it is money, possessions, or even children. Humans hold wealth in trust. *Zakat* therefore has the notion of giving back to God what belongs to him in a spirit of gratitude by giving to the poor. It is thus obligatory for all Muslims to give *zakat* from all their property. Again, *zakat* has the notion of a tax that each Muslim is obliged to pay once a year, and the rate is at least 2.5% of one's total income. According to Ahmed,

> At the end of year Muslims must give some of the wealth for good causes or to help the poor. The amount of *zakat* a Muslim pays varies with the individual's wealth. The rates are fixed: Muslims must give at least 2.5 of their money/assets; farmers at least 5 percent of their crops and a number of animals; traders at least 2.5 percent of the value of their goods.[91]

---

[90]   David Waines, *An Introduction to Islam*, 2nd ed. (Cambridge: Cambridge Press, 2003), 47.

[91]   Ahmed, *Islam Today,* 34.

Zakat is primarily for the poor and needy, but it is also meant for debtors who have fallen into difficulty which is not of their own making, for volunteers who fight for the faith and for travelers without means. This notion is expressed in the Qur'an:

> Alms are for the poor and the needy, and those employed to administer the (funds); for those whose hearts have been (recently) reconciled (to Truth); for those in bondage and in debt; in the cause of Allah; and for the wayfarer: (thus is it) ordained by Allah, and Allah is full of knowledge and wisdom. (Surah 9:60)

Islam distinguishes between obligatory alms (*zakat*) and voluntary charity (*sadaqa*). *Zakat* is obligatory; it is a legal almsgiving, while *sadaqa* is recommended of all Muslims, but not obligatory.[92]

Furthermore, in Islam, *zakat* and *salāt* have been associated from earliest time.

While salat implies the vertical relationship with God through worship, zakat implies the horizontal relationship with humans through almsgiving. Allah commanded all Muslims to "be steadfast in prayer (salāt); and practice regular almsgiving (zakat)." (Surah 2:83)

It is important to note that through the performance of Zakat, Muslims further mutual solidarity in the *Ummah* (Islamic community), and help to reduce the social contrasts by balancing things out between the well-to-do and the needy.

---

[92] Denny, *An Introduction to Islam*, 115.

2.2.2.4. Fasting: *Sawm.*

It is obligatory for all Muslims to fast, except for those who are legally exempt. Allah says: "O ye who believe! Fasting is prescribed to you as it was prescribed to those before you, that ye may (learn) self-restraint." (2:183) The exempt include the following, "Those who are very old or sick, or on a journey, or women in menstruation, and children who have not reached puberty."[93]

Fasting takes place during the ninth month of the Islamic (lunar) calendar, which is called Ramadan. According to the Qur'an:

> Ramadan is the (month) in which was sent down the Qur'an, as a guide to mankind, also as clear (Signs) for guidance and judgment (between right and wrong). So every one of you who is present (at his home) during that month should spend it in fasting, but if any one is ill, or on a journey, the prescribed period (Should be made up) by days later. (Surah 2:185)

This fast of Ramadan, as it is often called begins "with the sighting of the new moon,"[94] and it is from dawn to sunset throughout the period. The notion of fasting in Islam goes beyond refraining from food. As expressed by Ahmed,

> Fasting is not just refraining from food and drink; there must be no sexual intercourse, no tobacco, no backbiting, and no lying and

---

[93]   Ahmed, *Islam Today,* 35.

[94]   Andrew Rippin and Jan Knappert, *Textual Sources for the Study of Islam.* (Chicago: University of Chicago Press, 1986), 92.

so on. If, however, a Muslims eats or drinks something by mistake, then the fast may be continued as before and it is not nullified. If the fast is broken intentionally it must be compensated for by keeping a number of consecutive fasts or feeding poor people.[95]

After sunset, fasting is broken with prayer and celebration. The fast of Ramadan, apart from being a period of prayer, of contemplation, of good deeds and testing of self to the limits,[96] is also a time of celebration. As observed by Küng,

Ramadan is a time of feasting, full of countless religious and social activities in mosques, coffee houses [and homes]. It is a time of feasting and celebrating for the whole Muslim community, a great symbol of unity of Muslims all over the world and an invitation to non-Muslims to join the Ummah. Like its beginning, the end of Ramadan is established by the sighting of the new moon and the feast of the breaking of fast ('id al-fitr), one of the two main Islamic festivals.[97]

Muslims look forward to this period of the year with much enthusiasm.

---

[95] Ahmed, *Islam Today*, 34-35.
[96] Ibid, 36.
[97] Küng, *Islam: Past, Present and Future*, 135.

2.2.2.5. Pilgrimage: *Hajj.*

Hajj literally means to "set out for a place."[98] Religiously, *hajj* is the pilgrimage to Mecca, which every physically and financially able Muslim is expected to perform at least once in a lifetime. Millions of believers from all over the world participate in the ritual irrespective of their caste, color, creed or tradition. It tears down the difference of social status and brings all the Muslims on one platform. *Hajj,* as explained by Denny, is observed on the eighth through the twelfth days of the *Dhu al-Hijjah* (the 12th and the final month of the Islamic calendar).[99]

Muslims are not expected to borrow money for the performance of *Hajj.* The basic site of the *Hajj* is the Kaaba, but there are other sites like Arafat, and the Mountain of light. Before embarking on the *Hajj*, one's will is drawn and goodbye to ones family is said in case of death. This is a symbol of submission to the will of Allah.

Hajj is surrounded by a number of significant rituals. According to J. L. Menezes,

> As soon as the pilgrims arrive in the outskirts of Mecca, they put off their ordinary clothes, and after performing the ordinary purifications and prayers, put on the Ihram or pilgrim's gab consisting of two pieces of white cloth, one girding the waist and the other thrown over the shoulders,

---

[98] Ahmad, Kamal, *The Sacred Journey, Being a Pilgrimage to Mecca.* (New York: Duell, Sloan and Pearce, 1961), 45.

[99] Denny, *An Introduction to Islam,* 121

and with sandals on their feet, and head uncovered.[100]

The wearing of the *ihram* (the two of pieces of cloth) by the pilgrims is very significant. It reinforces basic Islamic principles of equality of all humans in the eyes of God. It further removes all worldly ranks. Again, the cloth reminds Muslims that they must be willing to give everything to God. It is also a reminder that dead people are wrapped in a similar sheet. After death, all fine cloths and wealth are of no value.[101] Women may wear their everyday clothes during the *hajj*,[102] but they must cover themselves from head to ankles. The hajj proper lasts for five days. As explained by Ahmed,

> On the first day, beginning at Makkah (Mecca), Muslims walk seven times around the Kaaba . . . The pilgrims then go to two small hillocks nearby. Here (the small hill) God had wished to test Abraham by ordering him to leave his wife Hagar and son Ismail, a progenitor to the Arabs . . . Then, the pilgrims spend the night at Mina. At dawn they move to the valley of Arafat. After sunset the pilgrims leave to spend the night at Muzdalifat. Part of the evening is spent hunting for small stones for the next

---

[100] J. L. Menezes, *The Life and Religion of Mohammad the Prophet of Arabia.* (New York: Roman Catholic Books, 2004), 134.

[101] Ahmed, *Islam Today,* 37.

[102] The wearing of every day cloths, mostly native attires, by women during the hajj is an expression of the rich cultural diversity and at the same time, unity that is found in Islam. Though, from many cultures, all are gathered together under Allah during the hajj.

part of the hajj, another ritual tracing back to Abraham. On returning to Mina, they set off for the three stone pillars which mark the place where the devil attempted to make Ismail disobey Abraham. Muslims believe that Ismail drove the devil away by throwing stones at him. In memory of that incident Muslims throw their stones at the pillars. It is symbolic of rejecting evil and wishing to follow God. The pilgrimage ends with the festival when animals are sacrificed. This custom again goes back to Abraham, who had been willing to sacrifice his son [Ismail] on God's command . . . Finally, pilgrims circle the Kaaba once more. Those who can afford it go on to Medina to visit the burial place of the Prophet and pray there.[103]

On returning home, a pilgrim is addressed as *Alhaji* or *Alhaja* (if a woman). In Nigeria, the federal, state and local governments sponsor about 75% percent of those who perform the *Hajj* yearly.

2.2.2.6. Jihad.

Some Islamic scholars include *jihad* among the pillars of Islam, making it the sixth pillar or act of worship.[104] This inclusion is perhaps because of the binding obligation of jihad (which is wrongly translated as "holy war") on all Muslims.

From the point of view of Islamic orthodoxy, and based on official teachings of Islamic authority, *jihad* does not

---

[103] Ibid, 37-38.
[104] Denny, *An Introduction to Islam*, 126.

mean war or holy war. According to Suzanne Haneef, "The Arabic word *jihad* means striving."[105] It is from the Arabic root of this word that its proper religious meaning is drawn in Islam. *Jihad*, therefore,

> In its primary religious connotation (sometimes referred to as the greater jihad), means the struggle of the soul to overcome the sinful obstacles that keep a person from God...However, because Islam considers this inward struggle for holiness and submission to be inseparable from the outward struggle for the welfare of humanity, jihad has more often been associated with its secondary connotation (the lesser jihad); that is, any exertion—military or otherwise—against oppression and tyranny.[106]

Expressed in another way, Haneef said,

> The greater jihad [is] within the self. Consequently, when we are serious about our religion, we are involved in a life-long struggle between our souls and its enemies: Satan, our *nafs,* its passions, and worldly attractions. Part of this struggle involves fighting against negativity and destructive energies, which are tools of Satan, both within ourselves and in our surroundings."[107]

---

[105] Haneef, *Islam: The Path of God*, 128.

[106] Reza Aslan, *No god But God* (New York: Random House, Inc., 2006), 81

[107] Haneef, *Islam the Path of God*, 128.

One thing that should be emphasized is that this striving or struggle is not for selfish purposes. For it to be a *jihad,* it must be in the cause of Allah. As such, "All everyday struggles in life to please God can be considered jihad. The struggle to build a good Muslim society is a kind of *jihad* . . . Self-control is also a great jihad. Taking up arms in defense of Islam is also a kind of jihad."[108]

Rather than meaning holy war as often times erroneously defined, *Jihad* could simply be defined as a holy striving towards perfection. Accordingly, Khaled Fadl writes,

> Jihad is a core principle in Islamic theology . . . In many ways jihad connotes a strong spiritual and material work ethic in Islam. Piety, knowledge, health, beauty, truth, and justice are not possible without jihad—that is, without sustained and diligent hard work. Therefore, cleansing oneself from vanity and pettiness, pursuing knowledge, curing the ill, feeding the poor, and standing up for truth and justice, even at great personal risk, are all forms of jihad.[109]

In the case of physical combat or lesser *jihad*, there are rules and restrictions.

According to Janin and Kahlmeyer,

> The classical medieval theory of jihad contained elaborate rules for the onset, conduct, interruption and cessation of war,

---

[108] Mark Water, *Encyclopedia of World Religions, Cults, and Occult* (Tennessee: A. M. G. Publishers, 2006), 121.

[109] Khaled Abou El Fadl, *The Great Theft: Wrestling Islam from the Extremists.* (New York: HarperCollins Publishers, 2007), 221.

for the use of weapons, and the treatment of prisoners. No war could be considered a jihad unless it was formally authorized and led by the legitimate religious leader. Islam's enemies were to be given fair warning before they were attacked.[110]

Highlighting some of the rules guiding the proper application of a *jihad* according to Islamic orthodoxy, Aslan said,

> Thus, the killing of women, children, monks, rabbis, the elderly, or any other noncombatant was absolutely forbidden under any circumstances. Muslim law eventually expanded on these prohibitions to outlaw the torture of prisoners of war; the mutilation of the dead; rape, molestation, or any kind of sexual violence during combats; the killing of diplomats, the wanton destruction of property, and the demolition of religious or medical institutions . . . [111]

Islam strictly forbids fighting and killing, except in self—defense, especially, in matters of faith, oppression and injustice. The Qur'an, 2:190 is quite clear on this, "Fight in the cause of Allah those who fight you, but do not transgress limits; for Allah does not love transgressors."[112] Consequently, "Acts of terrorism or attacks on civilians are

---

[110] Hunt Janin and Andre Kahlmeyer, *Islamic Law: The Sharia from Muhammad's Time to the Present.* (Jefferson: McFarland &Company, Inc., 2007), 108.

[111] Aslan, *No god But God,* 84.

[112] The Holy Quran, 2: 190.

strictly prohibited and detestable in Islam, even if they should be done by individuals claiming to be Muslims."[113]

In Islam, faith and good works go hand-in-hand. A mere verbal declaration of faith is not enough; it must be seen in action. Muslims consider everything they do in life to be an act of worship, if it is done according to Allah's guidance. They strike a balance by fulfilling the obligations of and enjoying this life, while always mindful of their duties to Allah and to others.

2.3 BASIC BELIEFS AND DOCTRINES OF CHRISTIANITY.

Christianity as a religion in Nigeria and the world-over encompasses a wide range of denominations and faith groups, and each subscribes to its own set of doctrinal positions. However, a look at the history of Christianity from its origin through the patristic period reveals a set of belief systems in the form of creeds. Creeds are the "foundational statements of normative Christian belief."[114] The two creeds that contain the deposit of basic Christian belief are the Apostles' Creed and the Nicene Creed. The Apostles' Creed is "the earliest known Christian creed, dating back to some time in the second, or even first, century AD. Though not written by the apostles, it is thought to reflect their teaching."[115] The Apostles' Creed reads:

I believe in God, the Father Almighty,

---

[113] Haneef, *Islam the Path of God*, 98.
[114] Anthony E. Gilles, *The People of the Creed: The Story Behind the Early Church.* (New York: St Anthony Messenger Press, 1985), 2.
[115] Mark Water, *Encyclopedia of World Religions, Cults and the Occult.* (Tennessee: AMG Publishers, 2006), 39.

the Maker of heaven and earth,
and in Jesus Christ, His only Son, our Lord:
Who was conceived by the Holy Ghost,
    born of the Virgin Mary,
    suffered under Pontius Pilate,
    was crucified, dead, and buried;
He descended into hell.
    The third day He arose again from the dead;
He ascended into heaven,
    and sitteth on the right hand of God the Father Almighty;
    from thence he shall come to judge the quick and the dead.
I believe in the Holy Ghost;
    the holy Catholic Church;
    the communion of saints;
    the forgiveness of sins;
    the resurrection of the body;
    and the life everlasting.
Amen.[116]

The Nicene Creed (325 CE) was formulated at the first ecumenical Christian Council to counter Arianism; a heresy propagated by Arius, a priest of Alexandria who denied the divinity of Christ.[117] It was established to identify conformity of beliefs among Christians, as a means of recognizing heresy or deviations from orthodox biblical doctrines, and as a public profession of faith.[118] The content of this creed was revised and expanded in the council of Constantinople

---

[116] Henry Bettenson, *The Early Christian Fathers*. (New York: Oxford University Press, 1982), 141

[117] Robert Broderick, *The Catholic Encyclopedia*. (New York: Thomas Nelson Publishers, 1976), 423-424.

[118] Gilles, *The People of the Creed: The Story Behind the Early Church*, 79.

(381 CE) to express belief in the divinity of Holy Spirit. The Nicene Creed reads:

> We believe in one God,
> the Father, the Almighty,
> maker of heaven and earth,
> of all that is, seen and unseen.
> We believe in one Lord, Jesus Christ,
> the only son of God,
> eternally begotten of the Father,
> God from God, Light from Light,
> true God from true God,
> begotten, not made,
> of one being with the Father.
> Through him all things were made.
> For us and for our salvation
> he came down from heaven:
> by the power of the Holy Spirit
> he became incarnate from the Virgin Mary,
> and was made man.
> For our sake he was crucified under Pontius Pilate;
> he suffered death and was buried.
> On the third day he rose again
> in accordance with the Scriptures;
> he ascended into heaven
> and is seated at the right hand of the Father.
> He will come again in glory
> to judge the living and the dead,
> and his kingdom will have no end.
> We believe in the Holy Spirit, the Lord, the giver of life,
> who proceeds from the Father (and the Son).
> With the Father and the Son
> he is worshipped and glorified.
> He has spoken through the Prophets.
> We believe in one holy catholic and apostolic Church.
> We acknowledge one baptism for the forgiveness of sins.

We look for the resurrection of the dead,
and the life of the world to come. AMEN [119]

These two creeds are the most widely accepted statements of faith among Christian churches. They contain the profession of faith common to the Roman Catholics, Eastern Orthodox, Anglican, Lutheran and most Protestant churches and denominations.

Extracting from the creeds, the following are the basic beliefs central to almost all Christian faiths in Nigeria. They are presented here as the core doctrines of Christianity. A small number of faith groups, who consider themselves to be within the framework of Christianity, do not accept some of these beliefs. It should also be understood that slight variances, exceptions, and additions to these doctrines could exist within certain faith groups that fall under the broad umbrella of Christianity in Nigeria.

a) Belief in One God.
b) Belief in the Trinity.
c) Belief in Jesus Christ.
d) Belief in the Holy Spirit.
e) Belief in the Authority of the Scripture.
f) Belief in Moral Integrity, and Community Life.
g) Belief in the Last Things (Eschatology): Death, Judgment, Heaven and Hell.

We shall proceed to explain each of these core beliefs in detail.

---

[119] Wilhelm Joseph, "The Nicene Creed," in *The New Advent Catholic Encyclopedia*. Vol. 11 (New York: Robert Appleton Company, 1911), 1106.

2.3.1. Belief in one God.

Christianity is a monotheistic religion that expresses belief in one God who alone is worshipped. The Apostles' Creed and the Nicene Creed both open with the statement of belief in One God who is the maker and creator of heaven and earth. This affirmation is the most fundamental belief in Christianity. The other articles of the Creeds are all dependent upon the belief in God. As expressed in the *Catechism of the Catholic Church* (CCC), "The confession of God's oneness, which has its roots in the divine revelation of the Old Covenant is fundamental to Christian belief. God is unique; there is only one God: the Christian faith confesses that God is one in nature, substance, and essence."[120]

Emphasizing the oneness of God, Francis Ripley writes,

> Not only that He is one in that He is absolutely indivisible, but also He is one in that there is no other like Himself, no other God. "The Lord, our God, is one Lord." (*Deut.6:4*). "I alone am, and there is no other besides Me." (*Deut. 32:39*).[121]

Christians believe that God had no beginning, and will have no end, for He is eternal. The Christian God has revealed himself through history: First to the people of Israel, and finally through Jesus Christ. In the words of Geoffrey Parrinder, "Christianity is a way of life centered on the

---

[120] *Catechism of the Catholic Church.* (CCC) (Vatican: Libreria Editrice Vaticana, 1994) n. 200. (Henceforth this is cited as CCC.

[121] Francis Ripley, *This is the Faith.* (Rockford: Tan Books and Publishers, Inc.,2002), 4.

worship of the One God revealed to the world through Jesus of Nazareth."[122]

The Bible in many passages attests to the belief in one God. Isaiah 44: 6 states: "Thus says the Lord: I am the first and the last; there is no other God besides Me." (cf. also Isaiah 43:10; 44: 8; Mk.12:29-30; John 17:3; 1 Corinthians 8:5-6; Galatians 4:8-9).

Besides being the creator of everything that exists (Genesis 1:1; Isaiah 44:24), God is omniscient (Acts 15:18; 1 John 3:20), God is omnipotent (Psalm 115:3; Revelation 19:6). God is omnipresent (Jeremiah 23:23, 24; Psalm 139), God is sovereign (Zechariah 9:14; 1 Timothy 6:15-16), God is holy (1 Peter 1:15), God is just and righteous (Psalm 19:9, 116:5, 145:17; Jeremiah 12:1), God is love (1 John 4:8), God is true (Romans 3:4; John 14:6). God is spirit (John 4:24). God is immutable and He does not change (James 1:17; Malachi 3:6; Isaiah 46:9-10).

It is this belief and faith in God that leads the Christian to turn to him (God) alone as his first origin and his ultimate goal, and neither to prefer anything to him nor to substitute anything for him.

2.3.2. Belief in the Trinity.

Christians believe that the One God who is truly one is at the same time a Trinity, that is "Three Persons in God: God the Father, God the Son and God the Holy Ghost."[123] Belief in the trinity has been one of the essentials and distinguishing doctrines of Christianity. The early Church fathers expressed this belief in their teachings and writings. According to Richard McBrien,

---

[122] Geoffrey Parrinder, *World Religions: From Ancient History to the Present*. (New York: Facts On File, Inc., 1985), 420.

[123] Ripley, *This is the Faith*, 102.

That God is triune is the clear and consistent teaching of the Church fathers and the official magisterium of the Church. The Council of Nicaea (325) testifies to the Church's official faith in "one God, the Father almighty . . . and in one Lord Jesus Christ, the Son of God . . . and in the Holy Spirit." The Council of Constantinople (381) confirmed the faith of Nicaea . . . The teaching of Constantinople was verified the following year at a provincial council in Rome from which appeared *The Tome of Pope Damascus* (d.384), which declared that there is one God of three, coequal, coeternal Persons, each distinct from the other, but not to the point where we have three separate gods.[124]

The doctrine of the Trinity is a mystery;[125] the most sublime mystery of the Christian faith.[126] Hence,

The mystery of the Most Holy Trinity is the central mystery of Christian faith and life. It is the mystery of God in himself. It is therefore the source of other mysteries of faith, the light that enlightens them. It is the most fundamental and essential teaching in the hierarchy of the truths of faith. The whole history of salvation is identical with the history of the way and the means by

---

[124] Richard P. McBrien, *Catholicism.* (New York: HaperCollins Publishers, 1994), 316-317

[125] By mystery, we mean a truth which is above reason, but revealed by God.

[126] Broderick, *The Catholic Encyclopedia*, 584.

which the one true God, Father, Son, and Holy Spirit, reveals himself to men.[127]

Attempting an explanation of Trinity, Ripley said,

> In the Trinity the term "one" applies to the nature; the term "three" applies to person ... In all things the three Divine Persons are equal, yet they are really distinct from one another. Each is God, each is infinitely perfect. Yet the Son comes from the Father, and the Holy Ghost from the Father and the Son. If we think only of the relationship between them, we can say of each Person what we cannot say of either of the other Two. Thus we can say of the Father: "He has begotten the Son"; of the Son, "He is begotten of the Father"; and of the Holy Ghost, "He proceeds from the Father and the Son".[128]

Though the word "Trinity" (first used by Tertullian—ca 155-230)[129] is not mentioned in the Bible, Christians believe that belief in the Trinity is referenced and expressed in the Bible. In the baptism of Jesus in the Jordan, the Father, the Son, and the Holy Spirit are mentioned (Matt. 3:16-17; Mk. 1:9-11; Luk. 3:21-22). The apostles are to make disciples of all nations, baptizing them: "In the name of the Father, and the Son, and of the Holy Ghost." (Matt. 28:19) Again, Christians are blessed in the name of the Trinity: "The grace of the Lord Jesus Christ, the love of God and the fellowship of the Holy Spirit be with you all." (2 Cor. 13:13)

---

[127] CCC, 234.
[128] Ripley, *This is the Faith*, 104-105
[129] Bettenson, *The Early Christian Fathers*, 133-134

Christians believe in a Trinitarian function[130] that sees the Father as the creator, the Son as the redeemer, and the Holy Spirit as the sanctifier.

2.3.3. Belief in Jesus Christ.

Jesus is at the center of the Christian belief. He is the corner stone of Christianity.[131] The most basic belief of the early Christian Church is in the Lordship of Jesus Christ. The statement "Jesus is Lord" (Greek: *kyrios*, Hebrew: *adonai*) is found throughout the New Testament and was one of the earliest Christian confessions of faith. According to Xavier Leon-Dufour,

> An ancient expression of Christian belief, probably the product of the Hellenistic churches is the confession of faith: "Jesus is Lord" (Rom. 10:9; 1 Cor. 12:3; Phil. 2:11), also proclaimed in the liturgical context. Here is no dry formula of faith, but an act of

---

[130] According to Iranaeus (one of the early fathers of the Church), "The Spirit prepares man for the Son of God; the Son leads man to the Father; the Father gives man immortality. Thus God was revealed: for in all these ways God the Father is displayed. The Spirit works, the Son fulfils his ministry, the Father approves" (*Adversus Haereses, iv. xx. 4)*, cited in Henry Bettenson, *The Early Christian Fathers.* (New York: Oxford University Press, 1982), 87.

[131] Robert Bumstead, "Christianity" in *The Religious World: Communities of Faith.* Robert F. Weir, Ed. (New York: Macmillan, 1982), 267.

recognition and of submission to the Lord, which is what Jesus had become.[132]

Christians believe that Jesus is not just Lord, but God. Thomas said to him [the resurrected Jesus], "My Lord and my God!" (Jon 20:28) Though Jesus is the Son of God and the second person in the Trinity, the Father referred to him (Jesus) as God: "But about the Son he [God] says, "Your throne, O God, will last for ever and ever." (Hebrews 1:8) He (Jesus) is God from all eternity: "In the beginning was the Word, and the Word was with God, and the Word was God." (Jon. 1:1). The eternal God (Jesus) in time became man to save man—the incarnation:[133] "The Word took flesh and dwelt among us." (Jon 1:14). Hence, Christians believe that Jesus is truly God and truly man. As stated in the *Catechism of the Catholic Church*,

> Jesus Christ is true God and true man, in the unity of his divine person ... [He] possesses two natures, one divine and the other human, not confused, but united in the one person of God's Son. Christ being true God and true man, has a human intellect and will perfectly attuned and subject to his divine intellect and divine will, which he has in common with the Father and the Holy Spirit. The Incarnation is therefore the mystery of the wonderful union of the divine and human natures in the one person of the Word.[134]

---

[132] Xavier Leon-Dufour, *Dictionary of Biblical Theology*, 2nd ed. (Boston: St. Paul Books and Media, 1995), 268.

[133] Incarnation is the taking of the human nature by the divine Jesus. In this, he became truly man as he is truly divine.

[134] CCC, 480-483)

In addition to the belief and worship of Jesus as God, Christians also believe that Jesus is the Messiah (*Christos* in Greek), the "anointed one" predicted in the Jewish Scriptures.[135] According to the Hebrew prophets, the Messiah is king-like figures from the line of David,[136] who will, among other things, rescue Israel from her oppressors, return Jerusalem to the Jewish people, and usher in an age of peace.[137] Christians believe that these messianic concepts are fulfilled in the person of Jesus, who is rightly, then, surnamed Christ. In the New Testament, affirmations of Jesus as the Messiah are found almost exclusively in the four Gospel narratives and the Acts of the Apostles. The Pauline and other epistles, many of which predate the Gospels, do not attempt to show that Jesus is the Messiah, yet they refer to him almost exclusively as "Christ."[138] In the Gospels, various people identify Jesus as the Messiah, and Jesus himself reinforces this perception. After meeting Jesus, Andrew runs to tell Peter that he has found the Messiah. (Jon 1:41) In a conversation with Jesus, a Samaritan woman says she knows the Messiah is coming. Jesus replies, "I who speak to you am He." (Jon 4:25-26) When Jesus asks his disciples who they think he is, Peter

---

[135] Oskar Skarsaune, *In the Shadow of the Temple: Jewish Influences on Early Christianity.* (Illinois: InterVasity Press, 2002), 305-307 Trinity

[136] Gershom Scholem, *The Messianic Idea in Judaism and Other Essays on Jewish Spirituality.* (New York: Schocken Books, 1995), 18.

[137] Harris Lenowitz, *The Jewish Messiahs: From the Galilee to Crown Heights.* (New York: Oxford University Press, 1998), 23

[138] The Pauline epistles are not theologies on messianism, nor are they an attempt to prove how Jesus is the messiah. They simply affirm and express the belief in Christ who is the Lord and Savior.

answers, "You are the Christ." (Mt 16:16; Mk 8:29; Lk 9:20)

It is also the belief of Christians that the name of Jesus is above every other name, and it is only through him that salvation is made possible, as he is the only way to the Father. (Phil. 2:9-10; Acts. 4:12; Jon 14: 6). Hence, the Christian prayer is made in and through Jesus Christ.

2.3.4. Belief in the Holy Spirit.

The early Christian Church expressed her faith and belief in the Holy Spirit (the third person of the Trinity) in the following words, "We believe in the Holy Spirit, the Lord, the giver of life who proceeds from the Father and the Son. With the Father and the Son he is worshiped and glorified. He has spoken through the Prophets."[139] It should be noted that historically speaking, the "filioque" (that is, the Holy Spirit as also proceeding from the Son) clause was not part of the original Nicene Creed, but was added later in the West.

A formal doctrine of the Holy Spirit did not begin to be developed until the early third century. Tertullian and the Montanist heresy[140] showed the need to distinguish between true and false activities of the Holy Spirit. In the 4th century, a heretical group known as the Pneumatomachi[141] or Macedonians accepted the divinity of Christ (against Arianism) but denied the full divinity of the Holy Spirit. This belief was refuted by St. Basil the Great in his *De Spiritu*

---

[139] CCC, 184

[140] Montanism is a heresy that was propagated by Montanus who proclaimed himself the Advocate, the spirit promised by Christ.

[141] Pneumatomachi is a heretical sect founded by Macedonius that denied the divinity of the Holy Spirit, hence the Pneumatomachi or Combators against the Spirit

Sancto ("On the Holy Spirit") and the Pneumatomachi were condemned by Pope Damasus in 374 and by the Council of Constantinople (canon 1) in 381. It was also at the Council of Constantinople that the divinity of the Holy Spirit was formalized. The doctrine of the Spirit was further elaborated by St. Augustine in his important work *De Trinitate* ("On the Trinity"), in which the Holy Spirit is seen as the bond of union and love between the Father and the Son.[142]

To believe in the Holy Spirit is to profess that the Holy Spirit is one of the persons of the Holy Trinity, consubstantial with the Father and the Son. The Holy Spirit, Christians believe, is at work with the Father and the Son from the beginning to the completion of the plan for our salvation. The Holy Spirit awakens faith in the believer and leads the believer to the Father through Jesus. Christians affirm, in accordance with the scripture that,

> No one can say Jesus is Lord except by the Holy Spirit (1 Cor. 12:3). God has sent the Spirit of his Son into our hearts, crying, Abba Father (Gal. 4:6). This knowledge of faith is possible only in the Holy Spirit: to be in touch with Christ, we must first have been touched by the Holy Spirit. He comes to meet us and kindles faith in us . . . Through his grace; the Holy Spirit is the first to awaken faith in us and to communicate the new life, which is to "know the Father and the one whom he sent, Jesus Christ." (Jon. 17:3)[143]

Again, Christians believe that the Holy Spirits who awakens faith confirms the faith and sanctifies Christians in holiness.

---

[142] Henry Bettenson, *The later Christian Fathers*. (New York: Oxford University Press, 1982), 74-83, 230-236.
[143] CCC, 683-684

He imparts grace and charisms for ministry and evangelism in the Christian community. His presence is active and permanent in the Church. According to Leon-Dufour,

> The principal agent in the sanctification of the Christian, then, is the Holy Spirit. He fills the [Christian] communities with gifts and charisms . . . The fullness and universality of His outpourings signify that the Messianic times have been accomplished since Christ's resurrection (Acts 2:19-38). On the other hand, His coming is bound up with baptism and with faith in the mystery of the dead and risen Christ (Acts 2:38; 10:47; 19:1-7). His presence is permanent, and Paul can affirm that the redeemed are "temples of the Holy Spirit" (1 Cor. 6:11, 20; 1 Cor. 3:16ff) and they have true communion with Him (2 Cor. 13:13). And as "all those whom the Spirit of God animates are sons of God" (Rom. 8:14-17), the Christians are children of God who have the source of the divine holiness always within them.[144]

The Holy Spirit, Christians believe, is the promised advocate, the helper and the comforter promised by Jesus (Jon 14:16, 26; 16:7). He is the promise of the Father (Acts 1:4) that was fulfilled on the great day of Pentecost (Acts. 2:1-13).

---

[144] Leon-Dufour, *Dictionary of Biblical Theology*, 238-284.

2.3.5. Belief in the authority of Scripture.

Christians believe that the Bible is truly the word of God and as such has an authority in the ways Christians relate with God and with one another. They believe that "through biblical stories and poetry the transcendent God is encountered. It is in this meeting with that which is ultimate that the kingdom of God becomes reality for us."[145]

In Christianity, both the Old and New Testaments are accepted as God's word. Jesus and the Apostles frequently cited the Old Testament, also known as Jewish Bible. The New Testament is a collection of twenty-seven books, which record the accounts of Jesus' life, death and resurrection, and the faith of his early followers. The Old Testament and the New Testament together comprise the Christian Bible to which Christians turn for instruction.[146]

The authority of the Bible is established by its own claims. Such declarations as, "Thus says the Lord," or its equivalent, occur so frequently in the OT that it can confidently be asserted that the whole account is dominated by the claim. The NT writers also refer to these Scriptures as having God for their source. In the NT itself both Christ and the gospel are spoken of as "the word of God" and so demonstrate the fact that the tie between the two is a vital and necessary one. As God's word, the Bible consequently carries in itself God's authority over Christians.[147]

---

[145] David Robert Ord and Robert B. Coote, *Is the Bible True? Understanding the Bible Today.* (New York: Orbis Books, 1994), 38.

[146] Eileen Flynn and Gloria Thomas, *Living Faith: An Introduction to Theology*, 2nd Ed. (Kansas City: Sheed and Ward, 1995), 118

[147] Karl Barth, *The Doctrine of the Word of God.* (New York: T. & T. Clark Publishers, 1956), 94

A basic Christian belief about the Bible is that is it inspired by the Holy Spirit (that is, written under the influence and guidance of the Holy Spirit). As expressed by McBrein,

> Inspiration signifies in general the divine origin of the Bible. Because the Bible is believed to be inspired by God, it has an authority equaled by no other written source. It is, in the theological sense, the *norma normans non normata* (the norm which is the standard for all other norms but is not itself subject to a higher norm).[148]

Stressing the inspiration of the Bible and the consequent authority that derives from it, the fathers of the Second Vatican Council (Vatican II) taught:

> The Church has always venerated the divine scriptures . . . It has always regarded and continues to regard the scriptures as the supreme rule of faith. For, since they are inspired by God and committed to writing once and for all time, they present God's own word in an unalterable form, and they make the voice of the Holy Spirit sound again and again in the words of the prophets and apostles. It follows that all the preaching of the Church, as indeed the entire Christian religion, should be nourished and ruled by sacred scripture.[149]

---

[148] McBrien, *Catholicism*, 60

[149] Vatican II, *Dogmatic Constitution on Divine Revelation, Dei Verbum*, 18 November 1965, 21.

The Bible itself in many passages attests to its divine inspiration. For example, in Mk.12:36, Jesus said that David, inspired by the Holy Spirit, referred to him (Christ) as Lord. The clearest statement on the inspiration of Scripture is found in 2 Tim. 3:16: "All scripture is inspired by God, and can profitably be used for teaching, for refuting error, for guiding people's lives and teaching them to be holy." The Bible is, then, the book of God's truth and has a divine authority in all things that pertain to life and godliness in Christianity.

2.3.6. Belief in moral integrity and community life.

The belief in morality and community life is an essential aspect of practical Christianity. This belief translates all the above-mentioned beliefs into action, and determines the state of one's life after death. The Christian concept of morality implies the notions of justice, dignity of human life, peace, love, and harmonious relations in the community. It is the Christian moral teachings that define relationships and obligations of Christians with God, with fellow humans, and within the community. Christian belief in morality has a two-fold dimension: making God's love and presence known in human relations and society, and the eschatological order and reward when the kingdom of God is made manifest. Thus, Christians believe that,

> When God reigns and his Spirit rules, things are right between us. We live relationally as gifts; we are in solidarity with all our brothers and sisters. When the kingdom comes, it marks the end of injustice, the end of destructive and evil relationships, the end of division and alienation, the end of lust and abuse, the end of domination and exploitation. It means that humankind will

be ordered and related as they should be, as they were meant to be, that is, in ways that evidently bespeak the covenant and the presence of God among us. But for that to occur, we have to put certain of our relations in order, our relations to God, to one another, and to the world.[150]

Morality defines the good that should be done and the evil that should be avoided. God made humans moral beings. As expressed in the Catechism of the Catholic Church,

> Deep within his conscience, man discovers a law which he has not laid upon himself but which he must obey. Its voice ever calling him to love and to do what is right and to avoid what is bad, sounds in his heart at the right moment . . . For man has in his heart a law inscribed by God.[151]

The source of the Christian belief and teaching on morality is the Decalogue (The Ten Commandments), given to the Israelites by God through Moses as recorded in the Book of Exodus chapter 20. A synopsis of the 10 commandments, as recited in the Catholic Church, is as follows:

I am the Lord your God; you shall not have strange gods before me.
You shall not take the name of the Lord your God in vain.
Remember to keep holy the Lord's Day
Honor your father and your mother.
You shall not kill.

---

[150] Dick Westley, *Morality and its Beyond.* (Connecticut: Twenty-Third Publications, 1984), 76.
[151] CCC, 1776

You shall not commit adultery.

You shall not steal.

You shall not bear false witness against your neighbor.

You shall not covet your neighbor's wife.

You shall not covet your neighbor's goods.

The Ten Commandments are divided into two groups: the first three deals with humans having a healthy relationship with God, whereas the last seven are about morality especially as it touches interpersonal human relationships. In the New Testament, responding to a Pharisaic question on which of the commandments is the greatest, Jesus summarized the commandments into two: The love of God above all things and the love of neighbor as one love one's self.[152] As expressed by Dick Westley, "As Christians we are always thought to have a very special vocation. First, we were supposed to come to know personally the God of love as revealed in Jesus and then we are to make that God and his love known to the world."[153]

Jesus, by his teachings and examples of life, laid a foundation for the Christian's moral life and commitment in the community. As expressed by Arnold Hunt and Robert Crotty,

> Jesus' ministry of forgiveness, his teaching, his healing, his bringing of light and peace to the needy, advocating for justice, his unremitting judgment of evil and falsity, and his example of holiness, became the exemplar for the lives of Christians. Jesus, throughout his life and in his death on the cross, had given himself totally in the battle of good against evil, in the final endeavor of the

---

[152] Cf. Matt. 22: 34-40.

[153] Westley, *Morality and its Beyond,* 87.

Father to bring about the rule of peace and righteousness upon earth. So, too, Christians had to re-enact the self-giving of Jesus by their own love and forgiveness, patience, mercy, holiness, and forbearance.[154]

A classical text on the moral and social teachings of Christianity is the golden rule of Matthew 7:12: "Always treat others as you would like them to treat you."

Again, Christians believe that morality and spirituality that centers on God alone without an extension towards improving the lot of suffering humans and for the improvement of the community is not an authentic morality or faith. On the last day, God will not judge on how many times one prayed, or attended Church service, but the actions one took for the good of humanity and society at large.[155]

The Christian moral principles largely affect and shape the Christian worldview. Expressing this view, Timothy O'Connell, a moral theologian, writes,

> The Christian vision of the world's meaning deeply affect our [Christian] ethical thinking in so far as it speaks of the dignity of the human race. Our human hopes are not dashed. The human drive for interpersonal union, for life shared in love, is not frustrated, because of our strong moral conviction. Indeed, these very human urges are but glimmers of the wonder God has in store in us. Thus there is a great reason for us to accept and cooperate with the call to human growth, to fidelity and

---

[154] Arnold D. Hunt and Robert B. Crotty, *Ethics of World Religions*. (Minnesota: Greenhaven Press, Inc. 1978), 39.

[155] Cf. Matthew 25:31-46; Luke 16:19-31.

generosity, and honor, that we hear within ourselves. Of course, it is not a matter of doing the "unpleasant good" in order to be rewarded at the end. Rather, it is a matter of knowing that the call to the good, a call that we sense as part of our human composition, is not the prelude of absurdity. It is not an invitation to develop ourselves only to be crushed into nothingness in the end. There is meaning to the best that is human. The Christian life is not a cosmic joke but rather a joyful cosmic gift. Thus human beings have a dignity and destiny that give the Christian a very special sense of meaning in the world; a meaning that calls for moral rectitude for the glory of the creator and advancement of human society.[156]

Charles Curran, expressing a similar view to O'Connell's has powerfully described how the central doctrines of the Christian faith shape the Christian's vision of the world and thereby serve as a basis for a distinctive approach to morality. As Curran sees it, there are five such doctrines. First, there is the doctrine of the goodness of creation; that grand truth proclaimed in the first chapter of Genesis. Second, there is the sad truth of sin also announced in Genesis, that potential for destructiveness that hides in the web of the human world. Paralleling these two doctrines of the Jewish Scriptures are two distinctively Christian doctrines. On the optimistic note, there is the doctrine of the Incarnation. Moreover, there is the doctrine of the cross: that salvation came only at the cost of Jesus' life, that when God became human we put him to death. Still, it is hope

---

[156] Timothy E. O'Connell, *Principles for a Catholic Morality*. (San Francisco: Harper & Row Publishers, 1990), 248-249.

that energizes the living of the Christian life. Therefore, as Curran views it, the doctrine of the resurrection, with its promise of a future fulfillment, is what ultimately grounds the Christian vision of moral living.[157]

Furthermore, the connection between the Christian faith, justice, equality, and right moral actions is expressed in the Book of James chapter 2:1, 9: "Brothers and sisters do not combine faith in Jesus Christ, our glorified Lord with the making of distinction between classes of people . . . as soon as you make distinctions between classes of people, you are committing sin, and under condemnation of breaking the law." Continuing, James said,

> Take the case, my brothers and sisters, of someone who has never done a single good act but claims that he has faith. Will that faith save him? If one of the brothers or sisters is in need of clothes and has not enough food to live on and one of you says to him or her, 'I wish you well; keep yourself warm and eat plenty', without giving him or her these bare necessities of life, then what good is that? Faith is like that: if good works do not go with it, it is quite dead. (James 2:14-16).

Faith, holiness, love and communal responsibility were among the marks of Christianity in the early Church (Cf. Acts. 2: 42-47), and these continue to be integral parts of the teaching and life of Christianity today.

---

[157] Charles Curran, *New Perspective in Moral Theology*. (Notre Dame: Fides Publications, 1974), 47-86.

2.3.7. Belief in the last things (Eschatology): Death, Judgment, Heaven and Hell.

Belief in eschatology—the last things—is an essential doctrine of Christianity. Defining eschatology, McBrien writes,

> Eschatology, in the traditional sense of the word, is that area of theology which is directly concerned with the study of the last thing(s). The "last thing" (*eschaton*) is God, or, more precisely, the Kingdom, or Reign, of God, i.e., the final manifestation of the reconciling, renewing, and unifying love of God. The "last things" (*eschata*) are various moments or stages in the final manifestation process: death, particular judgment, heaven, hell, Second Coming of Christ, resurrection of the body, general judgment, and the consummation of all things in the perfection of the Kingdom of God.[158]

We shall not be treating all these last things individually; we shall only concentrate on four of them (popularly called the four last things) that either include or imply the other, namely: Death, Judgment, Heaven and Hell.

2.3.7.1. Death:

Christians believe that all created things must die. The particular emphasis however is on human beings. Christians hold that we live once and die once; there is no second chance or reincarnation. The Bible is clear on

---

[158] McBrien, *Catholicism*, 1123.

this: "It is appointed unto men to die once." (Heb. 9:27) Specifically, "Death is the dissolution of the union between the soul and the body which must happen to every human being at end of his life."[159]

It is the Christian belief that God did not intend humans to die, but death came because of sin and the victory over death come from Jesus Christ, who by his own death and resurrection conquers death and gives it a new understanding for Christians. Death in Christ opens the way to new life. Explaining more on death in the Christian belief, McBrien writes,

> The New Testament is explicit and unequivocal about the origin of death: It is the consequence of sin and punishment for it (Rom. 5:12-14). Likewise in 1 Cor. 15:22, Paul asserts that we shall all die in Adam, but rise to life in Christ . . . The Christian experiences Jesus' victory over death by sharing in his death (Rom. 6:2-11). To die with Christ is to live with him . . . On the other hand; death is at once final and unique.[160]

After death judgment follows (Heb.9:27).

2.3.7.2. Judgment:

Christians believe that after death, all humans will appear before God to give account of all that they have done in life, good and bad (Matt. 25:31-46; Rom. 14:10-13; 2 Cor. 5:10). There are two types of Judgment that will come

---

[159] Ripley, *This is the Faith,* 378.
[160] McBrien, *Catholicism,*1158-1159.

upon all humans after death: Particular Judgment and Last or General Judgment.

Particular judgment implies that immediately after death, the soul stands before God and its fate is decided. As noted by Ripley,

> The common opinion of theologians is that the Particular Judgment will take place where death occurs and that it will be instantaneous. At the moment of death the soul will be internally illuminated as to its own innocence or guilt and will immediately, on its own initiative, make its way to heaven, to Hell or to Purgatory.[161]

The particular judgment underscores the uniqueness and particularity of every human person before God. We are individual persons and not just simply part of some larger, impersonal collective reality.[162] Though there is collective responsibility, there is still individual accountability.

The concept of the general judgment includes the second coming of Christ and the bodily resurrection of all the dead[163], as well as the end of history. According to McBrien,

---

[161] Ripley, *This is the Faith*, 381.

[162] McBrien, *Catholicism*, 1164.

[163] Belief in the resurrection of the dead has been an essential element of the Christian faith from its beginning. For just as Christ died and rose again, so shall it be with those who believe in Him. (I Cor. 15 12-14; Rom. 8:11; Phil. 3:10-11). Resurrection here implies that the human person whole and entire after falling to the power of death will rise again in an incorruptible nature. It is the revivification of the body and soul.

The general judgment applies to the consummation of the whole world and of history itself. It is connected with the Second Coming of Christ, or *Parousia*, of Christ [who will come again to judge the living and the dead]. Because it affects all it is called the "general judgment." Because it is the act, which terminates history, it is also called the "last" judgment.[164]

The *Catechism of the Catholic Church* states that, "The resurrection of the all the dead, both the just and the unjust, will precede the Last Judgment. This is the hour when all who are in the tombs will hear the Son of man's voice and come forth (1 Thess. 4:13-18) to the resurrection of judgment."[165] The Christian creeds and the early councils of the Christian Church attest to the Christian faith and belief in the final judgment at the second coming of Christ: In the Apostles' Creed—"He shall come again to judge the living and the dead." In the Nicene Creed (325)—"He ascended to the heavens and shall come again to judge the living and dead." In the Nicene-Constantinople Creed (381) from the Council of Constantinople—"He shall come again in glory to judge the living and the dead."

2.3.7.3. Heaven:

Christians believe in the reality of heaven as a place where God lives and where the righteous will live with him at the end of time. (Jon 14:2-3) After judgment, all those who lived virtuous lives (the saints) will be rewarded with the glory of heaven (Matt. 25: 34) where they will see

---

[164] Ibid.

[165] CCC, 1038.

God face to face. As stated in the *Catechism of the Catholic Church*, those who die in God's grace and friendship and are perfectly purified will live forever with Christ (in heaven). They are like God forever, for they "see him as he is, face to face." (Rev. 22:4)[166] Seeing God face to face in the glory of heaven is called the beatific vision, which is "the full union of the human person with God."[167] It is that toward which every Christian strives.

2.3.7.4. Hell:

In Christian belief, the contrast of heaven is hell where sinners will receive eternal punishment for their unrighteousness. (Matt. 25:46). The Church teaches that,

> Immediately after death the souls of those who die in a state of mortal sin descend into hell, where they suffer the punishment of hell and eternal fire. The chief punishment of hell is eternal separation from God, in whom alone man can possess the life and happiness for which he was created and which he longs.[168]

While not proving the location of hell, the Bible mentions the reality of hell in various passages. It is place of unquenchable fire (Mk. 9:43; Matt. 5:22; Jas. 3:6), a pit into which people are cast (Matt. 5:29-30; Luk. 12:5). It is the final destination of the wicked (Rev. 19:20; 20:9-15; 21:8). It is a place of weeping and gnashing of teeth Matt. 8:12;

---

[166] CCC, 1023.
[167] McBrien, *Catholicism*, 1166.
[168] CCC, 1035.

13:42; 22:13; 24:51; 25:30). It is place where the worm does not die (Mk.9:48).

The punishment of hell like the joy of heaven is eternal. It is not God who sends a person to the eternal punishment of hell, but the individual chooses where to go by his or her actions while living here on earth.

CHAPTER THREE

INTERFAITH RELATIONSHIP AMONG THE THREE RELIGIONS IN NIGERIA: AREAS OF DIVERGENCE AND CONFLICTS.

Nigeria is usually characterized as a deeply divided state in which major issues are vigorously—some would say violently—contested along the lines of the complex ethnic, religious, and regional political divisions in the country.[169] The issues that generate the fiercest tensions include those that are considered fundamental to the existence and spiritual life of the citizenry, over which competing groups tend to adopt exclusionary, winner-take-all strategies. Consequently, the Nigerian state tends to be fragile and unstable because almost by definition and doctrine, there are fewer points of convergence and consensus among the constituent groups than are required to effectively mitigate or contain the centrifugal forces that could tear

---

[169] Eghosa E. Osaghe and Rotimi Suberu, *A History of Identities, Violence, and Stability in Nigeria*: CRISE Working paper, n.6, 2005. (Center for Research on Inequality, Human Security and Ethnicity: CRISE Queen Elizabeth House, University of London), 4.

the society apart. Nigeria presents a complex of individual as well as crisscrossing and recursive identities of which the ethnic, sub-ethnic (communal) and religious are the most salient and the main bases for violent conflicts in the country. Above all, religion ties everything together. Hence, even what may seem to be ethnic, regional and political violence are always colored with and shaped by religious influences.

The category of ethno-religious identities initially owed its origin to regional formations. It has been useful for differentiating the predominantly Muslim North from the predominantly Christian South. The category has also helped to differentiate the dominant Muslim group in the North from the non-Muslim minorities in the region. Indeed, unlike the south where majority groups are distinguished from minority groups based on ethnicity, majority-minority distinctions in the north have been more religious than ethnic. Thus, a member of the Hausa/Fulani majority group in the north who is Christian is as much a minority in the overall scheme of things as say an Idoma or Igala, (both of which are northern minority groups) and is actually likely to enjoy fewer privileges than an ethnic minority person who is Muslim. In between the majority, Muslim North and majority Christian South are Traditionalists who cling to ethnic identity and their traditional religious ways of worship. This group forms the minority in the overall religious demography of Nigeria. Since the early 1980s, when the Maitatsine (a group of Muslim fundamentalists) riots ushered in a regime of religious fundamentalism in the Northern parts of the country, ethno-religious categories have been more frequently used to describe conflicts that involve an intersection of ethnic and religious identities. Again, for historical reasons, this has been truer of the North where, as has been pointed out, religious differences play a major part in ethnic and political differentiation.

This section of our work will carefully and in a detained manner examine the areas of divergences and conflicts among the three religions. These areas of conflict, violence and divergences are the most trumpeted aspects of religion in Nigeria in both the local and international media.

3.1 AFRICAN TRADITIONAL RELIGION (ATR) VERSUS ISLAM.

A striking divergence between ATR and Islam in Nigeria is the belief systems of both religions. While they agree in most aspects as already seen in the previous chapter, they sharply disagree on their concept of God. ATR is polytheistic, while Islam is strictly monotheistic. In Islam, polytheism, which means to associate (*Shirk*) someone or something with Allah's All-Perfect Self or with His attributes, is the greatest sin anyone can commit. Hence, Muslims see traditionalists in Nigeria as infidels, unbelievers, idolaters and pagan, and more often than not strictly and literarily apply this Quranic injunction on them: "When the sacred months are over fight and slay the polytheists wherever you find them. Arrest them, besiege them, and lie in ambush everywhere for them. If they repent and take to prayer and pay the alms-tax, let them go their way. Allah is forgiving and merciful. But if they violate their oath after their covenant, fight them and Allah will punish them by your hands, cover them with shame, and help you to victory over them, and heal the breast of the believers." (9:5, 14)

Muslims and Traditionalists had a long relationship of friendship and accommodation from the 9th century up to the 19th century. However, from the turn of the nineteenth century a new class of more puritan Muslim clerics arose who began to demand strict obedience to all of the Qur'an's dictates. When and where these demands were not met by the local Hausa rulers the clerics pressed for a jihad. One such *jihad* that ushered in the era of violence between the ATR and Muslims is the Sokoto (Fulani) *jihad* inaugurated by Uthman dan Fodio in 1804; a *jihad* that forged an Islamic empire, which reached throughout Northern Nigeria and into neighboring Cameroon, Benin and Niger. As recorded by Joseph Kenny,

> In spite of the long time they [the Hausa Kings] had been Muslims, up to the beginning of the 19th century the kings were expected to be the religious fathers or patrons of all their people, Muslims and non-Muslims. In the terminology of H. Fisher, they were 'mixers.' That is, they observed the rituals of both Islam and the traditional religion, as the occasion demanded. Against this background, Uthman dan Fodiye inaugurated his Jihad in 1804. His aim was the reformation of lax Muslims. He challenged the Hausa kings to accept his proposal of living strictly according to the Sharia [abandoning anything and everything of traditional religion]. When they refused, he overthrew them, setting up the Sokoto caliphate, a federation of emirates covering most of what is now the North of Nigeria.[170]

A good number of Fulanis, who were Muslims of the Qadiriyya brotherhood of the Sufi order, led by Uthman dan Fodio, were unhappy that the rulers of the Hausa states were mingling Islam with aspects of the traditional religion. Rallying around Fodio, they proclaimed him *Amir al-Muminin* (Leader of the Faithful), giving him the

---

[170] Joseph Kenny, "Sharia and Christianity in Nigeria: Islam and a 'Secular' State." *Journal of Religion in Africa,* Vol.26, Fasc. 4 (Nov., 1996), pp.338-364.

authority to declare and pursue a Jihad. He raised an army largely composed of the Fulani, who held a powerful military advantage with their cavalry. He led a widespread religious uprising in the North of Nigeria. Uthman dan Fodio declared:

> As for the sultans, they are undoubtedly unbelievers, even though they may profess the religion of Islam, because they practice polytheistic rituals and turn people away from the path of God and raise the flag of worldly kingdom above the banner of Islam. All this is unbelief according to the consensus of opinions. Therefore, you must fight and kill them for Allah has no rival.[171]

The *jihad* resulted in a federal theocratic state, with extensive autonomy for emirates, recognizing the spiritual authority of the caliph or the sultan of Sokoto. This was the first religious violence and intolerance against another religion recorded in the history of what is today known as northern Nigeria. The Arabian Islamic influence to 'purify' Islam in Nigeria and the West African regions of every 'impurity' occasioned by its interaction with ATR was a major reason behind this religious violence and conflict.

On the other hand, the traditionalists, who have been so tenacious and resilient in their traditional rituals, have on many occasions posed challenges to Islam all over Nigeria. One such example is noticeable in the South-East geopolitical zone where Islam is in the minority. For instance, coming to Igboland (Anioha) in the late 1950s, Islam was vehemently opposed by followers of ATR. Various

---

[171] Christopher Steed and David Westurland, "Nigeria," in *Islam Outside the Arab World.* David Westurland and Ingvar Svanberg, eds. (London: Palgrave Macmillan, 1999), 54.

methods of intolerance were carried out by followers of both religions against each other. On the part of Muslims, they destroyed some of the traditional religious symbols. In response, the traditionalists barred and ostracized the Muslims from active participation in community affairs; a heavy punishment in the traditional society. Native Chiefs who took to Islam were stripped of their titles. At times, there were verbal abuses and physical combats on both sides. The situation brought much rancor, division, and tension in a community that had known peace for decades. It also led to putting up a mat fence to separate the part of the village that professes Islam from the part that adheres to ATR.

Most communities like Nsukka in the East and Ijebu-Ode in West had similar experiences. It must be noted that in places where Muslims are in the majority, they seem to dominate and intimidate followers of ATR, while in places where Islam is a minority religion, ATR appears to take the upper hand to the detriment of Muslims. However, when compared to the scale of violence that have occurred between Christians and Muslims, or Christians and ATR, ATR and Islam have had minimal record of violence in Nigeria.

3.2 AFRICAN TRADITIONAL RELIGION VERSUS CHRISTIANITY.

Christianity has had a long history of interactions with ATR in Nigeria since its earliest attempt of taking root in the country in the 15th century, and its eventual success in the 19th century. Although these years of interaction have witnessed tremendous records of friendship, harmony and positive collaboration, it has also witnessed sad moments of conflicts, violence and intolerance against each other.

On the part of ATR, the natives and traditionalists tended to be skeptical and resistant to the missionaries whom they perceived as coming to upturn their traditional and cultural values. They also associated them with slave traders, and as allies of colonialism.[172] The slave trade factor played a role in the intolerable relationship between ATR and Christianity. On the one side was the common people, who were always victims of enslavement, seeing the missionaries as associates and brothers of slave masters and as such would not make friends with those who took and sent their relatives to foreign lands as slaves; on the other side, as the missionaries gained their footings and began to abolish the slave trade and to liberate slaves (from whose ranks most of their early converts came), they began to antagonize the chiefs who were middle men in slave trading—a major source of influence, labor and income to the chiefs. As reported by Elizabeth Isichei, quoting in part Bishop Knight Bruce in *The Hidden Hippopotamus,*

> Often a missionary presence created something like a class conflict, 'the chief cause of all these repeated and most annoying persecutions since 1874 is slavery—the fear of some of the Chiefs is that, should Christianity progress more than now . . . civilized ideas naturally will follow and more slaves will be set free and the trade will be abolished, and revolutionary ideas may take place among those who are still slaves.'[173]

---

[172] Richard F. Weir, ed., *The Religious World: Communities of Faith.* (New York: Macmillan Publishers, 1982), 49.

[173] Elizabeth Isichei, *A History of Christianity in Africa: From Antiquity to the Present.* (New Jersey: African World Press Inc., 1995), 156-157.

With this mentality, most of the chiefs who originally welcomed and extended arms of friendship to the missionaries began to do all within their powers to persecute them and to stamp out Christianity within their Chiefdoms. Among the various tactics they adopted to victimize Christians were:

- ❖ Excommunication of Christians from the community
- ❖ Imposition of heavy fines on Christians
- ❖ Denial of communal sharing of farm land and other rights
- ❖ Demolition of houses belonging to Christians and destruction of their properties.[174]

On the part of Christianity, the missionaries came with a message and style of evangelization, which to all intents and purposes set out to destroy the religious and cultural traditions of the Nigerian people. This was very vehemently and violently resisted. As reported by Oliver Onwubiko,

> Resistance to culture change has been part of the violence in Africa especially on the socio-spiritual level. People have seen their worldview challenged without proper substitution and in some cases the changes are so fast that some have seen their cultural values collapse and fall apart. Some, in consequence, have instituted themselves into a block of cultural immobility resulting into violent relationship (*sic*) between Christians and non-Christians on matters

---

[174] Ogbu U. Kalu, "The Dilemma of Grassroot Inculturation of the Gospel: The Case Study of a Modern Controversy in Igboland, 1983-1989." *Journal of Religion in African.* Vol. 25, Fasc. 1 (Feb., 1995) pp. 48-72

of traditional practices based on African Traditional Religion.[175]

This type of resistance, conflict and violence is often times unavoidable because, as observed by Vincent Mulago, "Any meeting of two different realities incurs the risk of conflict. We do, in fact, observe at times conflict between the cultural heritage of black Africa and Christianity."[176]

Christianity from its inception was very exclusive. It saw and described the Natives and non-Christians as the 'other' people, and as a darkness with which the light should have nothing in common. The traditional gods were described as fetishes, while the followers were dubbed pagans, heathens and animists.

Christianity came with a new teaching and ideology that looked upon everything traditional as ungodly; allegiance to the traditional institutions was seen as allegiance to the rulers of this world. As noted by Isichei, "As the number of converts increased, the [traditional] rulers became increasingly anxious about the existence of a rival center of authority especially when enthusiasts deliberately flouted traditional customs. All this led to conflict and persecution."[177] Converts to Christianity were required to change their native and traditional names as signs of their separation from an "evil" tradition to a "new" life in Christ. Even today, many Christian are dropping the native and middle names, which are connected with traditional religion. For example, a medical doctor by the name *Arunsi*, which means *god* (who happens

---

[175] Oliver Onwubiko, *Echoes from the African Synod*. (Enugu: Snaap Press, 1994), 129.

[176] Vincent Mulago, "Traditional African Religion and Christianity," in Jacob Olupona, ed., *African Traditional Religions in Contemporary Society*. (New York: Paragon House,1991), 128

[177] Isichei, *A History of Christianity in Africa*, 157.

to be my namesake), changed his name a couple of years ago to *Arisachi (Remember God)*. A recent example of a change of a traditional name to a Christian-based name which led to a violent clash that left 5 people dead and 15 injured along side with the destruction of properties occurred in Awka, Anambra State (South-East) Nigeria on September 3, 2009. The crisis started over the change of the name of the community from Nkerehi to Umuchukwu.[178] Nkerehi had been the original name of the community since its foundation by the forbearers. Christian fundamentalists in this community saw this name as traditional and therefore linked it with evil and lack of progress in the community. As an option, contrary to the wishes of the traditionalists and some "liberal" Christians, they renamed the village "Umuchukwu" (Children of God); a name, which they believe, is Christian enough to bring them God's "blessings" and to break the ties with their ancestral customs and traditions. Similar cases have occurred in other parts of the country especially in the South-East. Most of such cases have resulted to violent clashes and court litigations.

A very sharp difference that has remained noticeable between ATR and Christianity is the concept and practice of marriage norms. While ATR favors polygamy as well as monogamy as a matter of choice, Christianity is almost unanimously opposed to polygamy in favor of monogamy as the only lawful and holy matrimonial relationship. Describing the missionary teachings and attitude on marriage, a teaching and attitude that has remained the same till today, Isichei writes,

---

[178] Vincent Ujumadu, "5 Killed, 15 Injured in Anambra Communal Crisis," in *Vanguard.* September 4, 2009. http://www.vanguardngr.com/2009/09/04/5-killed-15-injured-in-anambra-communal-crisis/ (Assessed: September 25, 2009)

Missionaries in general expected Christians to be monogamous, while aware of the cruelty and injustice involved in disrupting polygamous unions. Plural marriage was deeply rooted in the social fabric. Kings cemented good relations with the subject provinces in this way, and the great value placed on the children, and the contributions made by wives meant that the more prosperous had overwhelming strong motives to acquire more wives . . . Once converted, people grappled in various ways with the relationship between their new faith, their cultural inheritance, and the needs and obligations of their immediate environment. One of the most enduring and complicated problem was plural marriage. Some new Christians renounced all their wives but one. For many, this was impossible . . . In 1917, ten leading laymen of a Lagos Methodist Church were indicted for polygamy. At a crowded meeting, fifty-five others said that they were guilty as well. Their dismissal led to the creation of the United African Methodist Church.[179]

An incident was reported by Jeffrey Peires of a polygamous traditionalist seeking to convert to Christianity who was required to send packing one of his wives as a condition. He replied, "I have long renounced idolatry, here are my two wives, from this I have gotten children, but she is poor; that one has no child, but she finds my daily bread. I have also suffered from a long sickness which has thus disabled

---

[179] Isichei, *A History of Christianity in Africa,* 96,159.

me."[180] The Yoruba Clergyman, Emmanuel Moses Lijadu, Peires continues, "told him to choose between Children and bread. He died before he decided."[181]

For many years, ATR and Christianity remained opposed and did not explore each other's positive sides and how they could benefit each other. Christianity in particular in most cases did not do her groundwork well to tap into the rich Nigerian cultural heritage and spirituality. Cultures and traditional religion were often times discriminated against and kept at bay. Looking at this phenomenon, David Ihenacho pointed out clearly,

> The result is that, rather than the Nigerian culture and tradition becoming partners with Christianity in the task of strengthening and reinforcing people's spirituality, they are made to look like competitors and adversaries. To the effect that while Christianity wins the public relations war with its gigantic structures and mammoth followers, cultures and traditional religion hunker down and manipulate people's consciences with uncanny laws and allegiances.[182]

The prognosis is that if something is not done to reconcile these two opposing religious forces, in a true and sincere spirit of interfaith dialogue and relationships, ATR, which is now lying low, may rise again and take the upper hand in the lives of the Nigerian people, particularly among the

---

[180] Jeffrey. B. Peires, *The House of Phalo* (Johannesburg: Jonathan Ball Publishers, 2003), 69

[181] Ibid.

[182] David A. Ihenacho, *African Christianity Rises*, Vol. 1 (New York: iUniverse Inc., 2004), 126.

Yoruba and Igbo. A traditional religion of a people hardly ever dies.

3.3 ISLAM VERSUS CHRISTIANITY.

The early history of Islam and Christianity in Nigeria was one of mutual tolerance but not of much collaboration. However, the scenario began to change after the Independence of Nigeria in 1960, when tribal, political and regional interests tainted with religious motifs began to play out in the Nigerian polity, reaching its peak in the 1980s. As succinctly articulated by Toyin Falola, "By the late 1980s, conflict between Muslims and Christians had become public, volatile and dangerous."[183] Since then, Islam and Christianity have been the major focus of religious violence, intolerance and conflict in Nigeria. Although this phenomenon cuts across the country, the North and South-East geopolitical zones have been the major theatres of religious violence. Articulating the religious situation in Nigeria, occasioned by Christian-Muslim relations, Jan Boer, writes, "The other major national problem in Nigeria is that of Christian-Muslim relations. If corruption has demonized the country, these relations have bedeviled it."[184] The relationships between these two great missionary religions in Nigeria have been characterized by suspicion and mistrust rather than concrete collaborations and cooperation. This suspicion and mistrust is clearly seen even at the government level and among the elite. For example,

---

[183] Toyin Falola, *Violence in Nigeria: The Crisis of Religious Politics and Secular Ideologies.* (New York: University of Rochester Press, 1998), 163.

[184] Jan H. Boer, *Nigeria's Decade of Blood, 1982-2002.* Vol.1. (Ontario, Canada: Essence Publishing, 2003), 14.

In 1986, the federal government established an Advisory Council on Religious Affairs (ACRA) to mediate between the two religions and to advise the government on religious matters. This Council immediately became embroiled in the crisis, as Muslim and Christian representatives found themselves unable to agree on a committee chair, or, for that matter, on much of anything, and they usually refused even to meet [because no group trusted the other]. The few meetings that actually took place, usually under pressure from the government, produced nothing or just a few concrete statements or decisions.[185]

The atmosphere has become so polluted that even the smallest issue can cause a major crisis. Verbal abuse and aggression towards each other has almost become a creed that followers of these religions learn and sing out in places of worship, open-door sermons, in popular culture and in politics, not excluding the media. In their efforts to convert people from the other faith, they present each other as dangerous.

For many Christians, Islam embodies the spirit of the Anti-Christ. Salman Rushdie's "notorious" book, *The Satanic Verses*,[186] a novel that portrayed some Quranic passages as inspired by Satan, and Islam as a diabolical religion that worships the three pre—Islamic Pagan Meccan goddesses (Allāt, Uzza, and Manāt), became popular among Nigerian Christians for its criticism of Islam. Falola noted that even

---

[185] Falola, *Violence in Nigeria*, 163
[186] Salman Rushdie, *The Satanic Verses*. (New York: Penguin Group, 1989).

those Christians who have never seen or read the book cited it with gusto.[187]

On the other hand, for many members of the Muslim intelligentsia in Nigeria, besides the West, Christianity is the major enemy of Islam. Many describe Christianity as a fictitious religion that worships a dead man Jesus. On one Good Friday, I read a car sticker boldly placed on a Muslim car that states: "Is your God dead; try Allah." This sticker was a way of mocking Christians for their belief that Jesus whom they call God died on a Good Friday, whereas the "true" God (Allah) can never die.

Preachers on both sides claim to be knowledgeable both of their religion and of the religion of their opponent, and have read and "understood" their sacred books. However, in seeking knowledge of the others' religion, they are not after the truth or common ground in most case, but differences and division. In their "ignorance" of the other's religion and traditions, they cite a few verses in their claimed knowledge out of context, without reference to history and scholarly commentaries. Young Nigerians too are not left out. They are socialized into conflict, learning to employ the words of adults in characterizing each other's religion. As noted by Falola,

> Steeped at home and in their schools with the language and values of hatred, teenagers learn hostility, resentment, and violence from adults around them. It is not surprising that they take part in virtually all the major outbreaks of violence [between Christians and Muslims in Nigeria].[188]

---

187 Falola, *Violence in Nigeria*, 263.
188 Falola, *Violence in Nigeria*, 261.

Below are some of the concrete areas that have created and produced divergences, conflicts, violence and tension between Muslims and Christians in Nigeria.

3.3.1. Belief and Doctrinal Issues

The issue of beliefs and doctrines has been a major source of divergence and conflict between Muslims and Christians in Nigeria. One major issue among these beliefs and doctrines is the belief in God, and its implications in Islam and in Christianity.

As a monotheistic religion, Islam believes in the absolute unity of God without equal or association. Quran 112:1-4, declares "Say: He is God [Allah], the One and Only; God, the Eternal, Absolute. He begets not nor is He begotten; and there is none like unto Him."

Christianity on the other hand equally believes in a monotheistic God, who is a Trinity; that is, three persons in one God: God the Father, God the Son and God the Holy Spirit. These three Persons are not three Gods, but One God.

Hence, while Muslims and Christians share a common belief in God, the Muslims consider it an abomination and offensive to say that there are three persons in God, and "many Muslims leaders and preachers maintain that Christianity cannot teach the true existence of a perfect God. To such Muslims, no one else can share in the nature and attributes of God."[189] Affirming the Islamic position, S. A. Ali, writes,

> The first major doctrinal difference is that of the Trinity which has puzzled the Muslim mind and has all along been a subject of hot

---

[189] Falola, *Violence in Nigeria*, 248.

debate. Some Muslims even think that this doctrine was invented three hundred years after Jesus and quote Christian scholars like Prof. Johan B. Hygen of the University of Oslo, who recognize that this doctrine is not found in the Bible. Perhaps I would not be wrong in saying that this doctrine has puzzled the Christian mind too.[190]

For the Muslims the doctrine of the Trinity clearly violates the absolute oneness of God, which forms the heart, and soul of Islam.

A follow up to the different notions of God between the two religions is the misunderstanding and differences surrounding the person of Jesus whom, Christians, contrary to Islamic belief, revere and worship not only as God, but also as the Son of God. In Islam, it is blasphemous to say that God is begotten, or that he begets a son. According to Muhammed Asadi,

> The major difference between Islam and Christianity revolves around the nature of Jesus. The Koran terms Jesus as a messenger of God, a mortal. It does not accept the Christian claim that God (immortal) becomes man (mortal), or that God begets offspring . . . Whereas the Koran states that Jesus was no more than a prophet of God, a

---

[190] S. A. Ali, "Christian-Muslim Relations: Ushering in a New Era," in M. Darrol Bryant and S. A. Ali, Eds, *Muslim-Christian Dialogue: Promise and Problems.* (Minnesota: Paragon House, 1998), 43

human being, Christian doctrine insists that he was in some way divine, a son of God.[191]

Another difference regarding the person of Jesus between Christians and Muslims is the cross. In Christianity, the Cross has a central place; it is an instrument of salvation upon which Christ by his crucifixion redeemed the world. This is unacceptable in Islam, and has been a major source of differences. As expressed by Ali, "The second major doctrinal difference [between Islam and Christianity] is related to the conviction of the Quran that Jesus did not die on the Cross. Instead, the Quran affirms that someone who resembled him was crucified and that Jesus was lifted up to the heavens."[192] The passage of the Quran being referred to by Ali is Surah 4:156-158 that states:

> That they rejected Faith; That they uttered against Mary a grave false charge; That they said (in boast): 'We killed Christ Jesus the son of Mary, the Messenger of Allah.' But they killed him not, nor crucified him, but so it was made to appear to them, and those who differ therein are full of doubts, with no (certain) knowledge, but only conjecture to follow, for of a surety they killed him not. Nay, Allah raised him up Unto Himself; and Allah Is Exalted in Power.

This teaching espoused in the Quran and strictly adhered to by Muslims is unacceptable and abominable to Christians, who believe and profess that Jesus, and not his resemblance,

---

[191] Muhammed A. Asadi, *Islam & Christianity: Conflict or Conciliation?* (San Jose: Writers Club, 2001), x, 31.

[192] Ali, "Christian-Muslim Relations: Ushering in a New Era," 44.

was truly crucified on the cross for the atonement of the sins of humanity and for the salvation of humankind.

The contrast between Islam and Christianity in Nigeria becomes clearer when we compare the Muslims' general attitude towards Jesus based on the Quran with the Christian attitude towards Muhammad (phup), the Prophet of Islam. Jesus has a very important place in Islam. He is called a prophet and messenger of God. He is also recognized in Islam as *Masih*, the messiah. His virgin birth is acknowledged and his mother recognized as being "chosen above the women of all nations." (Quran 3:42, 47) In all honesty, besides the doctrinal differences on the person of Jesus, I have never heard any Muslim use derogatory words about Jesus. On the other hand, Nigerian Christians towing the line of history have uttered many abusive words on Muhammad and have called him names. It was even suggested by a Christian journalist when Nigeria was about to host the Miss World pageant in 2002 that Muhammad may even take a wife among those ladies since he likes women a lot.[193] Christians do not believe that Muhammad was a prophet of God; if he is at all referred to as one; it is as a false prophet. He is referred to as a carnal man full of lust because he married 10 wives. The verbal assault on Muhammad by Nigerian Christians is not far from the teachings of Thomas Aquinas on Muhammad.

> He (Mohammed) seduced the people by promises of carnal pleasure to which the concupiscence of the flesh urges us. His teaching also contained precepts that were in conformity with his promises, and he gave

---

[193] John L. Allen, "Tough love with Islam—Church in Nigeria may be model of dialogue," in *Catholic Online* http://www.catholic. org/international/international_story.php?id=23597 3/30/2007. (Assessed: September 26, 2009)

free rein to carnal pleasure. In all this, as is not unexpected; he was obeyed by carnal men. As for proofs of the truth of his doctrine, he brought forward only such as could be grasped by the natural ability of anyone with a very modest wisdom. Indeed, the truths that he taught he mingled with many fables and with doctrines of the greatest falsity. He did not bring forth any signs produced in a supernatural way, which alone fittingly gives witness to divine inspiration; for a visible action that can be only divine reveals an invisibly inspired teacher of truth. On the Contrary, Mohammed said that he was sent in the power of his arms—which are signs not lacking even to robbers and tyrants. What is more, no wise men, men trained in things divine and human, believed in him from the beginning. Those who believed in him were brutal men and desert wanderers, utterly ignorant of all divine teaching, through whose numbers Mohammed forced others to become his follower's by the violence of his arms. Nor do divine pronouncements on part of preceding prophets offer him any witness. On the contrary, he perverts almost all the testimony of the Old and the New Testaments by making them into a fabrication of his own, as can be seen by anyone who examines his law. It was, therefore, a shrewd decision on his part to forbid his followers to read the Old and New Testaments, lest these books convict him of falsity. It is thus clear that

those who place faith in his words believe
foolishly.[194]

A teaching of this nature, which most Christians in Nigeria
hold unto against Muhammad and indirectly against
Muslims, is deeply offensive to Nigerian Muslims, and some
of them take to arms to fight against such teachings.

3.3.2. Legal Issues

Another major point of divergence and conflict between
Muslims and Christians in Nigeria is one that has to do with
the legal codes and systems that should operate in Nigerian
society. Muslims are demanding as a right the adoption of
the Islamic legal system, *the Shariah*, as the official system
of Law that should govern all Muslims in Nigeria. They
demand that Shariah be enshrined in the Constitution of the
Federal Republic of Nigeria. Christians reject such demand
as contrary to the article of secularity in the Constitution
since Shariah is strictly a religious legal system. Again,
Christians reject the adoption of the Shariah in Nigeria, as
that would lead to the Islamization of the Country. While
Christians and Muslims do find common grounds on many
public issues, they fundamentally disagree on the issue of
Shariah. As reported by John Allen,

> Archbishop Onaiyekan and his Muslim
> hosts found much common ground. Yet they
> sparred too, especially over Shariah. One
> Muslim argued that since Nigerian civil law
> is based upon English common law, Nigerian
> Muslims are already subject to a Christian
> legal code, so it's hypocritical of Christians

---

[194] Thomas Aquinas, *Summa Contra Gentiles*, Book 1, Chpt. 16,
Art.4.

to say that law and religion should not mix. When another Muslim said that Christians could take a case before a Shariah court, Archbishop Onaiyekan shot back, "That's not a right we recognize. . . . It's not a right we want."[195]

Writing on Christian-Muslim relations as it touches on the Shariah, Frieder Ludwig reports,

> For a long time, Nigerian Christians have been worried about being marginalized by Muslims. For an equally long time, Nigerian Muslims have worried about being dominated and undermined by the West [which Christianity represents]. The Shariah controversy is shaped by these fears, and there are clear antagonistic tendencies. Both sides have a well-developed arsenal of arguments at their disposal, and they do not agree on their views on the implications of Shariah or in their interpretation of Nigeria's history [as it concerns the Shariah and the history of the Nigerian legal system]. It is extremely difficult to organize public meetings or conferences which are more than a mere repetition of old arguments; the willingness to listen to the other side is severely limited at such gatherings.[196]

---

[195] Allen, "Tough love with Islam—Church in Nigeria may be model of dialogue," in *Catholic Online* 3rd March, 2009.

[196] Frieder Ludwig, "Christian-Muslim Relations in Northern Nigeria since the Introduction of Shariah in 1999," in *Journal of the American Academy of Religion*, September 2008, Vol. 76, No.3, 602.

Toyin Falola described a good example of such public meetings or conferences in Nigeria on the issue of Shariah that is characterized by argument, disagreement and suspicion of the others' religion and viewpoint. The federal government in 1998, prior to the introduction of the Shariah in 1999, set up a subcommittee of six Elders to deliberate over the feasibility of introducing Shariah into the Nigerian legal code. Most of what they said was repetitive, but they did produce a widely read document that stated quite clearly the concerns of both Muslims and Christians. Christians felt it would be unreasonable for them to accept any Shariah Court in the Constitution or to grant concessions that would contradict their own disbelief in state religion. Christians totally rejected the idea of a state sponsored religion, as the adoption of the Shariah Law would imply.[197] The main fear the Christian delegates expressed was what they called the progressive Islamization of Nigeria, articulated and evident in the following ways:

a) Nigeria's surreptitious entry into the Organization of Islamic Conference (OIC).

b) The face of Abuja: i) Abuja, the Federal Capital Territory, looks like a Muslim city with the architectural designs, especially the bus stops, designed like mosques. ii) The Federal medical center (hospital) in Abuja has no mortuary and nowhere can coffins be bought in Abuja. This denies non-Muslims the facilities for preserving and not burying their dead on the same day of death.

c) Utterances of Muslim religious and political leaders that political leadership of Nigeria is a monopoly of Muslims, that Muslims cannot voluntarily submit to leadership by a Christian.

---

[197] Falola, *Violence in Nigeria*, 89.

d) The effect on the Muslims to: i) Resist the declaration of Nigeria as a secular state where secularism is clearly understood as different from Godlessness. ii) Extend the provision of the Shariah Court beyond the 1979 limit that is the origin of the current controversy.[198]

The Muslim members of the committee also had their grievances. They stated that they have no intention of "de-Christianizing" Nigeria and the Christians should appreciate the concessions that Muslims had already made to them. Therefore, they demanded that, "Christians should at least, and without any cost to themselves, make a concession on the Shariah Court issue to enable the Muslims to live by the dictates of their religion, as provided for in the fundamental rights of the same constitution."[199] Like the Christians, the Muslims enumerated some of their concerns to include the following:

a) The Common Law and much of Nigeria's legal system derived from England is Christian inspired, the House of Lords has clearly declared Britain a Christian State, thus the laws and other precepts in England are not only consistent with Christian tenets but are indeed inspired by them. It is this Christian-based legal system that the Colonial masters imposed on Nigeria.

b) The Gregorian calendar, which is used in Nigeria, is Christian. The Muslim calendar is ignored so much that most non-Muslims do not know that it exists.

c) The Salute of the Nigerian Military Officers with sword or gun resembles the sign of the cross and

---

[198] Anthony N. Aniagolu, *The Making of the 1989 Constitution of Nigeria*. (Ibadan: Spectrum, 1993), 132-3.

[199] Falola, *Violence in Nigeria*, 90.

the cross is a Christian symbol. Yet Muslim soldiers have to observe the practice.

d) The signs at hospitals and other medical institutions denote the Christian symbol of the cross.

e) The observance of Sunday and Saturday as work free days is to respect the Christian religion.[200]

The protest from the Christians against the introduction of Shariah not withstanding, almost all the governors of the Northern states in Nigeria have introduced the Shariah legal system since the return of democracy in Nigeria in 1999. As one would expect, much tension has been generated in Muslim-Christian relationships because of this.

3.3.3. School System and Government Machinery

Another major area of rift is the control of the school system and the curricular role of religion. Since independence, Muslims have become opposed to the ownership and control of schools by Christians missionaries;[201] a control and ownership that made some Muslims describe Nigerian schools as "a breeding ground for Christians, and enemies of Islam."[202] It should be recalled that one of the strongest and most effective tools of evangelization used by the missionary was the establishment of schools. This issue led to a religiously masterminded take over of a number Christian mission schools in the North by the Muslim government. Most schools that were considered strategic for the advancement of the Christianity were taken

---

[200] Aniagolu, *The Making of the 1989 Constitution of Nigeria*, 133

[201] Falola, *Violence in Nigeria*, 171.

[202] Muhammad Sali, "Islam and Western Education in Nigeria," *Champions Newspaper*, May 15, 1990.

over and Islamized by government agencies. In Zaria, for example, Muslims have acquired the entire primary mission schools and their Christians names changed to Islamic ones. The famous St. Mary's College, Zaria, was changed to Queen Amina College, Zaria. In some other states, besides the acquisition of private Christian mission schools, it is difficult to teach Christian religious education in the Elementary and High Schools without facing Muslim, and at times government, opposition.

Some state own media houses like Radio and Television in Kano are not allowed to broadcast Christian religious programs, only Islamic ones are allowed. In some of these Northern states, Christians are not allotted land to build Churches, even when they do have land; they are denied issuance of the certificate of occupancy needed to ensure the approval of building plans. It is an unwritten offence for Christians to build churches in some parts of the northern states or for a Christian Church to rise higher than a Mosque in the same city. As narrated by Sukuji Bakoji, a religious crisis began to loom between September 18 and 20, 2008 at Kongo Campus, Ahmadu Bello University (ABU), Zaria, following a plan to build a chapel for Catholic students. Muslim youths from the host community staged a violent protest against the plan. For three days running, they chanted around the city "Away with Christians," "Zaria City is for Islam alone," "No more building of Churches in Zaria."

The initial Catholic Chapel, called Chapel of Salvation, located close to the Administrative block at the campus, was burnt and reduced to rubbles some years ago by some Muslim fundamentalists. Consequently, during the tenure of the sole administrator of ABU, Major General Mamman Kontagora, a plot was allocated to the Catholic community in the campus, which was approved and included in the general plan. Trouble started when the Catholic community decided to lay the foundations of the chapel. Apart from the violent protests, inciting leaflets in Hausa language were circulated, calling on Muslims to rise up in unison to defend their faith by stopping the building of churches in the area. One of the leaflets was addressed to the Zazzau Emirate; it stated that the ancient city of Zaria remained a citadel of knowledge and centre of Islam, but the Christians and other western institutions continued to violate the people's religion and culture with impunity. "We are warning our visitors, the Christians, against over-stepping their bounds under the auspices of CAN. It is better for them to understand that Zaria City is for Islam only."[203] However, in a swift reaction, the secretary of the Christian Association of Nigeria (CAN), Rev. Joseph Hayab, warned that Christians would no longer fold their arms and allow the unleashing of another bout of bloody terror on them in the name of defending Islam in the state. According to the CAN spokesman, it was one professor in the campus who went to the community and incited the youth to resist any attempt to build another church on the campus.[204]

With these types of situations, most Christian Churches in the North have been demolished as illegal structures. Such situations occurred even in Abuja (the Federal Capital Territory) where the Minister of the Federal Capital Territory, who was a Muslim, demolished some Christian Churches as illegal structures. It is interesting to note that no single Mosque was demolished in Abuja during that period. This did not and still does not go down well with the Christians. It breeds bitter and hateful feelings towards Muslims.

The South is not left out in the web of events that leads to violence within the school system. As observed by Falola,

---

[203] Sukuji Bakoji, "Religious Crisis Looms in Zaria over Church Building. Enough is Enough, CAN Warns," in *Sunday Independence*, September 21, 2008.

[204] Ibid.

If the south had managed to escape the devastating physical violence associated with the north, the University of Ibadan in the southwest became a most unexpected source of danger and volatility in 1985 and 1986. Christians and Muslims there were entangled in a bitter argument, with the Minister of Education intervening in the vice-chancellor's authority and the public preparing for a fight (*sic*). Even to outsiders, the cause seems like it should have been inconsequential to a community of scholars accustomed to grappling with complex intellectual issues. The controversy centered on a cross erected in the 1950s to denote places of worship in the university. The Church was first to be built, and a Mosque came much later. Christians originally predominated at the university, both as teachers and students, which accounts for the location of two prominent churches on campus. In 1985, Muslims complained that the location of the cross in front of the eastern side of their Mosque violated the Islamic requirement that Muslims *(sic)* not see a cross, idol, or effigy during worship. They demanded that the cross be moved or relocated closer to the Church.

The Christians were infuriated. They blamed two Muslim politicians and government officials who visited the university and advised Muslims to assert themselves by provoking a fight over the cross.[205]

---

[205] Falola, *Violence in Nigeria*, 175.

The Christians, backed by some authorities of the university, refused to remove the cross. The controversy was dragged before the public and the government in Lagos (then headquarters of Nigeria). A small 'cross' had become the object of a national debate, setting the stage for a violent confrontation in the major city of Ibadan. The Minister of Education, Jibril Aminu, a Muslim, took the side of Muslims. The Christians saw in the Minister a Jihadist bent on destroying Christians and their schools. For the Christian teachers, the cross provided an opportunity to fight Aminu; for the Muslims, an opportunity to rid the university of Christian association.[206]

In all, both Christians and Muslims have complained at one point or the other over different issues of government machineries advancing the cause of the other's religion to the other's detriment. This has created an unhealthy relationship between Christians and Muslims in Nigeria.

3.3.4. Foreign Policy

Ordinarily, religion should not be a determinant factor in shaping the foreign policy of a secular state as Nigeria. But in Nigeria, it does and it is as well a source of tension between Muslims and Christians in Nigeria. A good example of how religion is involved in the foreign policy of Nigeria and how it also creates religio-politico tension in Nigeria is articulated by William Pat and Toyin Falola: "Since independence, religion has affected the conduct of external relations in such areas as the definition of national interests, the preference of the north for Islamic

---

[206] Nereus I. Nwosu, "Religion and the Crisis of National Unity in Nigeria," in *African Study Monograph* 17(3), October 1996, 141-152.

countries, the role of foreign missionaries and relations with the West."[207] Stressing more the religious dimension of Nigeria's foreign policy, Alkali Nura and Adamu Adamu, write,

> Relations with Israel were a source of disagreement throughout the 1980s. CAN and many Nigerian Christians believed that the break in diplomatic relations between Nigeria and Israel from 1973 to 1991 was not politically motivated, but was instigated and sponsored by the Muslims as a gesture of spite against the Christians. CAN advised the government that relations with Israel were economically profitable, that Israeli companies were operating in Nigeria, and consular services were required to assist Christian pilgrims. The opposition of Muslims was based on the grounds that Israel was anti-Islam, anti-Arab, and in support of Nigerian Christians. They preferred to see the strengthening of relations with Islamic countries and more cautious relations with the west.[208]

While most Christians in Nigeria oppose strong ties and diplomacy with Saudi Arabia, most Muslims also oppose and question Nigeria's diplomatic relations with the Vatican City, which they see as a model of a Christian theocratic state. These relations have often raised public

---

[207] William Pat and Toyin Falola, *Religious Impact on the Nation State: The Nigerian Predicament.* (London: Avebury, 1995), 54.

[208] Alkali Nura & Adamu Adamu, *Islam in Africa: Proceedings of Islam in African Conference.* (Ibadan: Spectrum, 1993), 178.

and verbal conflict and aggressiveness between Muslims and Christians in Nigeria.

3.3.5. Mutual Suspicion

Relationships between Muslims and Christians have been characterized by mutual suspicion over the years. Every action, even friendly action, is often times looked upon by Muslims and Christians as having some ulterior motive. Crises that are not clearly religious are suspected of having a hidden religious agenda, and are traced to the other's religion. For example, in the recent political crisis that took place in Jos, the Christians suspected and alleged that Muslims terrorists from neighboring countries were hired by Muslims to unleash terror on innocent Christians under the cover of a political crisis. Reporting the suspicion and accusation, Hassan Ibrahim writes in the *Nigeria Tribune*,

> The Christian Association of Nigeria (CAN) in the Northern states rose from its meeting in Kaduna on Wednesday, alleging that hired terrorists were used to unleash terror on innocent people during the recent Jos crisis where six pastors were killed.
> The body also condemned the replacement of a Christian commissioner of police in Plateau State with a Muslim officer, leaving a Muslim State Security Service (SSS) director and a Muslim military intelligent officer to investigate the crisis.
> The chairman of CAN in the Northern states and Abuja, Archbishop Peter Jatau and the secretary, Elder Sa'Idu Dogo, in a communiqué read to newsmen in Kaduna, said they were shocked following their

discovery that most of the killings were carried out by hired terrorists who operated in police and military uniforms.

The Christian body said its findings showed that about 500 of these terrorists, who were not Nigerians, were in various police detentions in the state for their connection with the crisis.

"We are equally shocked that the killings and wanton destruction of properties were carried out spontaneously in different places.

This is an indication that the riot was premeditated and pre-planned and that the perpetrators just hid under the guise of local government election to execute their long-time plan," it said.

It expressed with dismay that the security agents failed to report to the appropriate authorities, which it alleged was because of religious bias.

It [CAN] described as callous and malicious the call for the resignation of the Plateau State governor or a declaration of state of emergency in the state, while calling on the Federal Government to employ a diplomatic means to find out the level of involvements of neighboring countries in the crisis.[209]

One such suspicion was displayed during the visit of Archbishop John Onaiyekan to the Abuja National Mosque on the March 29, 2007. As reported by Allen,

---

[209] Hassan Ibrahim, "Terrorists Killed 6 Pastors in Jos Crisis—CAN," in *Nigerian Tribune*, December 18, 2008.

After the meeting broke up, one of the Muslims escorted his Catholic guests on a tour of the enormous domed mosque, just as afternoon prayers were ending. Archbishop Onaiyekan was dressed in a red-and-white clerical gown with a pectoral cross. As the group stood in the center of the mosque, a knot of men approached the guide. They angrily demanded to know by what right Christian clergy had to be invited into the mosque. One of them spit out a Hausa word, which means, roughly, "abomination." Before things could get out of hand, Archbishop Onaiyekan made a quick exit. [210]

This suspicion pervades even the daily relations of Christians and Muslims in cities across the country. In Christian dominated towns and cities, like the South-East, Muslims are careful about what they say and do, in a similar manner, in Muslim dominated towns and cities, like the North, Christians are extremely careful of their utterances and actions, because everyone sees his neighbor of the other religion as a *sabo* (a spy and or a betrayer).

3.4 ATR, ISLAM, AND CHRISTIANITY

Strained religious relationships, divergences and conflicts in Nigeria are not limited to the interactions of just two religious faiths: Islam against Christianity or Christianity against Islam and or Christianity against ATR. They at times involve the three religions simultaneously. In some cases, it is the three religions against each other

---

[210] Allen, "Tough love with Islam—Church in Nigeria may be model of dialogue."

as individuals. In some other cases, it is two religions teaming up as 'partners in crime' against one religion. For example, there is a joint effort by Christians and Muslims in collaboration with the government to undermine and to relegate ATR to the background despite the official recognition of ATR in Nigeria. Certain benefits given to Christians and Muslims are not extended to ATR. For example, in Abuja, the Nigerian Federal Capital, the federal government funded the building of the Muslim national Mosque and the Christian National Ecumenical Center. Whereas not even a piece of land has been allocated for the building of a shrine, be it ecumenical or not, and no fund has been appropriated for the building a Shrine for ATR by the federal government.

The areas of divergence, conflicts and tensions between ATR, Islam and Christianity in Nigeria include:

3.4.1. Belief Systems

The major source of divergence among the three religions in Nigeria is the belief in God. Although all three profess faith in a God who is supreme, eternal and creator of the universe, they differ in their concept and nature of this God. Muslims and Christians, with some limitations, are a bit closer in the concepts and nature of God, but collectively diverge and abhor the gods of ATR. In the words of David W. Shenk,

> Although African traditional faith agrees with Islam and Christianity that God is the creator of the earth and the life giver, Muslims and Christians believe that the creator in African religions is no longer and has never been dynamically present sustaining the earth and life. Those functions are left for the

lesser gods and spirits that are powerless
and figments of the imaginations, Muslims
and Christians maintain.[211]

Christians and Muslims see the traditional deities
as dead gods with mouths that cannot speak or eat,
hands that cannot move, and ears that cannot hear. The
Muslims see the Christians as not worshipping the true
God (Allah) because they worship Jesus, who is merely
human and whom they represent in images and symbols
in their places of worship. On the other hand, ATR sees
the Christian and Muslim Gods as gods who are far from
their people, whereas their gods live side by side with
them. They see the Christian and Muslim Gods as gods too
slow to act and to restore order in the society. Hence, ATR
accuses Islam and Christianity of being responsible for
corruption and moral decadence in the society, because
their Gods are slow to anger thereby condoning evil. In
traditional religion and society, the gods are the police and
the 'chief security officers.' In fact, many in Nigeria believe
that when all worshiped the native gods there was order
and justice in the society. They believe that things began
to change for the worst since the introduction of Islam and
Christianity when many abandoned the traditional gods to
submit to foreign gods. In the words of a Christian minister,
Rev. Canon B.M. Obiukwu of Emmanuel Anglican Church
Ezinifite, as reported in *The Nation Newspaper*,

> The Church and even Islam are preaching
> morality, but many Christians and Muslims
> are looking the other way. The behavior of
> people is far from what Christianity and

---

[211] David W. Shenk, *Global Gods: Exploring the Role of Religions
in Modern Societies*. (Waterloo, Ontario: Herald Press, 1995),
73.

Islam expect, but there is hope. People listen to the world and the material things it offer. They don't listen to what the Bible and the Quran say. That is the major problem we have in the society today. The deviation from the gospel and the Quran is responsible for many evils in the society and the society will not find its footing unless people turn back to God and stop worshipping the world.[212]

Followers of ATR respond to such emphatic statements as Obiukwu's that the God people need to turn back to and worship is the Native and traditional gods whom they abandoned to worship the Christian and Muslim gods. In fact, many, including some Christians and Muslims in Nigeria today, suggest that if public office holders were to take their oath of office with African gods and traditional religious symbols rather than using the Quran or the Bible, corruption would disappear among politicians and public office holders. This belief is held because traditional gods are believed to have struck dead those who violated oaths taken before them or in their names. Muslims and Christian respond by saying that the ATR worship demon gods who delight in killing their people while they serve a living God who is merciful to his people.

In general, Muslims and Christians forbid their followers from showing any tolerant attitude or accommodation to traditional gods, which they call idols, even though they may and have allowed certain aspects of the religion that worships these "idol." As reported in the *Associated Press*,

Early missionaries to Nigeria had condemned most traditional practices as pagan. The

---

[212] Michael Umudu, "Slaughter of the gods," in *The Nations.* September 21, 2008.

two mainstream groups, the Catholic and the Anglicans, gradually came to terms with most of them, even incorporating some traditional dances into church liturgy. But there was no room for the local gods, which were left stranded and unprotected once their erstwhile worshippers became Christians. Similarly, Muslim preachers in the predominantly Islamic north of the country forbade any interaction with figures and figurines dedicated to local idols. But many cultural dances featuring traditional masks are still tolerated in the north. Most converts are in constant tension over how much of the old beliefs can be taken into the new faith, said Isidore Uzoatu, a specialist in the history of Christianity in Africa affiliated with Nnamdi Azikiwe University in southeastern Nigeria.[213]

The divergences on the concept and notion of God and the war of words surrounding the belief in God have been a source of tension and disharmony in Nigeria. Such have led to the burning of native shrines and symbols of native deities, as well as the burning of Churches and Statues and Mosques.

---

[213] "Christianity vs. the old gods of Nigeria." *Associated Press.* September 4, 2007. http://wwrn.org/sparse.php?idd=26135 (Assessed: October 1, 2009).

3.4.2. Physical Violence, Discrimination and Verbal Abuse

Craig Nessan defined violence as "the attempt of an individual or group to impose its will on others through any nonverbal, verbal, or physical means that inflict psychological or physical injury."[214] Informed by Craig's definition, one can therefore unequivocally say that the three religions together in Nigeria have witnessed and are still witnessing lots of violence, intolerance, discrimination, physical and verbal abuses towards each other and their followers. As recorded by Joseph Awolalu,

> Christianity and Islam, when they came in contact in with traditional religion caused a disruption and a division. Both divided the community into two camps—the converts (either Christians or Muslims) who looked down upon the old traditional religion and the loyal adherents of the traditional religion. Thus it can be asserted that from the middle of the 19th century to about the middle of this century, there was a big struggle between the imported religions and the indigenous religions held by Nigerians. As a result of the encounter, the indigenous culture was badly shaken. Many Nigerians became so westernized, Christianized and Islamized that they came to look down on [and abuse] things indigenous and traditional.[215]

---

[214] Craig L. Nessan, "Sex, Aggression, and Pain: Sociological Implications for Theological Anthropology," *Zygon*, 33 (1998), 451.

[215] Joseph Omosade Awolalu, "The Encounter between Traditional and other Religions in Nigeria," in Jacob Olupona,

Reporting on some of the physical violence, Adebayo Waheed writes,

> The incident of Muslims who destroyed shrines of traditional worshippers in Offa, Kwara state is fresh in people's memories. So is the case of Christians in Calabar who did the same. This is not to say that the traditional worshippers are saints. A Christian evangelist was recently manhandled in a Lagos suburb while a leading chief, who abandoned African Traditional Religion for Islam had his property seized by the traditional worshippers. Yet no religion teaches violence or hatred.[216]

Citing an example of the verbal abuses that have characterized the presence of the three religions in Nigeria, Michael Umudu reports that:

> Amaekwulu situation represents a miniature of what has become a common phenomenon in most parts of Igboland, Nigeria and indeed the rest of Black Africa. The raging war against Africa's traditional institutions was launched by Christian Missionaries as well as Islamic Jihadists [sponsored] from Arab (*sic*) and since then 'the centre could no longer hold'. These major world religions did not only exert efforts at converting the indigenous Africans to their faiths but labeled virtually

---

ed., *African Traditional Religions in Contemporary Society.* (New York: Paragon House, 1991), 115.

[216] Adebayo Waheed, "Nigerians are too far from God," in *Nigerian Tribune.* Monday, 20th August, 2007.

everything about Africa evil. Their economic, political and social powers enabled them to sweep through the soils of the Black World with little or no resistance. Though not entirely without resistance, the remaining traditionalists went on with the worship of their indigenous gods; they retained their holy sites and lived side-by-side with Christian converts who grew in number day-by-day. The remaining traditionalists in this part of Nigeria saw Christianity as a strange visitor that would soon go back to where it came . . . One of the problems we have in this society is that Christians think that if you are not their member then you are not worshiping God. To Muslims, they call Muhammedans and "Alakubas", and traditionalists they call pagans and heathens. The Muslims in return group Christians and traditionalists as infidels.[217]

Continuing, Michael Umudu gave a brief synopsis of the origin of the physical and verbal wars between the religions in Nigeria, and especially how it has taken shape presently in Igboland:

The struggles for the souls of Africans were not for the sake of enshrining Christianity, Islam or any other imported religion. The proponents of these religions told the indigenous Africans that the light has come and hence they should no more wallow in darkness. When they came they brought their social, political and indeed religious

---

[217] Umudu, "Slaughter of the gods."

systems and told the Africans to accept them and do away with what they referred to as Africa's primitive ways of life. The Africans embraced the systems and now propagate them by themselves. In Igboland today, the war is no longer between the traditional religion and Christianity as the former has almost gone extinct. The battle is now among different extremes in the Christendom (*sic*), while traditional religion remnants fold their arms and watch.[218]

Apart from violently and verbally abusing each other, the three religions in Nigeria discriminate against each other. They show love and care only to those who are of their religion. Such discriminations are noticeable in the labor market, admission into tertiary institutions, the award of government contracts and elections and appointments into political offices or posts. A Muslim in Zaria, Kaduna State and in Sokoto, for example, with a very low score in an entrance examination is considered first before a Christian indigene of the same states. Election to the highest office in Nigeria is determined by religious affiliation. The first question that comes out of people's lips is: is the candidate Christian or Muslim or Traditionalist? Appointments to political office are made in line with religious identifications. In some parts of the country, a person has to strongly manifest a tendency towards a particular religion before he is offered a job or employment. Reporting on this ugly incident, Frieder Ludwig in research on the relationships between Muslims and followers of other religions in Zamfara State of Nigeria since the introduction of Shariah in the state in 1999 writes,

---

[218] Ibid.

Among other things, there were accusations of discriminations by the followers of Christian faith [and African Traditional Religion] in the distributions of goods and services. The chairman of the Zamfara State Chapter of CAN (Christian Association of Nigeria), Reverend Father Linus Mary Awuhe told *Weekly Trust* in 2002 that the government [headed by a Pro-Shariah governor] has exhibited itself in discriminatory action particularly against persons that are of different faith [from Islam] . . . "Take, for instance, the governor has spent a lot of resources building mosques everywhere in the state. Tell me one shrine the governor has built," Rev. Awuhe pointed out.

In the interviews conducted by Musa Gaiya in Zamfara in 2003, it was pointed out that if a Christian wants to buy a piece of land to build a house he must sign a clause that the place would not be turned into a church or a hotel.[219]

Such discriminations in Zamfara extends to mandatory imposition of a particular dress code considered as decent in Islam and the use of public transportation that forbids men and women to ride on the same bus or motor-cycle popularly known as *kabu-kabu* in Northern Nigeria and *Okada* in the South. It must be emphasized that these discriminatory tendencies in Zamfara affect not just the Christians who complain aloud, but painfully affect more the small minority of traditionalists in the state who suffer in silence.

---

[219] Frieder Ludwig, "Christian-Muslim Relations in Northern Nigeria..." 621

3.4.3. Education and Literacy

All three religions appreciate the place and importance of education in transmitting religious norms and customs to future generations and for the development of society, but they differ on what should be taught, who should teach, and how to teach what should be taught.

Traditional religion in Nigeria and Africa as whole is not a religion of the book (although scholars of African traditional religion have done much in articulating the basics of ATR in their various works, there is still no codified doctrinal handbook of ATR as we have the Bible/Catechism and the Quran/Hadith); it transmits its teachings and norms through oral tradition, proverbs, mythical stories, and songs. While Christians and Muslims appreciate and borrow some aspect of their teaching methodology like songs and proverbs from ATR and incorporate them into Christian and Muslim teachings and rituals, they condemn the totality of African traditional literacy as uncivilized and barbaric. African Traditional Religion is not the subject of study in any elementary or high school in Nigeria. The religious curricula is still that which was inherited from or which was influenced by the Christian and Muslim missionaries that presented native and traditional religion as evil and sinful, and the followers as pagans and heathens.

Furthermore, Muslims reject not only traditional literacy but also western education that they closely link with Christianity. Hence, in some Northern states, it is forbidden to teach Christian religious knowledge. Some Muslims fundamentalists, like the Boko Haram that rejects everything western, forbid teaching Muslim kids in English or in any other language except in Arabic. As recorded by Falola,

Muslims rejected western knowledge that did not teach Arabic and Islamic religious knowledge. They fought these curricula in 1976 . . . In addition, they succeeded in minimizing the teaching of Christian religious knowledge in northern schools and in removing African traditional religions from many schools so as not to promote "paganism." In the 1980s, Yoruba Muslims sought to put an end completely to Christian domination of the educational system. As far as they were concerned, the purpose of those schools was to evangelize the youth, taking them away from Islam.[220]

Christians in turn equally forbid not only the teaching of ATR; they as well forbid the teaching of Islam and Arabic in mission schools nation-wide and in public schools in the South-East and South-South zones.

There is an exclusivist tendency in religious education in Nigeria that breeds and leads to religious hatred, contempt and intolerance among Nigerian kids of school age, who will be the leaders of tomorrow.

3.4.4. Struggle for Polictical and Social Identity

Politically and socially, all the three religions struggle to assert their self-importance in Nigerian society. It is not uncommon in political and social gatherings to see an Imam (Muslim), a Bishop (Christian), and a Traditional ruler (ATR) struggling and lobbying for who should be acknowledged first and who should act on behalf of the other religious leaders. Acknowledging anyone before the

---

[220] Falola, *Violence in Nigeria*, 172.

other breeds feelings of resentment from followers against the individual and religion of the one who "was made" to look more important than the other.

In an effort to boost their social importance, to the envy of one another, these religious leaders ascribe to themselves bogus titles, either in imitation of the other or to out shine the other. For example, the Sultan of Sokoto, besides his Royal Highness, is now addressed as His Eminence, the Sultan of Sokoto. The idea behind the title "his eminence" is to imitate the Catholic Cardinals, and to exalt him far above all other Christian leaders and traditional rulers. The title of "Your or His Eminence" has never been an Islamic title. Similarly, most Christian ministers have arrogated to themselves the title of "His Holiness" and "King of Kings" to boost their social status and to appear above Muslim and traditional leaders in rank and holiness. Equally, traditional rulers are now addressed as "His Majesty", placing them in a position almost or next to God. All these have led to bickering, jealousy, and backbiting and even open confrontations among the religions in Nigeria, especially when the leader is not properly addressed in his proper "title" by followers of other religions.

Furthermore, Peter Lewis and Michael Bratton in a survey that touched on identity, violence and the stability in Nigeria reported that,

> Religious identities in Nigeria are usually classified into three—Christian, Muslim and Traditional. Of the three, traditional religions is the least politically active; numbering several hundreds of ethnic groups and subgroups, villages, clans and kin groups; and, involving the worship of different gods and goddesses. However, in parts of the Kogi, Kwara, and Nassarawa states, masquerade activities associated with traditional religion

have been a major source of conflicts. In effect, Christian and Muslim identities have been the mainstay of religious differentiation and conflict, with Nigerian Muslims much more likely to evince or articulate a religious identity than Christians.[221]

3.4.5. Ethno-Religious Differences

Another area of visible differences and conflict among the religions in Nigeria is what can be described as Ethno-Religious differences. Partly because of their tendency to spill over from their initial theatres into other localities, states, or even regions of the federation, ethno-religious clashes have proved to be the most violent instances of interfaith crisis in Nigeria. They have occurred mainly in the Middle-Belt and cultural borderline states of the Muslim north, where Muslim Hausa-Fulani groups have been pitted against non-Muslim ethnic groups in a "dangerous convergence of religious and ethnic fears and animosities ... [in which it] is often difficult to differentiate between religious and ethnic conflicts as the dividing line between the two is very thin."[222]

Major examples of violent ethno-religious conflicts in Nigeria have included the Kafanchan-Kaduna crises in 1987 and 1999, Zangon-Kataf riots of 1992, Tafawa Balewa clashes in 1991, 1995 and 2000, Kaduna Shariah riots of 2000, and the Jos riots of 2001 and 2010

---

[221] Peter Lewis and Michael Bratton, *Attitudes toward Democracy and Market in Nigeria: Report of a National Opinion Survey.* (January—February, 2000), 5.

[222] "Nigeria: Continuing Dialogues for Nation Building," in *International Institute for Democracy and Electoral Assistance (International IDEA)* (Stockholm, 2000), 296.

The connection between religion and ethnicity in Nigeria as a major source of divergence, conflicts and tensions in Nigeria is not far fetched. One only needs to understand the notion of ethnicity to see this connection. Ethnicity is generally regarded as the most basic and politically salient identity in most Nigerian tribes. This claim is supported by the fact that both in competitive and non-competitive settings, most Nigerians are more likely to define themselves in terms of their ethnic affinities than any other identity. Indeed, according to the authoritative 2000 survey on *Attitudes to Democracy and Markets in Nigeria*, ethnicity "is demonstrably the most conspicuous group identity in Nigeria."[223] In essence, close to two-thirds of the population see themselves as members of primordial ethnic, regional, and religious groups. What is more, "religious and ethnic identities are more fully formed, more holistic and more strongly felt than class identities as evidenced in the fact that whereas those who identify with religious and ethnic communities are almost universally proud of their group identities... those who see themselves as members of a social class are somewhat more equivocal about their pride."[224] In some communities ethnicity comes first before religion, while in some, religion comes first (especially among dominant Muslim communities). Which ever way, ethnicity and religion are intertwined in Nigeria in such a way that ethnic violence translates easily into religious violence and vice versa.

---

[223] Lewis and Bratton, *Attitudes toward Democracy and Market in Nigeria*, 27.

[224] Ibid, 26.

CHAPTER FOUR

INTERFAITH RELATIONSHIP AMONG THE THREE RELIGIONS IN NIGERIA: AREAS OF CONVERGENCE. *(A DIALOGICAL APPROACH).*

It has not been all violence and conflicts in the interaction among the three religions of Nigeria. Much has been done in areas of convergence, friendship and interfaith actions towards improved relationship. This part of our work examines from a dialogical perspective (this perspective—dialogical—places side-by-side one religion with another) the moral values, beliefs and doctrines, and ethical principles on which the religions in Nigeria agree enough as a basis or starting point of interfaith relationships and to take action together on the socio-religious problem facing the nation. It will also point out evidence of mutual existence and cooperation among the religions. The importance of this chapter is underscored by a simple belief that if we can identify the depth and breadth of convergence that already exists in the ethics, doctrines, and teachings of these religions, then we will discover the basis for promoting the common good of all in the society through interfaith relationships. This approach is in line with the teaching of Vatican II:

> In our day, when people are drawing more closely together and the bonds of friendship between different peoples are being strengthened, the Church examines more closely its relations with non-Christian religions . . . it reflects at the outset on what people have in common and what tend to bring them together.[225]

Keeping in mind these points of convergence is not only important, but also essential for people for whom religion is a basic component that informs their individual and social life. They are essential for the believer who through his religiosity intends first to worship God and to express individually and socially his fulfilling dependence on God, as well as seeking a just way to enhance relationships with people of other faiths. They are important for those who study the place of religion in society and for those who are called to mediate in religious conflict resolutions.

4.1 AFRICAN TRADITIONAL RELIGION (ATR) *VS* ISLAM.

African Traditional Religion is the basic structure upon which the Islamic faith was built in Nigeria. ATR has shown various levels of openness and interaction with Islam since its inception in Nigeria. Similarly, Islam, which was introduced to Hausa and Fulani lands in northern Nigeria

---

[225] Vatican II, "Declaration on the Relation of the Church to Non-Christian Religions" *(Nostra Aetate)*. 28 October 1965, no. 1.

by Muslim itinerant traders,[226] has examples of a wide range of interaction with African traditional belief systems and practices. According to Toyin Falola,

> Indigenous religious practices were still very much alive in the Hausa state [along side Islam]. In Kanem-Borno, the King continued to maintain the age-long practice of seclusion. Other Hausa Kings, not wishing to offend powerful cult priests, continued to practice the ancient rites. Many Muslim converts tolerated indigenous practices, and most of the rural areas were probably unaffected by Islam. The majority of the political leaders did not seek full-scale application of *al-Shari'a*, and certainly no state could be described as a theocracy. Political leaders of the Muslim faith compromised with traditionalists and involved them in government. Conversion efforts existed, but usually on a small scale. The minority Muslim elites were generally tolerant of non-Islamic practices.[227]

Evidently, when Muslims constituted a minority, a pluralist response to other cultures and religions occurred. Commenting on the pluralistic response, Nehemiah Levtzion and Abdin Chande write,

---

226 Joseph Omosade Awolanu, "The Encounter between African Traditional Religion and Other Religions in Nigeria" in *African Traditional Religions in Contemporary Society*, edited by Jacob K. Olupona. (New York: Paragon House, 1991), 114.

227 Toyin Falola, *Violence in Nigeria: The Crisis of Religious Politics and Secular Ideologies*. (New York: University of Rochester Press, 1998), 25.

The cross-cultural trade in many parts of Africa, apart from reinforcing cultural self-identity and nurturing religious commitment, fostered a pluralist structure in which commerce, Islam, and the indigenous system supported the urban network. In this way a balance was established between local ritual prescriptions and those of universal Islam.

Islam, which for many centuries coexisted well with traditional African religion, gradually over time attempted to replace it as the dominant faith of some regions. What made this possible was that the Islamic faith was much more adaptable in Africa, with minimum requirements for new members, including at the very least a change of name after reciting the testimony of faith. The observances of Islamic duties along with the understanding of the faith were supposed to follow later. For the first generation of Muslims, introduction to Islamic cultural values was what came first whereas Islamization itself could take generations to realize. At this level, there was accommodation to social and political structures of authority. This was the period when the learned Muslims, as in West African kingdoms, played a key role in administration and diplomacy. Eventually, however, a number of these African rulers adopted Islam and in doing so may partly have undermined the basis of their legitimacy as guardians of African ancestral religious traditions. Nevertheless, they did not completely renounce ties with the African traditional religion, which continued to be the religion of many of their subjects. This arrangement assisted in maintaining order although it did not please some West African Sūfī leaders of the eighteenth and nineteenth centuries who launched their jihāds and reform movements of Islamic revivalism, some of which had Mahdi and messianic overtones, to establish Islamic states.[228]

Muslims took the view that different forms of primal religion could exist side by side with them in the same society. Coupled with this was the recognition that the social and political structure of the wider society could be accommodated. Individual Muslims and whole communities throughout Nigeria have incorporated into Islam to varying degrees different aspects of traditional life.

In many regions of Nigeria Islam has gradually substituted itself for the traditional religion, sometimes under the influence of external factors and in the overwhelming majority of cases without any violence. One could cite a whole series of factors that show a degree of religious, cultural and sociological proximity between these two religious faith communities in Nigeria. Such areas of interaction and convergences between ATR and Islam in Nigeria include the following: Religious belief, Rituals, Spirits and their powers in human affairs, Treatment of illness, Socio-cultural solidarity, and Authority and norms.

---

[228] Nehemiah Levtzion and Abdin Chande, "Islam: Islam in Sub-Saharan Africa" in *Encyclopedia of Religion.* Lindsay Jones, Ed. Vol. 7 2nd ed. (Detroit: Macmillan Reference USA, 2005), 4600-4612.

4.1.1. Religious Belief:

ATR and Islam share many common religious beliefs, prominent among which is the belief in a creator God, who is transcendent and yet immanent, who is omnipotent, omniscient and omnipresent. Although referred to by different names and titles, God in both religions deserves the worship and absolute reverence from the adherents. He has the power to reward and to punish, and he directs human life. John Mbiti, describing the similarities between the religious belief systems in ATR and Islam, said,

> Concerning purely religious beliefs, there are elements of contact between Islam and traditional religions. As we have seen, the concept of God is universally acknowledged by African traditional religious people. This [concept of God] is the Ethno-Religious differences key doctrine of Islam: 'There is but one God, Allah, and Muhammad is his prophet'. Here then, there is no need for Islam to stress the concept of God or the oneness of God, as far as traditional religions are concerned.[229]

Islam did not teach the African who God is; every African knows him and relates to him with great awe, reverence and devotion, just as Muslims do. Both religions believe that the surest medium of communion and communication with God is prayer. Thus, in ATR one wakes up with prayers on his lips, kola nut and wine in his hands for pouring libation while uttering the words of prayers of thanksgiving, protection and blessing. In Islam also, prayer stands out as

---

[229] John S. Mbiti, *African Religions and Philosophy*, 2nd ed. (Ibadan: Heinemann, 1990), 244.

138

the one pillar that every Muslim adheres to. Both religions believe worship and prayer requires a fundamental attitude of strict discipline and reverence.

4.1.2. Rituals:

Ritual actions and practices in worship and in life as a whole is another area where ATR and Islam in Nigeria interact and converge. One such ritual practice is the place of animal sacrifice in both religions. At certain points in Islam, e.g., after Ramadan, the celebration of the Id El-Kabir or Sallah, as it is called by Nigerian Muslims, goats and rams are ritually slaughtered as a sacrifice to Allah and in commemoration of the sacrificing of the ram by Abraham in place of Ismail. In ATR, various sacrifices to the gods are done with animals of different kinds. Thus, coming to Nigeria, the Muslims saw a common ground between them and ATR in the area of animal sacrifice as a way of expressing worship to God.

Islam in Nigeria does not reject as false every aspect of belief and practice found in indigenous religion. Islam with qualification and modification recognizes a number of important traditional rituals and practices, like divination, or magic accepted as sihr, as legitimate. [230] Practitioners of divination and experts on traditional spiritual categories bridge the gap between Islam and primal religions by 'chiseling' out all the edges of Muslim orthopraxis to create a form of popular religion. Explaining the interaction that exists in the ritual life and practices of ATR and Islam, Mbiti writes,

---

[230] Peter B. Clark and I. Linden, *Islam in Modern Nigeria*. (Munchen: Entwicklung und Frieden, 1984), 138.

Another area of ready agreement between Islam and traditional concepts and practices is in matters of ritual, divination and magic. Islamic practice encourages divination and the use of good magic . . . Islam approves and sanctions magical rituals which are directed towards such legitimate ends as the cure of disease, the prevention and curtailment of misfortune, and the assurance of prosperity and success; even if in the background the people retain hope in God. Some Muslims use divination to impress and win converts, but justify the use of sorcery and witchcraft only when employed to protect the rights of people and trap wrongdoers.

Islamic ritual connected with birth, marriage, and burial are fairly readily assimilated into existing traditional ideas and practices [especially in Northern Nigeria]. In funeral matters, the Islamic rituals and practice of washing the dead agrees with the traditional practices. Points of similarity emerge in ritual mourning, which includes washing, cleansing, seclusion, and purification.[231]

Although Muslims have strong faith in God, some of them still rely on traditional rituals and magic and charms for protection against enemies and against evil spirits; a belief that is dominant in traditional religion. Affirming this fact, Benjamin Ray writes,

Although Islam is a universal religion focused on a transcendent God, it has been fairly tolerant of elements of African

---

[231] Mbiti, *African Religions and Philosophy*, 245.

religions that deal with the microcosmic level of existence. Islam has never renounced the means of handling a concern that is central to traditional African religions: the explanation and control of personal fortunes and misfortunes.[232]

A good Muslim friend of mine never travels without his charms around his waist or as a ring on his finger. As a kid, I remember a good number of Muslims who would pray in our village square to Allah and after prayers would go around the village selling charms and amulets for various uses. The traditionalists in my village never saw any difference in their belief and worldview that every body should have his or her *chi* (charm, spirit, amulets, talisman) that helps and guides him or her through life, between that of Muslims who were selling the *chis* to natives and were also using them as well. This combination endeared the natives to the Muslims, and so instead of attacking them and chasing them away, they offered them much hospitality. Again, in one of the religious riots that occurred in the South-East of Nigeria, which I witnessed, many Muslims evoked the magical powers of their charms that enabled them to disappear, thus escaping death. On the other hand, cases abound where oils and perfumes from Arabia are highly sought after by traditionalists, who believe these oils and perfumes coming from Arabia, especially Mecca, have magical powers.

There is therefore a well-blended interaction between ATR and Islam in Nigeria in areas of ritual practices as can be seen in the daily lives of followers of both religions.

---

[232] Benjamin C. Ray, *African Religions: Symbols, Rituals, and Community*, 2nd ed. (New Jersey: Prentice Hall, 2000), 159.

4.1.3. The Spirits and Their Powers in Human Affairs

In ATR the world is full of spirits, good and evil. The good spirits are intermediaries between humans and the Supreme Being. Likewise, Islam affirms the existence of many spiritual beings, including angels, jinns and the devil, which are easily assimilated into the traditional religious milieu. Islam in Nigeria does not ask its new converts to abandon their accustomed confidence in these spirit and mystical forces or beings.

Thus some Muslim clerics in different parts of Nigeria permit the practice of consulting spirits and spirit possession. One such spirit that exercises much influence among Muslim is Northern Nigeria is *Bori*. *Bori* is a Hausa noun, meaning the occult force, which resides in physical things. The *Bori* cult is both an institution of spiritual forces, and the performance of ritual, dance and music by which these spirits are controlled and which heal illness. It is an aspect of the traditional Maguzawa Hausa religious traditions. *Bori* became a state cult led by ruling class priestesses amongst some of the late pre-colonial Hausa States. At this period (late pre-colonial Hausa—1800s-1902) the Bori spirit priestesses communed with spirits through ecstatic dance rituals. A corps of Bori priestesses and their helpers was led by a royal priestess, titled the 'Inna', or 'Mother of us all'. The Inna oversaw this network, which was not only responsible for protecting society from malevolent forces through possession dances, but also provided healing and divination throughout the kingdom.[233]

Before the Jihad of Shehu Uthman Dan Fodio of the early 19ᵗʰ century (a jihad that overran the northern traditional institutions and leaving many dead), almost

---

[233] Adeline Masquelier, "Lightening, Death and the Avenging Spirits: Bori Values in a Muslim World," in *Journal of Religion in Africa*, Vol. 24, n.1, Feb., 1994, pp. 2-51.

all Muslims of the Northern region were initiated into the Bori indigenous deity or cult. Some Muslims were proud to be called "sons" and "daughters" of Bori. These initiates performed public possession dances, exhibiting the personality and the behavior of the spirits, and received offerings made to the spirits. After Shehu's jihad, the *Bori* cult was officially banned and was displaced to the margins of Muslim Hausa-speaking society. The *Bori* cult became a cult of Hausa-Muslim women, whose social and religious status had been significantly diminished by mainstream Muslim control. These women exhibited a wide range of social roles involving status, power, and display in public life, all of which are normally denied to Muslim women. Although some Muslim clerics, following the example of Uthman Dan Fodio, discredited and condemned the *Bori* cult as unlawful, they recognized the reality of the spirits behind the Bori cult. Some Muslim clerics even regarded these traditional spirits as local forms of Arabic jinn spirits which are recognized in the Qur'an.[234] Despite the criticism from fundamental and zealous Muslims, the Bori spirits and other such spirits continue to influence the life of Muslims and their interaction with followers of ATR, even to these modern times. According to Nehemiah Levtzion and Chande,

> Despite Muslim efforts to purge African elements from their faith, Islam continued to display a level of indigenization or Africanization in Nigeria and other parts of West Africa. In spite of producing such well-known major religious Fulani reformers of the nineteenth century, including Shehu Usuman Dan Fodio, in northern Nigeria,

---

[234] Ray, *African Religions: Symbols, Rituals, and Community,* 157-158.

women still tend to follow the traditional cults, including the bori spirit cult, even with the sustained impact of Islam in Hausaland for centuries. According to some scholars, there must be a level of affinity between the two religious systems which allows this to happen. For instance, the belief in mystical powers (jinn or invisible supernatural creatures) allows Islam to be accommodated to the African spirit world, which is important to understanding the African religious universe.[235]

Habila U. Dan Fulani gave a good example of the integration of the traditional spirit possession among Hausa Muslims of Northern Nigeria as part of their faith and religions. According to his report, at about three thirty p.m. on the 24th of February, 1990, the Bauchi Radio Corporation was playing its program on "Peoples and Events" in Hausa, the first words the presenter used were *Ikon Allah Baya Karewa*, "God's wonders and miracles never end". He continued, 'A girl of nine in Ungwan Jahun here in Bauchi town has now become the center of attraction, for she and her parents believe that a spirit *Iska* had appeared to her and had given her medicine for all sorts of ailments.' The reporter then went on to say that, while he was interviewing the girl who claims that she can cure different types of ailments, about fifty women and twenty men were waiting for the girl to prescribe medicine for them. While discussing *Ikon Allah*, the "wonders of God," exhibited in the life of a spirit possessed Muslim girl and priestess, the Muslim reporter saw no contradiction at all between the power of *Iska*, a *Bori* spirit, and the power of Allah, God.

---

[235] Levtzion and Abdin Chande, "Islam: Islam in Sub-Saharan Africa," 4603.

Such a paradox, where Hausa Muslims react thus to the sporadic appearance of Bori spirits in human society is not surprising, especially when viewed from the backdrop of the traditional Hausa worldview. The Hausa worldview exhibits a strong belief in the existence of spirits and their interaction with human beings.[236] It is this strong belief among Hausa people in the influence of spirits on human affairs that forms one of the bedrocks of belief in spirits among Nigerian Muslims and upon which the survival of the Bori cult in a predominantly Muslim environment hinges. When spirits appear, the phenomenon is referred to as *Ikon Allah!* (God's power/miracle) They are thus tacitly accepted in an Islamic environment as coming from Allah, God himself. This paradox serves to emphasize the existence of the institution of Bori as a contemporary cult in the predominantly Hausa-Muslim societies of Northern Nigeria.

One African writer who affirms Islamic accommodation to Africa's indigenous spiritual heritage among Nigerian Muslims is Ibrahim Tahir in his novel the *Last Imam*.[237] Tahir's narrative tells of a reformed-minded Alhaji Usman, the Imam of the Bauchi Emirate of Nigeria, who strives to abolish some of his community's pre-Islamic beliefs and practices. The Imam, who belongs to the same lineage of scholars as the Fulani reformer Shehu Uthman Dan Fodio, rejects the accommodating approach of his father, his beloved predecessor, and gradually but sternly suppresses several popular customs. These changes begin to alienate the people from the practice of Islam in Bauchi. The story reaches its climax with the occurrence of violent

---

[236] Habila U. Dan-Fulani, "Factors contributing to the survival of the Bori Cult in Northern Nigeria," in *Numen.*, Vol. 46, n. 4, 1999, pp 412-447.

[237] Ibrahim Tahir, *The last Imam*, (London: Routledge & Kegan Paul, 1984), 15-35.

lightening storms and a harsh drought, which cause death and suffering in the community and which persist in their severity despite the Imam's prayer. He refuses to respond to the people's urging to offer a sacrifice to a local spirit called the Great Hyena. Instead, he preaches fervently about the absoluteness and the universality of God's will by which all things happen in the world. He urges acceptance of the situation as God's will. As the drought deepens, the community begins to see it as God's judgment against their Imam's strict orthodoxy. In the end, the practical minded Emir of Bauchi, acknowledging the voice of the people against the Imam, dismisses the imam from office. The Emir does so in full recognition that his kingdom will never again have an Imam of Alhaji Usman's learning and purity of faith. Hereafter, future Imams appointed to the office will be both less learned and more accommodating to the local indigenous belief and religious environment. With this there was peace and harmony between followers of both traditions and faith in Bauchi for years and years to come. The action of Imam Usman reveals the trend of thought that sees a strict dichotomy between Islam and ATR, whereas the action of the Emir of Bauchi in this report clearly portrays that, though Muslims, the traditional natives still owe much allegiance and reverence to their indigenous beliefs and practices.

Ancestral spirit beliefs in ATR have been recombined with Muslim practice to form a new "folk" religion with emphasis on the veneration of recognized leaders and holy people, which popular Islam and Sufism reinforce and which approximate to local ancestor veneration. Traditional heroes and forebears, some of whom occupy the position of intermediaries, fit into the Muslim concept and recognition of holy men and women who are respected and revered in most cases in Islam.

4.1.4. Treatment of Illness:

Another common aspect of interaction between followers of ATR and Muslims in Nigeria is their belief that certain illnesses are supernatural and are treated not with orthodox medicine but with traditional and native medicine. Some of the healers (traditional and Islam) practice a combination of rituals involving both Indigenous and Islamic practices of sacrificing and atoning the spirits, invocation of the Ancestors, and use of amulets as well as herbs believed to have potent powers. In such cases, followers of ATR patronize Muslim healers just as Muslims patronize traditional religious healers. There is no discrimination on the part of the healers based on religion towards their patients; their aim is to heal and restore balance to the human person and to the society irrespective of religious affiliations. Such interactions abound in many communities in Nigeria especially in the North and South-West zones of Nigeria. Commenting on this, Nehemiah Levtzion and Chande said,

> The diagnosis and treatment of illnesses attributed to occult forces in Africa have provided an opportunity for Muslim healing traditions to flourish and allowed for the services of Muslim healers and holy men, who provided additional healing choices to local practitioners, to be in high demand. The appearance of new epidemic diseases such as smallpox and cholera, which arose in the nineteenth and twentieth centuries in the hinterland of Africa and which the local people could not adequately deal with, led people to turn to the Muslim healing system that combines with it indigenous practices.[238]

---

[238] Levtzion and Abdin Chande, "Islam: Islam in Sub-Saharan Africa," 4605.

4.1.5. Socio-Cultural Solidarity:

One of the central points where ATR and Islam interact in Nigeria is in the area of social solidarity and emphasis on community life.

In ATR, the individual is located and is relevant only as part of the community. Likewise, in Islam, the *Ummah* (community) is the basis of social life and the integration of the individual within the larger community. The community instills moral teaching, generally from the older to the younger members through words and examples. The process of initiation ceremonies (some of which may last several years) are the formal communal occasions for instilling moral values in young people and passing on to them important traditional values. Stories, proverbs, wise sayings and taboos are employed in the teaching of morals as well as for entertainment. Where the basic philosophy of life is "I am because we are", it is extremely important that the two dimensions of "I am" and "We are" be carefully observed and maintained for the survival of all. The individual is very much exposed to the community and anonymity is virtually out of the question. Human relations are largely oriented horizontally.

Because of the emphasis on socio-cultural solidarity in ATR and Islam, followers of Islam do not see themselves as aliens in matters of community development and cultural identity. A Yoruba Muslim for example will always dress in traditional Yoruba attire even as he/she goes to the Mosque for prayer. Male and female Muslims take traditional titles indigenous to their people even as they fulfill their religious duties and take religious titles. During traditional communal ceremonies they take their proper places among the elders as a 'sons/daughters of the soil' while still maintaining their identity as Muslims.

In the Northern zone, there is a commingling of religious communal ceremonies with traditional dances and outfits. One such example is the *Sallah* celebration. The *Sallah* day, as it is called in Nigeria, marks the celebration of *Eid el-Kabir* (the day of sacrifice). It is a day on which Muslims worldwide celebrate the end of the year's annual *hajj*. In Nigeria this celebration is a community celebration that brings both traditionalist and Muslims together in a joyful mood of dancing and feasting. On such occasions, traditional dances are featured. Below is Kanuri traditional dance, as part of the entourage that accompanied the Emir at a Sallah celebration.

In Arochukwu (South-East), during the *Ikeji Aro* (New yam festival), the Muslims always identify with the traditional ruler of the Aro Kingdom by paying him a courtesy call and in some cases presenting him with the gift of a cow.

Giving an example of what obtains in Nupe Kingdom, Mbiti narrates that Islamic convention among the Nupe of northern Nigeria started with their King, Jibiri around 1770. By the end of that century Islam was well entrenched in the Kingdom. It provided the people with new religious-cultural ceremonies in addition to, but not in place of, their traditional ones. There was an integration of the old and the new, so to say. Nupe Muslims, Mbiti states, do not follow strict Islamic tradition. They observe only those feasts and ceremonies that already find expressions in their culture and tradition, such as three out of the seven major Muslim festivals among Nigerian Muslims. The three they observe are New Year (Muharram), Id el Fitr (at the end of the fast month, Ramadan), and Id el kabir or Id el Azha (the great feast in the pilgrimage months which ends the year).[239] The reasons for accepting these three is not far from the culture and native tradition of the Nupe people that employ dancing and great feasting on every occasion. Islamic traditions that have little or no joyful mood and

---

[239] Mbiti, *African Religions and Philosophy*, 239-240.

celebration are not in consonance with the Nupe culture and tradition and are therefore not 'parts' of Nupe Islam.

As observed by Joseph Stamer, the long cohabitation of Islam with traditional African religion has also had an effect at the cultural level. The African languages are in general languages with a concrete vocabulary, rather limited in the expression of more abstract realities or more developed reflections. With the Arabic language, Islam has been able to fill a gap. Many African peoples, some scarcely touched by Islam, have borrowed a complete abstract, and especially religious, vocabulary from Arabic, with no more than changes proper to the structure of each language. The actual Islamization has come later, confirming and assembling within a coherent structure these scattered modes of thought and expression that were from Islam in the first place. Thus, the inculturation of the religious message has in many cases preceded islamization itself.[240]

The followers of ATR and Muslims have on various occasions taken action together to respond to the social needs and concerns for the poor and society at large. They have arisen together to condemn social vices and together praised and rewarded honesty and hard work in Nigerian society.

4.1.6. Authority and Norms:

In Nigerian traditional societies, religion and politics were always combined. The King or the Oba or Chief was said to be divinely appointed by God and his authority in matters of religion and governance was always final. This traditional institution provided a good basis for Islam to mingle, integrate and interact with the different political kingdoms in the North and South of Nigeria. This was

---

[240] Josef P. Stamer, *Islam in Sub-Saharan Africa* (Estella, Spain: Editorial Verbo Divino, 1995), 125.

possible because among Nigerian Muslims, the king or Emir is both the political and religious authority. The native kings saw a good playing ground and accommodation within Islam in contrast to Christianity, which substituted the religious authority of the native ruler with that of the missionary or ordained priest. Hence, in those kingdoms where the traditional rulers were at the same time Muslims, and having both political and religious powers, Islam and ATR lived harmoniously and collaborated with each other in daily lives. Commenting on this, I. M. Lewis said,

> On the political scene, African traditional rulers have been more inclined to receive elements of Islam and Muslim culture and organization which can be applied to reinforce and extend their established authority. They also added Muslim regalia and ritual elements to their traditional outfits and royal rituals.[241]

Aside from authority, there have been many interactions in the area of norms. Both Islam and ATR are religions that have laid down laws and norms for worship, for the ordering of society, and for individual life. They both believe that there is an ethical order given by God, for the wellbeing of persons and nature. They attempt to live by it in form of laws, rules, customs, and taboos. What is right or wrong is judged normally in terms of interpersonal relations—in the family, in the community, towards the surroundings, and towards the departed. Such norms that are seen as taboos in the society include willful homicide, adultery, abortion, and stealing. Again, commenting on this, Lewis said,

---

[241] I. M. Lewis, *Islam in Tropical Africa* (London: Oxford Press, 1966), 20.

When it comes to the contact between Islamic law (shariah) and traditional African norm, there are levels of interactions. In matters where the two systems correspond, such as concerning illicit sexual relations, theft and restitution, they uphold and strengthen each other.[242]

On marital, family and dietary norms, Mbiti, using Nupe as a case in point, describes certain levels of interaction between ATR and Islam. Accordingly,

> Marriage rules, especially concerning marriage gifts and easy divorce, circumcision, kingship rites and prohibitions to eat pigs, are points of similarity, and therefore immediate contact, between Nupe and Islamic traditions, so that here Islam fits well into the Nupe traditional thinking and practice, without conflict.[243]

In most Nigerian communities, when conflict of interest arises over marital laws and inheritance, preference is given to native traditional norms over Islam, and followers of both religions adhere to such preference without conflict or violence. Affirming this position, Lewis said, "In matters of inheritance of land, livestock, property and family, traditional procedures are followed more often than Islamic policy."[244] Corroborating Lewis' point, Mbiti, again, using Nupe as an instance, writes,

---

[242] Ibid.

[243] Mbiti, *African Religions and Philosophy*, 240

[244] Lewis, *Islam in Tropical Africa*, 20

Whereas in some countries Muslims practice sororate marriages, this is completely forbidden among Nupe Muslims who, however, strictly adhere to their tradition concerning levirate marriages.[245] In matters of inheritance, Nupe traditional practices prevail over Islamic law (without conflict among followers). This has prevented the fragmentation of the land which would ensure if Islamic rules were followed.[246]

It must be noted that the most obvious marital practice that ATR and Islam share in common, and which, actually, drew many Africans to Islam rather than missionary Christianity is polygamy. Islamic religion allows the marriage of more than one wife, if so desired and if able to do so, even up to four.[247] ATR always allows more than one wife. In fact, in traditional societies, marrying more wives is a mark of honor and respect. This is a point that is clearly expressed by Chinua Achebe in *Things Fall Apart*, in the story of

---

[245] Sororate marriage is a marriage in which a husband engages in marriage or sexual relations with the sister of his wife, usually after the death of his wife, or once his wife has proven barren. Levirate marriage, on the other hand, is a marriage in which a widow marries one of her husband's brothers.

[246] Mbiti, *African Religions and Philosophy*, 240.

[247] In Islam there are conditions for allowing polygamy. Among them are: The wife (s) must not have raised any objection about polygamy during or before the marriage contract. If such was raised and the husband disregards that, the wife has the right challenge him at the Islamic court; all the wives must receive equal treatment from the husband, and the number of wives must not exceed four.

Okonkwo who, among the outstanding qualities that made him great, famous and wealthy, had three wives.[248]

The interaction and convergence between ATR and Islam, or what J. S. Trimingham described as assimilation of Islam into the African religio-cultural society, is expressed in three stages. Explaining these three processes, Trimingham wrote,

> In the first phase, the people merely adopt 'superficially' certain elements of the material culture of Muslims such as dress, ornaments and food habits. In the second phase, actual religious elements of Islamic culture are assimilated, especially the recognition or awareness of an impersonal power resident in and working through persons or things. This recognition is, as we have seen, found in African traditional societies. As such it is not peculiarly Islamic but forms a point of contact. The third phase is characterized by a genuine belief in the efficacy of Islamic sanctions, and involves actual change in customs and habitual conduct. Yet, even at this stage, old beliefs do not lose their validity to the African Muslim's life; on the contrary, certain beliefs gain a renewed vitality by acquiring an Islamic orientation. Such beliefs are the continued respect for the living-dead [the ancestors], belief about spirits associated with natural objects, the use of charms and fear of witchcraft.[249]

---

[248] Chinua Achebe, *Things Fall Apart.* (New York: Anchor Books, 1994), 8.

[249] J. S. Trimingham, *Islam in the Sudan,* (London: Oxford Press, 1949), 248.

The result is therefore a new synthesis that fosters harmonious relationships between ATR and Islam in Nigeria. Thus, what is characteristically "African" in Nigerian and Sub-Saharan Islam is therefore a question of local cultural and religious forms. Indigenous spirits like Oshun among the Yoruba, and Bori among the Hausa are still worshiped today by Muslims. Systems of divinations and charms are still being employed; healing rites with traditional undertones continue to be performed. Rather than replacing these practices, Islam in Nigeria retained them within a broader religious vision.

Such is the picture of Islam in traditional African and Nigerian societies. On a purely religious front, it has done little to add or alter radically African religiosity, except in some ritual aspects where Islamic practices have overall introduced or strengthened existing practices. Deeper issues of great value remain traditional, even if they might gain Islamic guises. One can therefore say that Islam, in its traditional Nigerian form, is entirely a part of the African cultural heritage and thus an African reality.

These points of interactions and convergences between ATR and Islam in the areas of belief, ritual, social, cultural and daily life, paradoxically facilitate a quick or smooth conversion from one religion to another, but more importantly hinder the process and manifestation of a deep and radical Islam or ATR. It means then that ATR accommodates Islam and Islam accommodates ATR. The lack of radicalism and violence that has characterized the longer history of the two religions gives a bright hope that with better understanding interfaith relationships will advance the peace and unity of the religious bodies in Nigeria.

4.2 AFRICAN TRADITIONAL RELIGION *VS* CHRISTIANITY.

Christianity has had a long history of interaction and relationships with ATR in Nigeria. At the beginning, the encounter revealed a hostile attitude from ATR and the domineering attitudes and prejudicial views that Christian missionaries had against the indigenous religion and culture. This was a state of monologue, when the validity of Christianity stood over and against any belief system. European agents believed they were bringing civilization, superior culture, and belief to unfortunate and primitive savages. However, this stage gradually gave way to the stage of mutual relationships, understanding and interaction. According to Jude Aguwa, "Transition from the monologue stage to the most rudimentary form of dialogue occurred with the first generation of converts whose practice of Christianity involved blending some practices of the Indigenous Nigerian culture and Christianity."[250] Expressing the same view, Geoffrey Parrinder pointed out:

> It must not be supposed that the convert leaves all his beliefs behind and comes to Christianity with a blank mind. Sometimes the first generation of convert makes a great break with the past [but not in all cases], but his successors conform more to the pattern of life around him. Even when objects of worship are changed, images broken, charms

---

[250] Jude C. Aguwa, "Christianity and Nigerian Indigenous Culture," in *Religion, History, and Politics in Nigeria: Essays in Honor of Ogbu U. Kalu.* Chima J. Korieh & Ugo Nwokeji, eds. (New York: University Press of America, 2005), 14.

(sometimes) thrown away, it is difficult to adopt a completely different world view.[251]

However, the first concrete positive manifestations of interaction between ATR and Christianity in Nigeria was made by the Indigenous churches. In these churches, allegiance to Nigerian culture is foremost, strong and overt. As observed by Parrinder, "The effect of traditional religion may be seen in the independent (indigenous) churches, which are often most successful in proselytization by joining Christian and African practices."[252]

On the side of missionary or orthodox Christianity, especially in the Catholic Church, the initiative and efforts towards positive encounters between ATR and Christianity was occasioned by the change in the ecclesiology of Vatican II, which has been very open and positive toward ATR. As noted by Christopher Ejizu,

> The Second Vatican Council remains both the culminating point as well as the point of departure for bold and positive developments that we witness currently in inter-religious relations [especially towards African Traditional Religion]. Up until the Vatican II, the official policy of the Church in relation to other religions and their millions of adherents was, to put it mildly, unchristian. That was the protracted era of *extra ecclesiam nulla salus* (outside the Church there is no salvation). Incontestably, the negative attitude reflected the dominant mind-set and extreme ethnocentrism of the

---

[251] Geoffrey Parrinder, *Religion in Africa*, (London: Pengium Books, 1969), 228-229.

[252] Ibid, 229.

age in the West. Social analysts and writers like Auguste Comte and George J. Fraser, inspired by Darwin's theory of evolution of species have suggested a similar unilineal evolutionary trend for human society and culture. Black sub-Saharan African races, if at all human, were thought to be at the lowest stage of the evolution ladder. The cultures and religions of the "so-called savages" were "barbaric" and in dire need of civilization and conversion.[253]

A more concrete impact was made by a 1993 letter addressed to all the Bishops of Africa and Madagascar on the need and urgency of positive encounter and interaction between ATR and Christianity, by the Nigerian born Cardinal, Francis Arinze, then the Prefect for the Secretariat for Non-Christians (Pontifical Council for Inter-Religious Dialogue). The letter urges a serious pastoral attention to African Ttraditional Religion incorrectly called "animism."[254] The letter reaffirms the Church's respect for the religions and the cultures of peoples, and wishes in her contact with them to preserve all that is noble, true and good in their religion and their cultures. It also envisages a fruitful dialogical encounter between Christianity and African Traditional Religion, with promises of a mutual enrichment for both in the measure where the messengers

---

[253] Christopher I. Ejizu, "The Influence of African Indigenous Religions on Roman Catholicism: The Igbo Example" in *African Tradition Religion* Webpage maintained by Chidi Denis Isizoh http://www.afrikaworld.net/afrel/ejizu-atrcath.htm (accessed: August 24, 2009).

[254] John Paul II, The Church in Africa: Post Synodal Apostolic Exhortation, *"Ecclesia in Africa."* (Rome: Vatican Press, 1995), 8.

of the gospel will better understand traditional religion, and Christianity will also be presented to Africans in a more appropriate fashion. It also encourages the study of traditional religion as a means to identify the underlying felt needs of Africans, and to clarify the manner in which Christianity can respond to them. This way the Church will be at home in Africa, and Africans will feel more and more at home in the Church. The letter thus recommends dialogue with traditional religion to take place at two levels: first, with the people who adhere to traditional religion and who do not yet desire to become Christians. With such persons, dialogue has to be understood in the ordinary sense of encounter, of mutual understanding, of respect and a mutual search of the will of God. Second, with those who desire to become Christians, and with Christians converted from traditional religion, the dialogue has to be understood in a wider sense of a pastoral approach to traditional religion, with a view of presenting the Gospel of Jesus Christ in an appropriate manner, so that the Church takes deeper roots on African soil. As part of the pastoral attention to traditional religion, the letter calls for appropriate research centers to be established for research purposes into traditional religion, to discern the 'principal tenets of its beliefs: particularly God the Creator, the place of the spirits of the ancestors, the fundamental rites in this religion, sacrifice, priesthood, prayer, marriage, the human soul, life after death, religion and the moral life'. The letter strongly recommends that ATR be part of the curriculum and study program of seminaries and religious houses of formation.[255]

This letter from the President of the Pontifical Council for Inter-Religious Dialogue is the first of its kind to come

---

[255] Francis Arinze, *Pontificum Consilium Pro Dialogo Inter-Religiones*, Bulletin, 1996/2: Pro Dialogo, Plenary Assembly, 20-24 Nov. 1995, Rome, 1996.

from very high ecclesiastical circles, a Vatican central office. It pronounces directly and elaborately on the need for the Church, particularly in Africa and Madagascar, to take ATR seriously, to give it urgent pastoral attention, to study it, and to enter into dialogue with it. It gave birth and greater impetus to efforts already contemplated or initiated in research work on ATR by theological faculties and ecclesiastical institutes of higher learning such as at Kinshasa, Nairobi, Abidjan and Port Harcourt, as well as the teaching of ATR in major Seminaries. The letter is a main inspiration for the various dialogue commissions on the diocesan, provincial, national, inter-regional and inter-national levels.

The ongoing encounter with ATR reveals the many values which are common to both Christianity and ATR, and which can serve as a *"praeparatio Evangelica,"* as stepping stones for introducing African adherents of ATR into the full acceptance of the Christian faith and or accommodation of the Christian faith within the traditional society and religious practices. The value common to both religions unveiled through dialogue are indispensable for inculturation, and for harmonious coexistence of all within the society. The Christian church itself gains from this, for inculturation helps the African Christians to live an integrated life, which is truly Christian and truly African.

The following are areas where positive relationships, convergences, and interactions are most visible between ATR and Christianity in Nigeria.

4.2.1. Belief System:

One of the basic areas of convergence between ATR and Christianity in Nigeria is their common belief systems, especially the belief in God, spirits, ancestors/saints, and the exalted place of prayer in both religions as the only medium of communication between the Divine and humanity.

Belief in God is the most central tenet in ATR. In traditional religion God or the Supreme Being, as it is commonly called, is the creator and ruler of the universe. He has unlimited power over all in everything. This is the same concept that Christians express about God. Hence, in Nigeria, followers of ATR did not see any contradiction with their notion of God and that of the Christians. ATR believes that the Supreme God dwells in heaven, hence the invocation of God among the Igbos as *Obasi di n'elu* (God who is above in heaven). The same is true of the Christians, who always invoke God as *Heavenly Father.*

Again, Christianity believes in the existence and ministry of spiritual beings, who are often called Angels. These spiritual beings are messengers of God and can guide Christians in their day-to-day life. Scripture testifies to this belief thus: "He will command his angels to guard you in all your ways. They will lift you up with their hands so that your foot may not hit a stone" (Psalm 91:11-12; Matt. 4:6). "Suddenly an Angel of the Lord stood there (where Peter was in prison) and light shone in the prison cell. The Angel tapped Peter on the side and woke him saying . . . Put on your belt and your sandals . . . Then Peter recovered his senses and said, now I know that the Lord has sent his Angel and has rescued me from Herod's clutches and from all that the Jews had in store for me." (Acts: 12:7-11).

There are bad spirits in Christian belief also. These bad spirits are the devil and fallen angels. On the other hand, belief in spirits—good and bad, is dominant in ATR. There are spirits everywhere in ATR, in the air, tree, and water, human spirits, and ghosts (spirits of dead people). The spirits are also intermediaries and messengers of God in ATR. The teaching on the Holy Spirit and other spirits by Christians was not foreign at all to the natives, who were already familiar with the existence and workings of the spirits in traditional religion and culture. For example, an old woman attending catechetical class to receive the sacraments in one of the parishes in Igbo land was asked by the Catechist: *Uzo otu nmuo ole di?* (How many types of spirit are there?) The old woman answered: *Ha buru nnukwu ibu. Kedu ebe aga ebido-ebido guba? Aga ebido na Ulaga, m'obu Ike-udo, m'obu Ijele, mobu na Nw'-ikpo?* (They are legion, where would one begin to enumerate? Would I mention Ulaga, or Ike-udo, or Ijele, or Nw'ikpo?)[256] Ulaga, Ike-udo, Ijele, Nw'ikpo are some famous masquerade[257] spirits in Igboland. Therefore, the woman answered the question not from her Christian background of just mentioning two types of spirits: good and bad spirits, but she rather began to enumerate all the traditional spirits that she is familiar with.

Another outstanding area in the belief systems of the two religions is the place of and role of the departed holy men and women in the religious life and temporal life of the living. These men and women in ATR are called the ancestors, and in Catholic, some Orthodox and Protestant Christianity, they are called saints. Both religions have a firm belief in the communion with the ancestors and saints, who can intercede on their behalf with God and or with the spirits. Hence, in Nigeria, especially among the Yorubas and Igbos, the Catholic celebration of All Saints and All Souls on November 1st and 2nd respectively, is seen as a day when both Christians and traditionalists offer special prayers and offerings to their departed ones. When I was in Bigard

---

[256] This story was told by Bishop A. G. Nwedo in 1985 at St. Mulumba's Parish, Ihechiowa during a Catechetical Instruction for those preparing for the Sacrament of Confirmation. I was one of the confirmati.

[257] In Igboland, masquerades are the living spirits of the ancestors. They are believed to come out publicly only during festivals and important celebrations.

Memorial Seminary, Enugu, Nigeria, one of the masses for All Souls was celebrated at an old public cemetery, thus giving the traditionalists and Nigerian Christians a reason to celebrate and venerate their departed ancestors, especially at their graves sites.

Furthermore, prayer occupies a central place in both religions. In Nigeria, it is now very common to hear and to see prayers that have a flavor or combination of ATR elements and Christian elements. Such prayers are usually said in ceremonies involving peoples of both faiths and in private devotions. An example of such prayers for private devotion is the prayer to the Seven African Spirits. It reads:

> Oh seven powers that are the Saints among Saints; I humbly kneel before your miraculous picture to ask your intercession before **GOD, loving Father** that protects all creation, living and dead, and I ask in the **most sacred name of JESUS,** that you accede to my plea and return to me spiritual peace and material success, reseeding from my house and removing from my path the dangers that are the cause of my evils without ever being able to torment me again. My heart tells me that my wish is just and if you accede to it, you will add more glory to the blessed name for years and years of our GOD, from whom we have received this promise. So in **the name of the Father, the Son and the Holy Ghost!** Listen to me, **Chango! (Sango)** Hear me **Ochun! (Osun)** Pay attention, **Yemala!** Look at me with good eyes, **Obatala!** Do not forsake me, **Ogun!** Act favorably towards me, **Orula,** Intercede for me **Elegua!** Grant me what I am asking for, for the mediation of

the Seven African Powers, Oh Saint **Christ of Olofi.** Forever, be blessed. Amen.[258]

The highlighted words represent the divinities or deities from the two religions combined into one prayer. God, loving Father, the most sacred name of Jesus, and in the name of the Father, the Son and the Holy Ghost, are all Christian concepts of God, while Chango (Sango), Ochun (Osun), Yemala, Obatala, Ogun, Orula (Orumila or Ifa), and Elegua are among the Pantheons of Yoruba gods and goddesses. It is common to find Christian religious items like the images of Mary, Jesus, St. Michael, and other saints in the altars and shrines of ATR, especially practitioners of Mami Wata and Voodoo. Mami Wata (mother of the sea) or Voodoo as it is called in some places is a pantheon of water spirits or deities, venerated in West, Central, and Southern Africa, and in the African Diaspora in the Caribbean and parts of North and South America. It is believed by devotees to be the oldest religion in the world, older than Hinduism. According to Mama Zogbe, Vivian Hunter-Hindrew,

> In ancient Sumerian mythology, Mami (Mammi, Mamma, Mammitum) is a sacred name of worship and endearment for the great mother-goddess known as Ninhursag. Mami was the creatress (*sic*) of the first human beings known affectionately to Her as 'the black-headed people' or 'those who come (*sic*) out of [her] great womb.' Her own mother was Mami Nammu, great goddess of the primeval sea and the one who gave birth to heaven and earth . . . The Mami [Wata]

---

[258] Philip J. Neimark, *The Way of Orisha: Empowering your Life through the Ancient African Religion of Ifa.* (New York: HarperCollins Publishers, 1993), 167.

ancestral tradition is perhaps one of the oldest survival remnants of what was once a powerful, matrilineal priesthood of healers, seers and prophetesses, known during the ancient times as the Sibyls, and in more contemporary times as Amengansies and Mamaissiis. They were the first consecrated body of a holy order of priestesses who served as sacred bearers of the original logos universally recognized as Isis (divine wisdom) . . . . In African the Sacred pantheon of water deities collectively known as Mami Wata and its Sibyl priestess tradition, is matrilineally inherited through the blood of the African Mother . . . Known only as "Mami" amongst her devotees, Mami Wata is a sacred generic name of respect and personal affection to describe a specialized pantheon of ancient female and male deities, who are Cosmo-genetically and spiritually linked to the African people.[259]

4.2.2. Rituals.

This is another area that has experienced much interaction, collaborations, and convergences between ATR and Christianity in Nigeria. The Christian Church has recently become aware that the life of the Church in any given community depends on rites and rituals, expressed

---

[259] Vivian Hunter-Hindrew, *Mami Wata: Africa's Ancient God/dess Unveiled. (Reclaiming the Ancient Mami Wata Vodoun history and Heritage of the Diaspora)*. Vol. I. (Martinez: Mami Wata Healers Society of North America Inc., 2007), 49, 37-40.

in liturgical celebrations. These rites and rituals make present and celebrate the faith and belief of the community. In them teachings and doctrines are translated into life and action in what is called liturgy. The Vatican II *Constitution on the Sacred Liturgy*, therefore, called for the revision of the liturgy to reflect particular rites and rituals of mission lands like Nigeria. The Council here affirmed that:

> Anything in people's way of life which is not indissolubly bound up with superstition and error the Church studies with sympathy, and, if possible, preserves intact. It sometimes even admits such things into the liturgy itself, provided they harmonize with its true and authentic spirit ... In mission countries, in addition to what is found in the Christian tradition, those elements of initiation may be admitted which are already in use among every people, insofar as they can be adapted to the Christian ritual ... [260]

With this directive, Christianity and ATR in Nigeria have interchanged and enriched each other with rituals from each other's tradition. Rituals within the context of our work include sacrifice, divinations and use of charms or sacred symbols, Church dedication, kingship coronation and religious ordinations.

ATR is a religion of sacrifice. Almost, if not all the ceremonies start with one form of sacrifice or the other. Individuals frequently offer sacrifices to the gods, spirits, and ancestors either for blessings, thanksgiving or for atonement. One of the basic elements of sacrifice in ATR is the offering of animal and food items among other

---

[260] *Sacrosanctum Concilium* nn. 37, 65.

things. Similarly, sacrifice is a very important element in Christianity; among Catholics, it is the Eucharistic sacrifice. With the Protestants, it is the sacrifice of praise or spiritual sacrifice. (Cf. 1 Pt. 2:4-5). Nigerians who converted to Christianity, especially Catholicism, see in the Christian sacrifice elements of ATR, and thus they approach it with the same reverence as they would the native sacrifice. When I was young boy attending Catechism class to receive Holy Communion, one of the things that we learnt from the Catechism was the concept of sacrifice and the Eucharist as a sacrifice. The first question on the section on the Holy Mass was this: "*Gini Bụ Mass Di Asọ?* (What is the Holy Mass?) *Mass di asọ bụ Aja arụ na ọbara nke Jesu Kristi, nọ na olta n'ezie n'ụdi achicha na mmanya.*" (The Holy Mass is the sacrifice of the body and blood, truly present on the Altar in forms of bread and wine.) Another question that follows was: *Gini Bụ Aja?* (What is Sacrifice?) *Aja bụ ihe erunyelụ so Chukwu site n'aka ụkọ chukwu, ka owe gosi na ya bụ Chukwu, na-osebuluwa nke ihe nile.* (A Sacrifice is something that is offered to God alone, through the priest, to show that he is truly God, and the creator and lord of all.)[261] As one who had being going to the native shrine to offer sacrifices with my grandfather, I began to see the role of the Catholic priest with the eyes of my grandfather, who was the chief priest of our native deity. I began to see the bread and wine as the fowl and yam that people used to bring to our shrine. I began to see the Holy Communion as the sacrificial meal that we used to share in our shrine. More importantly, I began to appreciate why my grandfather and other elders in my town said that the only "true" Church is the Catholic, because they both offer the same sacrifice. This concept of traditional sacrificial ritual did not influence my thinking alone; in fact, it conditions and shapes the attitude of

---

[261] Anthony G. Nwedo, ed. *Katikisim Nke Okwukwe Nzuko Katolik n'asusu Igbo.* (Onitsha; Imico Press, 1964), 35.

Christians in Nigeria. For example, individual Christians go to their priests to request that the sacrifice of the mass or prayer be offered on their behalf, as they use to do with their native priest. On the day such sacrifice of mass is offered, they come to the Church with the same items like goat, fowl, even cow, and yam, which they used to carry to the native shrine. With this practice, Catholics and many other Christians do not feel alienated from the traditional religious way of worship; though Christians, they still feel part of their cultural heritage.

The traditional ritual of divination and use of charms for protection, security and to ward off evil spirits in traditional religion is dominant among Christians in Nigeria in many ways. Christians still consult native diviners for answers to question in their life. Many Christian Churches have diviners, seers, visionaries, and prophets who perform the same role as traditional priests and seers. These Church diviners, seers, visionaries, and prophets employ the rituals of ATR, with some modifications, to satisfy the quests of their clients. They equally prescribe rituals that must be performed by the client for success or to achieve results. Some of the prescriptions at times include offering sacrifices and taking a bath in river, as the traditionalists would prescribe.

As a substitute to native charms, most Christians use religious items blessed and consecrated by their priests or pastors. Such items used for protection and deliverance include holy water (for sprinkling, drinking and bathing), the wearing of chaplets and scapular, the use and keeping of holy pictures and bibles at homes and in cars and even under the pillow, and the use of olive oil. Some Christians still use a combination of both the traditional charms and Christian items together for 'more power and effectiveness.' As remarked by Nathaniel Ndiokwere, referring to those Christians who combine native charm with Christian sacraments; "Oh Christians, Mass in the morning, witch doctor in the evening. Amulet and Charm in the pocket, bible in the hand and scapular/medals around the neck."[262]

A good example of this interaction and combination of both religious ideals in the daily existential life of Nigerian Christians is seen in the life of one of the parishioners in one of the parishes in Igbo land. This man has a strong background of African Traditional Religion but he is now a Christian. He takes to Christianity some of the best values of the traditional religion. He holds on to the worldview given him by the African Traditional Religion. In Christianity, he acquires another worldview. In the course of his life as a Christian, he runs into trouble. He says that a witch or evil spirit is regularly attacking him. Being a Christian, he first turns to Christianity for solution. He goes to his parish priest or pastor to ask for his help. Unfortunately, the parish priest or pastor is too much an intellectualist. It is often the case that because of the large population of the Christian faithful in a parish, individuals are lost in anonymity. The parish priest or pastor has no time to listen to his pagan stories. He dismisses him without ever listening to him. The troubled man fails to get adequate and profound answers to his questions. He has no choice but to return to traditional religion for a solution. He consults a diviner and follows his advice to perform some rituals in the shrine of the traditional religion or somewhere else. When the problem is over, he returns to Christianity and continues from where he stopped. This shuttle between Christianity and African Traditional Religion is a form of internal dialogue, which is going on inside some converts to Christianity. It is non-verbal and its primary purpose is

---

[262] Nathaniel Ndiokwere, *The African Church, Today and Tomorrow,* Vol. I (Onitsha: Effective Key Publishers, 1994), 53.

"to integrate the two world views so as to give the African Christian an integrated religious personality."[263]

Another visible area of ritual interaction and relationship between ATR and Christianity is in the Dedication of Churches, especially in Igboland. In 2000, the Mater Dei Cathedral, Umuahia was dedicated. The ceremony featured rich cultural and ritual interaction together with a good number of traditional rulers that graced the occasion. In 2006, I dedicated my then Parish Church of St. Thomas Catholic Church, Amuvu Arochukwu. Again, the ceremony featured many rituals borrowed from ATR, e.g., the ritual processional or dance into the Church, a dance performed only by Elders in traditional religion during very important ceremonies, the pot of fire with yellow palm fronds and incense placed in front of the Altar to depict the sacredness and awesomeness of the Altar, seen as a powerful native shrine in Igboland, and other aspects of ritualizations. Another example in this area is the dedication of churches in the Catholic Diocese of Orlu, Nigeria. As reported by Ndiokwere,

> The dedication of a Church took a new momentum with the creation of the Catholic diocese of Orlu in 1980 with Most Rev. Dr. Gregory Ochiagha as its first Bishop. Since he assumed office in the diocese, the bishop has used each occasion of dedication of a parish to show the significance of such rituals in the lives of Christians and that of the Church in Africa . . . The rituals have African color: the famous Igba Eze cultural dance features prominently throughout the celebrations, the

---

[263] Chidi Denis Isizoh, "A Critical Review of the Lineamenta," *The African Synod Documents, Reflections and Perspective*, Maura Brown, Ed. (New York: Orbis, 1996), 37.

profuse burning of incense in the traditional African earthenware, the lavish smearing of the altar with consecrated oil, the lighting of candles at various corners of the Church, the Sacred Dance of *Igba Muo* (dance or drum of the spirits) by the congregation including the bishops and concelebrating priests, are all reminiscences of African cultic celebrations, cherished by the people. The Sacred Dance is graceful and the entire ceremony which takes up to five hours can be moving indeed. The dedications of St. John's Church, Urualla, April 1991, and Sacred Heart Parish Church, Orsuihiteukwa, 6th February 1993, saw the climax of the richness of inculturated Para-liturgical ceremonies in the Diocese of Orlu. The entire community of Urualla (Christians and non-Christians) was there. The various cultural groups led by the Igba Eze were there to grace the occasion.[264]

Another area of interaction between ATR and Christianity is seen in the coronation of the Kings in Igboland. Below are two examples of such coronation ceremonies that I was personally involved in. The first was the coronation of His Royal Highness Eze (*King*) Paul Ifeanyi Ekwuruonu of the Amomukwu Community in Ikwuano, Abia State. I was the Pastor of the Parish Church in the community, and Eze Ekwuruonu was my parishioner and a Knight of St. Mulumba. The ceremony began with the traditional ritual of breaking of Kola nut and the pouring of the libation by the 'crowning' Chief in his *Obu* (the ancestral spot in the house of an elder believed to be

---

[264] Nathaniel Ndiokwere, *The African Church, Today and Tomorrow*, Vol. II. (Enugu: Snaap Press, 1994), 203-204.

a point of contact with the ancestors). Then there was a procession with traditional dance that accompanied the Eze-Elect to the coronation venue. The ceremony proper was performed with the celebration of Catholic Mass (using the Catholic ritual of blessing and installing a new king) presided by the Catholic Bishop of Umuahia, Bishop Lucius Iwejuru Ugorji. At a certain time within the Mass the royal regalia and paraphernalia of the Eze-Elect was presented to the Bishop for blessing by the Chief (majority of who were traditionalists). After the ritual of blessing by the Bishop, the elders led by the *Oke Nze* (the oldest among the elders) performed the actual coronation of the king using traditional rituals, language and gestures. After that, the Bishop gave the final blessing to all assembled at the ceremony.

The second coronation was that of His Royal Highness, Eze Linus Nto Mba of Umuzomgbo, Ihechiowa (my home community). Eze Mba is catholic and was recently made a Papal Knight of St. Sylvester (one of the highest honors conferred upon laymen in the Catholic Church by the Pope). The ceremony took the same pattern as described above and was presided over by the same Bishop Lucius Ugorji. Both Kings are Christians and yet traditional rulers and custodians of the people's culture and tradition. The essence of combining both the ATR rituals and the Christian rituals in their coronations was to give them legitimacy, recognition and loyalty by both followers of ATR and Christians within the community and beyond. They in turn will be a point of unity, collaboration and harmonious living among followers of ATR and Christians in their respective communities.

4.2.3. Cultural Interaction.

One of the most visible areas that have experienced collaboration, relationships, and interaction between ATR and Christianity in Nigeria is the area of culture. Occasioned by a positive change of attitude and understanding from both religions, this has led to better appreciation of each other's culture. Oliver Onwubiko observed that this change of attitude toward the culture of each other "has influenced positively the method of the Christian mission to elements of African Traditional Religion and culture, and the openness of traditional religion to integrate elements of Christianity within its system."[265]

What has contributed to this mutual understanding is the shift of emphasis from the sole theology of redemption and evangelization that sees the Christian message as a privileged message of redemption to a hopeless and dammed people of Africa to a theology of inculturation that recognizes that the Africans have a religious system and a rich culture that can mingle, interact and enrich the Christian message, making it more relevant to African Christians. Inculturation simply means "the ongoing dialogue and interaction between faith and culture. More fully, it is the creative and dynamic relationship between the Christian message and a culture or cultures."[266]

The cultural interaction between ATR and Christianity is affirmation of the Second Vatican Council's call that Christians should not look down on the indigenous cultures of any people, but take whatever is good and noble in that culture as part of its own expression of the message of

---

[265] Oliver A. Onwubiko, African Thought, Religion, and Culture. (Enugu: Snaap Press, 1991), 150.

[266] Aylward Shorter, *Towards a Theology of Inculturation.* (New York: Orbis Books, 1997), 11

Christ.[267] Vatican II, in its various documents like *Ad Gentes Divinus*, sets out what can be considered the blue print of the Church's attitude toward the cultures of indigenous people. As Aylward Shorter puts it,

> It is difficult to exaggerate the importance of *Ad Gentes* for the development of modern mission theology . . . From the outset stress is laid on human communities and their socio-cultural traditions as the focus of missionary interest. In this context the analogy of the Incarnation is used for the first time (in the Council's documents).[268]

In all, the interaction between Christianity and ATR in the area of culture has truly enriched Christianity in Nigeria, making it acquire a surplus of meaning in loyalty and conformity to its tradition,[269] and at the same transforming the culture and practices of ATR without confrontation. The Christian transformation of culture is not a take-over bid, a form of cultural imperialism. Rather it is a reinterpretation of that culture, which results in the enhancement of its authentic meaning. I will now give some examples of this inculturation, both general and particular.

African ethnic religions are typically "religions of nature." That does not mean that they are "nature religions," in which natural phenomena are objects of worship. It means that created nature offers both an explanation of the divine and at the same time the means of contact with divine reality. In African religion, the physical environment is not only sacred, but it is also an organic universe. In other words, nature is biologically continuous with humanity, and

---

267 *Lumen Gentium*, n. 13, 16, 17; *Ad Gentes*, n. 10, 22.
268 Shorter, *Towards a Theology of Inculturation*, 195
269 Shorter, *Towards a Theology of Inculturation*, 13

it connects human beings with the world of spirit. Such a conceptual scheme can be Christianized, with reference to an ascending Christology. Christ has ascended through all the cosmic spheres and "has placed all things under his feet" (Ephesians 1:22). In other words, by becoming human and through the mystery of his death and resurrection, Christ has brought about a cosmic rebirth. In this new world order, humanity and created nature—which is the setting of human life—have been reattached to God. The physical environment can therefore speak to us, not only about God the Creator, but also about the redemption wrought for us by Christ. The cosmic Christ can be discerned both in the human community and in the natural environment.

Another example of an ascending Christology is provided by the experience of base communities in Nigeria. From their reading of the Bible, members of these communities understand the humanity of Jesus from their own experience of being human. In their concern for social justice and in their compassion for the poor and the sick, they celebrate the compassion and the healing activity of Jesus. From their experience of realities in the towns and villages, and the consideration of what it means to be human in conditions that are inhuman, they rise to an intuition of the divinity of Jesus. Christology, therefore, illuminates and reinterprets this experience of the local culture.

A particular example of the Christian transformation of an African organic universe is provided by Thomas Christensen's theology and catechesis of the African Tree of Life.[270] Christensen is an American Lutheran missionary, who has worked for a number of years in Cameroon and Nigeria among the Gbaya people, who are also found across the border in the Central African Republic. A semiotic analysis of the structure of Gbaya signs revealed that the

---

[270] Thomas G. Christensen, *An African Tree of Life*. (New York: Orbis Books, 1990).

root-symbol of the Gbaya is the *Soré* tree. The whole web of meaning that underlies Gbaya culture is centered on this ordinary little tree, which is called by them "the cool thing." A branch from the *Soré* tree is used ritually to help Gbayas overcome the threat of death in cases of blood feud or the breaking of taboos that entail the sanction of death. It helps them cope with their consciousness of sin and takes them through the threat of death into a new life. It is therefore very much a "tree of life." Both Christensen and the Gbaya saw in the *Soré* an analogy with the cross of Christ as the means of salvation in Christianity. They therefore reinterpreted the whole Soré symbolic complex in the light of a Christian theology of the Cross. Gbaya Christian preachers themselves first made the association of Soré with the crucified Jesus. It was a search for theological meaning evoked by evangelization. This led to the reflection: "What does Jesus have to do with *Soré*?" The answer is that the cross links Jesus with *Soré.* They see it as the symbol of all that God has done for them in and through Jesus. The cross is the fulfillment of *Soré*, transforming it and enhancing its meaning.

Christensen examined all the Gbaya life contexts in which *Soré* played a role. These included ritual meals and sacrifices, purification in life-crisis rituals, blood-pacts, marriage, dancing, hunting, conflict resolution and reconciliation, justice and peace, vows and promises, exorcisms, funerals, prophecy and moving house. He then examined biblical and patristic tree symbolism, and particularly the tree of life image as applied to the cross. When the Gbaya *Soré* meanings are applied to the cross of Jesus, they bring a metaphorical newness to Christian teaching, but they are themselves transcended by the reality of salvation wrought by Christ. The Gbaya believe that God is at work in *Soré*. The application, therefore, of this symbol to Jesus draws attention to his divinity. *Soré* is the symbol of life and the transmission of life through the covenant of love, which is marriage. It is therefore an apt symbol of the love of God revealed in Jesus Christ, the Word of Life. The use of *Soré* in the washing rituals at Gbaya funerals are the means by which the bereaved return to normal life. Christensen shows their relevance to the "water of life" in Christian Baptism, through which a person dies and rises to eternal life. The prominence of *Soré* in meals of reconciliation, lends itself to a Eucharistic application with the "Bread of Life."

Many parallels can therefore be found between Gbaya culture and Christian salvation theology. Moreover, this transformation of Gbaya culture by Christian faith sets the scene for particular Gbaya inculturations of the image of Jesus himself and of the Christian sacraments.

Another example is that of Bernard Mangematin, a missionary in Nigeria who made a plea to take catechetics out of the classroom, to jettison blackboard and chalk, and to abandon the traditional printed catechism or religious syllabus.[271] Mangematin, an acknowledged expert in the language and culture of the Yoruba, preferred, in the spirit of inculturation, to use a form of traditional praise prayer known as *oriki*. He argued that catechesis through prayer would give the student a true religious sense and a real conviction that was impossible to achieve through explanatory and discursive lessons. Adapting the words of Jesus in the Bible, Mangematin stated, "My Father's House is a House of Prayer. Do not change it into a classroom." For him, it is in and through prayer that the unlearned native Yoruba will know more about God than in a classroom type of catechesis.

---

[271] Bernard Mangematin, "Oriki: Yoruba Prayer and the Future of Catechesis in Nigeria," in *Catechesis for the Future: Theology in the Age of Renewal*. Adios Muller, ed. (New York: Herder and Herder, 1970), 147-159.

The *Oriki* has been called a form of prayer by which the Yoruba praise their gods in a manner that is in complete conformity with their culture. It is a poetic hymn, chanted in honor of an *Orisa* (divinity), or of an important person. It can be addressed to a divinity either in the privacy of an early morning offering or in regular cult meetings and festivals. It is a series of epithets or appellations addressed to the subject by the devotee, which is both expressive and efficacious. Not only does it encapsulate the essence of the subject, but also it enhances its (orisa) presence. It empowers, it propitiates, and it augments the reputation of the subject. It strengthens the bond between the praise-singer and the subject and it spreads healing and harmony in the community. *Oriki* praise poetry constitutes a shared, protean repertoire; with an infinity of manifestations. The *Oriki* is essentially oral, spontaneous and imaginative. It recruits ideas and images from a wide spectrum of sources, and appeals as much to the emotions as to the intellect. In this way, it mirrors the world, natural, human and divine. Like the Yoruba divinities themselves, the poems, which praise them, are inconsistent, fragmented and merging. This is not an accidental or deplorable untidiness; it shows a faithful reflection of the fluidity and dynamism in relationships, both human and divine. Although Yoruba traditional religion has declined, the Oriki still flourish vigorously, especially among women. In fact, the principal praise-singers and carriers of Oriki are women, because through marriage they are also the primary sources of social differentiation and social linking.

Mangematin insists on the use of proverbs, aphorisms and images derived from the Bible and the Liturgy in combination with the *Oriki* even if they are not fully understood at first. The *Oriki's* power to generate conviction rests on the ability of symbols to question or disturb the hearer. Mangematin's sample of *Oriki* is a catechesis on the mystery of God's holiness. It begins as a praise greeting to God, and then develops images of light, fire, lightning, swiftness and sharpness. After this, the poem uses symbols of purity, lucidity and innocence. These qualities are contrasted with the sinfulness and weakness of humanity, and the poem ends with a prayer for salvation. The reciprocity of God and humanity emerges in every stanza and the hearer is progressively involved, as the poem develops: "Take the shoes from thy feet;" "Rise from the dead and Christ will enlighten thee;" "And we are but dust and ashes;" "Pray for us sinners, now and at the last hour;" "Alas, I must keep silent." It is in this reciprocity that the poem's efficaciousness consists. The inculturated prayer poem of *Oriki* was a very powerful method of drawing the Yoruba culture and Catholic Christianity together, with much appreciation and without conflict. In Yoruba land, the *Oriki* is used, for example, at Catholic funerals after the departure of the priest. The *Oriki* tradition is an aspect of the Yoruba cultural heritage, which unites Christians of every denomination, and it is clear that it has considerable catechetical and liturgical potential of continuously bringing ATR and Christianity together in very strong harmonious relationships.

4.2.4. Social Interaction.

Many of improved relationships have been recorded in Nigeria between Christians and followers of ATR. However, the areas that these interactions and relationships have occurred differ according to geo-political zones in Nigeria. Much of what shall be discussed here is peculiar to the South-East (Igbo land) geo-political zone.

In Igbo land the traditional age-grade system,[272] as also other types of cultural practice, have left their impact on the Church. In some cases, the titles and practices have been adopted whole scale into the Church, while in some others, there have been varying degrees of modification, especially where religious rituals are involved. The prestigious *Ozo* title initiation (which posed a protracted headache to the Church in the north-western Igbo sub-culture), the *Otu Ogbo* (age grouping), the *Iwa Akwa* initiation in Mbano area, the *Mgbuli* (fattening ritual) for young ladies for marriage in Uli-Mgbidi axis, are some typical examples of areas of mutual collaboration between both religions. Initially, Christians were forbidden under the penalty of excommunication to belong to these groups, but today they are allowed to do so. Even the voluntary religious associations in the Church, like knighthood, become more acceptable to the people helped by a traditional background that is familiar with cultural institutions like secret societies and prestige clubs, e.g. *Otu-Odu, Ekwe/Lolo, Ekpe, Okonko, Odo*, etc.[273] During priestly ordination in Igbo land, the age grade system plays a vital role in the organization of events (as was the case in my own ordination, the age grades—my parents age grades and my own age grade were given a special place of recognition).

In the dynamic area of social and human organization within the Church, the influence of the indigenous culture has been significant as well. The Local Church, no doubt,

---

[272] The age-grade system is a practice where people born within the age range of 1-5 years apart are grouped together as culturally sharing the same age. They are given a cultural name (eg, *Ikemba* age grade. Ikemba means the strength of the community), rights and responsibilities in the community.

[273] Emefie Ikenga-Metuh and Christopher Ejizu, *Hundred Years of Catholicism in Eastern Nigeria: The Nnewi Story.* (Nimo: Asele Publishers, 1985), 15-16.

has drawn inspiration, and enjoys the added support of such indigenous cultural patterns as the age-grade system *(Otu Ogbo, Otu Umu Ada,* etc.) in the arrangement and functioning of its current statutory bodies of the Catholic Men's Organization (CMO), Catholic Women's Organization (CWO), Catholic Boys' Organization (CBO), and Catholic Girls Organization (CGO), and at the station, parish, deanery, diocesan and inter-diocesan levels. Lately, some dioceses in Igboland have begun to organize their members' resident in other towns within and outside the country. This type of structure and arrangement is related to and influenced by the old idea of Igbo Unions, a cultural, social and political association that flourished in several parts of the country prior to the civil conflict. In addition, the offertory dance of young maidens, which is gradually gaining ground in several dioceses, is directly descended from the indigenous dance of young virgins (girls) at shrines of local deities during the *Isi-ebili* festival in parts of Igboland. At times, the influence of the indigenous religious culture is perceived as a major problem that Catholics, particularly innovative pastors, feel sufficiently challenged by to create rites in the Church in response to a felt-need. This appears to be the case for funeral/burial rituals, naming of babies, churching of women after childbirth, marriage practice, new yam ritual, widowhood practice, outing of new dance. Currently, some pastors that I know are seriously concerned with how to respond to the serious threat they feel among their flock from a number of indigenous religio-cultural practices such as membership and performance of major masquerades like *Ozo-ebunnu, Odo*, and possession of lineage *Ofo* symbol.

4.2.5. Festivals and Celebrations.

Parts of the cultural and social interactions and relationships between ATR and Christianity in Nigeria that have advanced interfaith relationships and mutual co-existence are festivals and celebrations. The Igbo are people of festivals and celebration. Every event in life, from birth to death, involves festivities and celebrations. In every celebration, there is drumming, music, singing, and dancing. According to Ndiokwere, "During such moments of joy and mourning like thanksgiving and funerals, music and dancing feature as important integral elements of the celebrations. They constitute the most important elements of all festivals and these attract mammoth crowds."[274] For Africans, music and dancing is in the blood and is part of every public gathering, be it religious, cultural, social and even political.

Writing on the sense of festivity and celebration in Nigeria, Peter Schineller, an American Jesuit who has spent much of his life in Nigeria, said,

> A celebration without song, and dance, without a deliberate unrushed atmosphere, is no celebration at all. When Nigerians gather to celebrate, as they frequently do, the occasion is most often remarked by joy and festivity. Traditional dances with traditional costumes link the present with the past, and unite the entire community in a shared celebration. The sacred and the secular intertwine; the formal dance of those in costume invites the active participation of the onlookers . . . While there are occasions

---

[274] Ndiokwere, *The African Church, Today and Tomorrow,* Vol. II, 180.

for elaborate, stylized ritual and traditional dance and music, more spontaneous songs and dance also have their time and place.[275]

The Christian Churches in Nigeria have realized the power of traditional dance and music in celebrations and uniting the entire community in an atmosphere of peace and joy, and the religious import of active participation and communion with the divine, inherent in traditional dancing. Consequently, the churches have begun to adopt them in their various religious worships, festivities and celebrations. As observed by Awolanu,

> Christianity is already adopting some aspects of traditional religion like the use of extempore prayer, drumming, singing, and dancing during worship. In this way, there is now healthy interaction between one religion and another in Nigeria. And this is expected because in natural life people of diverse faiths live together under the same roof. In other words, brothers and sisters in Nigeria profess different faiths; but they do not cut one another's throat. They instead accommodate one another, upholding the philosophy of "Live and let live."[276]

Hence, as a means of collaboration and enrichment between ATR and Christianity, instead of the colonial and foreign melodies of Bach, Handel, and Mozart, and the Gregorian Chant that do not inspire or resonate with the Nigerian

---

[275] Peter Schineller, *A Handbook on Inculturation*. (New York: Paulist Press, 1990), 77.

[276] Awolanu, "The Encounter between African Traditional Religion and other Religions in Nigeria," 117

people, Nigerians now bring in their traditional local instruments and hymns (that were initially considered fetish and instruments of idol worshipping by Christian missionaries) into the Christian worship and liturgical celebrations to make them more lively, enriching and enjoyable. The rhythmical movement of the body can often be 'infectious.'

Another area of festivals and celebrations that has brought much interaction between ATR and Christianity in Nigeria and thus helped tremendously in enhancing relationships among followers of both religions, especially in Igboland, is the New Yam festival, known as the *Iri ji* (the eating of Yam), *Iwa ji* (the cutting of Yam), or *Ike ji* (the harvesting of Yam). In Igbo land, Yam is the king of all crops, and the importance, which the Igbos attaches to it, cannot be underestimated. The New Yam festival offers an interesting occasion for the social, cultural and religious development of the Igbo people. *Ahiajoku or Nfijoku* is traditionally the god of Yam in Igboland. The New Yam festival is therefore *Nfijoku's* festival, which heralds the harvesting season. It is a time of thanksgiving in which sacrifices are offered to the god of Yam for better harvest. Describing the importance of the New Yam festival, Donatus Anyanwu writes,

> The actual impact of the Ikeji annual festival is better experienced than described; it confirms the Aro's belief that culture is not opposed to true belief in worship of God. The festival also demonstrates that the people are excited to have come to the end of the toils of the farming and famine period and can now begin to enjoy the products of their labor with the arrival of the New Yam. It is altogether a celebration of success and one

in which the people pay homage to God, the author of their success.[277]

The New Yam today has assumed so many Christian features that Christians and followers of ATR express positive surprise and happiness at the rate by which the traditional elements have been incorporated into the Christian practices. Christians do not feel any more qualms celebrating the festival with relatives, without fear of being accused or condemned of taking part in unlawful practice in the Church. Most towns have a fixed date for their new yam festivals. In the parishes where I have been, the celebration begins with a Christian liturgy of the Mass, parishioners and traditionalists present at least two yams each to the altar. The elders present a goat also to the altar. The priest blesses the yams and each person takes one leaving one behind as his or her offering of thanksgiving to God. The priest, who represents God (as very much understood by the people from their native religious background), takes care of the yams offered to God. At a particular time (in most communities, afternoon), all the community gather at either the town square or the Eze's palace for the actual cutting and eating of the yam *(Iwa Ji/Iri ji)*. The Christian priest or pastor will say the opening prayer of blessing over the yam to be cut and eaten. I have always said this prayer and been part of the eating in all my parish communities. After the prayers, the Eze (King) or his *Eze Ji* (the one who holds the spirit of yam) pronounces the traditional blessing with the pouring of libation over the yam, and cuts the yam. Every body is invited to have of a piece of well-roasted or cooked yam. It is a joyful celebration in every community. People travel from everywhere to be part of the festival. It offers members of the community, ATR and Christians alike,

---

[277] Donatus Anyanwu, *The Imo Cultural Heritage.* (Owerri: Assumpta Press, 1989), 47-48

an opportunity to meet together to plan for the welfare and development of their community. Community projects like rural electrification, pipe-borne water, hospitals and scholarship funds have been undertaken at the instance of New Yam festivals.

4.2.6. Indigenization of Language, Music and Art.

In Nigerian Churches today the Africanization or indigenization of liturgical texts, music and costumes is very much evident. With the call of Vatican II to revise the liturgical texts to reflect local customs and situations, especially by changing the language of the mass from Latin to the vernacular,[278] missionaries devoted many efforts toward creating literary forms of indigenous languages. While this accomplishment immediately permitted translation of the Bible and Catechism books into the vernacular, it also factored significantly into the development of a pattern of dialogue in the relationship between Nigerian culture and Christianity.[279]

In spite of their disdain for the indigenous religious culture, pioneer Christian missionaries in general (whether Roman Catholic or Protestant) knew they had to depend on the indigenous language to communicate the gospel message to the people. While the doctrines and principal religious ideas remained those of their respective Christian traditions, the local language became the primary medium of communication with their host and provided the bulk of the concepts, terms and linguistic symbols and imageries.

Connected to language is music and art. The level and degree of influence of the three may not be even. Nevertheless, the overall impact of the Igbo language, music

---

[278] *Sacrosanctum Concilium,* n.35.
[279] Ajuwa, "Christianity and Nigerian Indigenous Culture," 23.

and art on Roman Catholicism, particularly since Vatican II, is huge and highly significant. Serious commitment on the part of the local Church since 1970 to the use of the Igbo language in the administration of the sacraments and sacramentals, including the bearing of Igbo names by candidates at baptism, has brought about the greater influence of the indigenous language in the Church. The initial objection and protest that formed part of the novel practices in the 1970s quickly died down. Thus, the Igbo language gradually has become accepted as the ordinary language of liturgical worship and sacramental administration in the Catholic Church in Igboland. The successful translation of basic religious texts into the indigenous language, especially the Bible, the Roman Missal and sacramental rites, is very positive and relevant. The greater usage of the Igbo language in the Church's liturgy naturally brings with it the employment of many indigenous religious concepts, idioms, and expressions into the lexicon of the Roman Catholic Church in Igboland. This, in turn, brings into the Catholic tradition certain orientations in spirituality and moral attitude from the Igbo indigenous religious and cultural background.[280]

The account of the influence of the Igbo language on Roman Catholicism today would be incomplete without mentioning the significance of the *Odenigbo* series (lectures and colloquiums). This is a recent special pastoral cum academic initiative of Archbishop A.J.V. Obinna of the Archdiocese of Owerri. Its primary goal and design is to use the Igbo language and culture to spread the message of Jesus Christ to the Igbo people. *Kristi Odenigbo* is fast gaining popularity within and outside Imo State. Archbishop Obinna and his collaborators in the series

---

[280] N. Omenka, "The Role of the Catholic Mission in the Development of Vernacular Literature in Eastern Nigeria," in *Journal of Religion in Africa*, XVI, 7, 1986, p.10.

are determined to avail of the unique opportunity of the Odenigbo to translate and render properly most, if not all, alien religious terminologies and jargons that are still found in Igbo Catholic literature. The project is proceeding well. One needs time, however, to be able to correctly assess its real impact on the Igbo religious terrain.

The influence of the indigenous religion on the Church's liturgical music in the post-Vatican II era is equally significant, thanks to the continuing effort of the different Diocesan and inter-Diocesan Liturgical Music Commissions. Through their effort, the Catholic Church in Igboland has been able to mobilize and encourage talented individuals to use their skills in order to blend indigenous rhythms, tunes and motifs into the Church's musical ensemble. Worthy of special mention is the evident rhythmic appeal and gusto of many contemporary musical pieces for specific aspects of the liturgy in the Igbo Church today; particularly songs for Offertory, Holy Communion, and choruses.

Some people have wondered as to the source of their special appeal. I suggest that a good measure of it comes from the indigenous religious and cultural background of the Igbo. As observed by Ikenga-Metuh and Ejizu,

> The indigenous religious culture has a rich tradition of joyful rituals and thanksgiving to ancestral and other benevolent spirits, special offering and dedication of animals and things, (human beings occasionally), to patron deities and nature forces. Some examples that readily come to mind include the Ikwuaru festival in the Nnewi-Ozubulu area during which fat bulls are purchased, paraded and offered to honor local patron arch-deities, the practice of commissioning Mbari art gallery in the south-central zone, or artfully-decorated Ikenga sculptures

in the Anambara sub-culture area, the performance of special musical lyrics and dance by minstrels, and/or prestigious and highly decorated masquerades like Ijere, Oka-nga, Ozo-Ebunu, Ikpirikpi Ogu/Iri-agha, by adult males, etc. The indigenous religious culture is partly responsible, therefore, for the emerging rich collection of soul-stirring liturgical pieces. Indeed, the achievement of the Catholic Church in Igboland in the area of liturgical music must rank among the best the African Continent has produced in recent times.[281]

In the field of art, the degree of influence may not be as elaborate, but it is no less striking. Gifted Igbo carvers, sculptors and other art-creators have been able to employ local materials as well as indigenous religio-cultural ideas, symbols and motifs to express some important Christian themes and values. Beautifully carved doors rich in indigenous art forms and other religious ritual symbols today adorn several churches and Catholic religious centers in Igboland. In addition, considerable inspiration has been drawn by fabricators of Church vestments, particularly in the areas of design and color, from the rich indigenous heritage of Igbo symbolism. Onitsha Archdiocese occasionally organized public exhibition of religious art-works which attracted talented art-creators, including carvers, sculptors, painters, and designers. Such occasions are a good opportunity not only for the display of finished products, but also for cross-fertilization of religious ideas among artists; Catholics as well as non-Christians.

---

[281] Ikenga-Metuh and Ejizu, *Hundred Years of Catholicism in Eastern Nigeria,* 15-16

4.2.7. Intellectual Interaction.

Recently, there has been on-going interaction and dialogue between followers of ATR and Christians at the level of the academia. This has tremendously helped in re-shaping the various thinking and notions that people have towards ATR. Christian scholars and elites who either studied or read an aspect of ATR have become more enlightened and thus came to appreciate the beauty of the religion and the need to collaborate more with the followers in pursuing a common course for the overall good of all Nigerians.

The intellectual dialogue started with the adoption of African religion as a subject in the university. It began with the appointment in 1949 of Geoffrey Parrinder to teach African Religion in the University College of Ibadan, Nigeria. [282] As Adrian Hastings wrote about this: "In a real way he created the subject and christened it too: 'African Traditional Religion.'"[283] Since the time of Parinder, African scholars, many of whom are Christians, have developed interest in studying and researching ATR, and have published notable works in this field. Most of them have occupied top academic positions in various Nigerian Universities and beyond and have academic honors in the field of ATR. Among such notable personalities are, Ogbu U. Kalu, John Mbiti, Jacob Olupona, Emmanuel Bolaji Idowu, Oliver Onwubiko, Denis Chidi Isizoh, and Emefie Ikenga-Metuh, to mention but a few. In addition, almost all Nigerian Universities have a department on Religious Studies, with ATR as an integral part of it.

The recognition of ATR within academia had tremendous significance for the religion, which hitherto had been

---

[282] Ajuwa, "Christianity and Nigerian Indigenous Culture," 23.
[283] Adrian Hastings, "Geoffrey Parinder," *Journal of Religion in Africa* XXXI, 3, 2001, p.355.

dismissed as superstition by European missionaries and western scholars. A lot of seminars and workshops have been put in place to bring elites from both religions to reason together on issues with religious undertones. This has advanced better understanding and relationships between ATR and Christianity in Nigeria. The result of this intellectual relationship between ATR and Christianity has been beneficial to both Christianity and Nigerian culture. The message of Christianity is more deeply and clearly understood in light of African thought, religion and culture, giving it more relevance to the lives of African Christians.

The interactions and relationships that have existed between ATR and Christians have resulted to such terminologies as "indigenization," "adaptation," "acculturation," and "inculturation." Christians and followers of ATR have come to appreciate the values of each other's faith and contribution to the growth and development of Nigerian society. The Christian Churches have begun to include necessary steps in the training of priests and evangelizers so that they are no longer alienated from their culture but rather have an authentic sense of cooperative dialogue and collaboration with other religions, including ATR.

Overall, Christianity has become an integral part of the Nigerian cultural society, with features of the religion and culture of the people, rather than an imported religion or an imposition on Nigerians. On the other hand, Christianity has also affected Nigerian culture and native religion in many positive ways. Thanks to Christianity, twins are no longer killed; human sacrifices are no longer practiced. However, the relationship is dynamic, and the best neither in Christianity nor in ATR has yet been fully explored. Constructive dialogue, in greater refined form, remains an imperative, in order to deal with intruding forces such as Christian fundamentalism and Nigerian culture and religious revivalism. As Chibueze Udeani noted,

Today many Igbo converts maintain a dual relationship. Though converted Christians, they remain consciously and unconsciously deeply rooted in Igbo traditional religion. The fact that irrespective of the conversion into Christianity, the Igbo still flock to their traditional religion should be indicative of the ambiguity existing in their religious life. This shows clearly that there is need for dialogue between Igbo traditional culture and the message of Christ.[284]

4.3 ISLAM *VS* CHRISTIANITY.

Islam has a longer history in Nigeria than does Christianity. As Islam was spreading in the second half of the nineteenth century, Christianity was just laying its foundation. Whereas in the north, Christianity had to confront Islam as an established religion, the story was different in many Yoruba towns, where both religions appeared around the same time. Christianity's appropriation of Western education was to give it an edge, especially in those areas where education became highly prized.[285]

Historically, therefore, Islam and Christianity reveal a long presence in Nigeria and have mutually interacted and converged with each other in many ways. Nigeria's regional and geo-political differences have equally played a role in this mutual interaction and relationship. In the East,

---

[284] Chibueze Udeani, *Inculturation as Dialogue: Igbo Culture and the Message of Christ.* (Amsterdam: Rodopi, 2007), 214

[285] Toyin Falola, *Violence in Nigeria: The Crisis of Religious Politics and Secular Ideologies.* (New York: University of Rochester Press, 1998), 27.

the predominance of Christians has ensured that Islam poses little or no threat or even a rivalry to Christianity. In the West, both religions have a long history of peaceful coexistence, although competition is not uncommon. For most of the nineteenth and twentieth centuries, Muslims sent their children to Christian schools. 30 % of students in Loyola Jesuit College, Abuja, Nigeria (a Catholic school) are Muslim. Again, about 90 percent of teachers in the Islamic education center in Enugu, Nigeria are Christians. Presently, one of my brothers is a teacher (as a youth corp) in a predominantly Muslim school in Kano state, which is a core Muslim state. Muslims use Christian hospitals, maternity centers and dispensaries.

Relationships between Islam and Christianity are as old as Islam itself. The Holy Qur'an is full of verses directed toward Christians, at times confirming the truths shared between the two religions, and calling for a meeting on common terms between both of them. It is said that Muhammad (peace be upon him) the Prophet of Islam freely and without conflict held discussions with the priests and monks of Najran for three days when they stayed as his guests in the mosque.[286]

The Christian openness and collaboration with Muslims in Nigeria is informed by the shift of emphasis and ecclesiology of Vatican II from an exclusivist approach to an inclusive approach towards other religion.

As noted by Paul Knitter,

> To understand how Vatican II and contemporary Roman Catholic thought form a watershed in Christian relationships with

---

[286] Izz al-din Ibrahim, "Islamic-Christian Dialogue: A Muslim View," in *Muslim-Christian Dialogue: Promise and Problems.* M. Darrol Bryant & S. A. Ali, Eds. (Minnesota: Paragon House, 1998), 15.

other religions, we must have some idea of what went before.[287]

The uniqueness of the Church (the exclusion of all other religions), outside which there is no salvation, dominated the ecclesiology of the Christian Church for many centuries. It came to its heights at the Council of Trent (1545-1563) in reaction to the Protestant Reformation; it was further reaffirmed by Vatican I (1869-1870). Vatican II came with a theology of aggiornamento[288] that permanently realigned the ecclesiology of the Church; bringing about the openness and relationships towards religions and ecclesial communities.

On the Muslim side, the relationship with Christians in Nigeria is also in line with the call of King Abdullah, the King of Saudi Arabia, on all Muslims to have cordial relationships through dialogue with the monotheistic religions.

For the practical purpose of relationship between Muslims and Christians in Nigeria, apart from the general similarities of belief in one God and a common ancestral heritage from Abraham that Muslims and Christians share, there are four aspects, which offer us good elements to affirm important convergences, interactions and relationships. These aspects are capable of motivating encounter and collaboration among Muslims and Christians in Nigeria, both at the individual, community and national levels.

---

[287] Paul F. Knitter, *No Other Name? A Critical Survey of Christian Attitude towards the World Religions.* (New York: Orbis Book, 1986), 121

[288] Aggiornamento literally means to bring up to date. It was name given to the pontifical program of Pope John XXIII in a speech he gave on January 25,1959, and was one the key words used during the Second Vatican Council both by bishops and clergy attending the sessions, and by the Media and Vaticanologists covering the Council.

4.3.1. Collaboration at the Leadership Level.

Recently Christians and Muslims leaders in Nigeria have awakened to the responsibilities their position as religious leaders bestow on them. One such visible area is the coming together of these leaders to discuss ways of mutual collaboration and averting crises between the two religions. The coming together of such leaders in an atmosphere of peace is a good example to their followers who look to them for guidance and direction. A joke was cracked when I was in the Seminary on the need for peace: "We are here killing ourselves in the name of religion, whereas Jesus and Muhammad are in heaven enjoying together a bottle of Apple Juice. If those who are our guide and model in faith can share a bottle of Apple Juice without fighting, then why can't we enjoy a bottle of Champagne together without violence?"[289] An example of such gatherings of Muslim and Christian leaders in Nigeria was held in October 2007 in Abuja, Nigeria, with fifty religious leaders in attendance. As narrated by Mohammed Lawal Shaibu: Fifty Muslim and Christian religious leaders met in Abuja to explore ways of achieving enduring peace and harmony in the country. An equal number of Muslim and Christian leaders met at the Transcorp Hilton Hotel under the auspices of the Nigeria Inter-religious Council (NIREC) to map out strategies on how to avert crises before they occur. The Sultan of Sokoto Alhaji Muhammadu Sa'ad called on Nigerians to eschew religious intolerance and imbibe the spirit of harmonious coexistence in the interest of Nigeria's growth and development. The Sultan said that no meaningful development could be achieved in a country where there is crisis and instability. He urged Muslims and Christians in the country to extol the virtues

---

[289] I made this joke in 1991 during a gathering of Nigerian Federation of Catholic Student at Ikot Ekpene, Nigeria

of tolerance, charity, respect and forgiveness as well as to promote the universality of the common bonds, which joined them together as Nigerians. The Sultan said that the issue of peace and religious harmony constitutes one of the cardinal principles that underlie the essence of our collective existence. Peaceful co-existence remains one of the key ingredients of nation-building and socio-economic development. He emphasized that religious harmony and the respect for the life and property of one another embody not only our commitment to these national goals but also express our common humanity and the affirmation of the benevolence of our Creator who, in His infinite wisdom, has put us together in this common abode.

Sultan Sa'ad, who is also the president general of the Nigeria Supreme Council for Islamic Affairs (NSCIA), said Nigerian religious differences should serve as a source of its national strength, stressing that its people should live, work and co-operate with one another to resolve any misunderstandings, which might arise in their day-to-day activities. The Sultan also called on religious leaders in the country to rededicate themselves to the noble cause of peace-building and mutual co-existence among religious groups. In his words,

> We must, as religious leaders, champion the cause of truth, honesty, accountability and justice and ensure that our followers embody these virtues and put them into effect. We must serve as a source of succor to the weak and the poor in our societies and provide hope and confidence to our people to face the social, economic and moral crises,

which they are bound to encounter in their collective existence.[290]

4.3.2. Healing the Wounds of the Past.

Muslims and Christians in Nigeria have taken various initiatives together to heal the wounds that religious violence from both sides has left on the nation, the faiths and on individuals. Various religious groups and individuals have stepped out to heal these wounds by actions, support and assistance to one another and to those most affected by such violence irrespective of their religion. A practical and most encouraging example of this is the efforts of Iman Ashafa and Pastor Wuye, popularly known as *the Imam and the Pastor,* who in the past were warlords 'fighting for and defending their faiths'. Many religious conflicts in the North are traceable to these two people. Today, both of them have come together to create what could be described as a bridge over the troubled waters.

Tracing the past lives of Ashafa and Wuye, and their transition from being war—lords to peacemakers and bridge-builder between Muslims and Christians in Nigeria, an analyst observed that in recent years, Nigeria has been plagued with an alarming frequency of violence between its Muslim and Christian communities. One of the worst hit regions was Kaduna State in 1995. The cofounders and national coordinators of the Muslim-Christian Dialogue Forum of Kaduna are two men ("The Imam and the Pastor") with deep roots in the opposing communities, both of whom have turned away from violence and militancy and instead embraced nonviolence, reconciliation, and the advocacy

---

[290] Muhammed Lawal Shuaibu, "50 Leaders Met in Abuja," in *Daily Trust,* October 18, 2007. http://allafrica.com/stories/200710180440.html (Assessed: August 27, 2009).

of peaceful relations between their communities.[291] Once they were bitter rivals, but now they consider themselves brothers. In fact, at one time, they each tried to have the other killed. James Wuye and Muhammed Ashafa are living proof that people can change, and that the urge for revenge can be replaced by an urge to foster reconciliation and peaceful coexistence. The project that the two men launched, which consists of both the Muslim-Christian Dialogue Forum and the Inter-Faith Mediation Centre, aims to prevent the recurrence of violent conflict and to contribute to an increase in the level of trust and tolerance between Christians and Muslims in Kaduna State. With trust, tolerance, and an absence of violence, reconciliation can begin through the development over time of collaborative relationships and cohesive peace constituencies in both communities. At the same time, as such reconciliation takes root, the communities' capacity to resolve conflicts will also be enhanced. Five specific objectives of the Muslim-Christian Dialogue Forum and the Inter-Faith Mediation Centre have been identified:

1. To reestablish relationships that has been damaged due to recurring violence over the last five years;
2. To minimize the reoccurrence of violence amongst various groups in the community;
3. To initiate programs and projects that require and encourage the involvement of Christians and Muslims (including dialogues, workshops, cultural events, and the establishment of a resource center);

---

[291] James Wuye and Muhammad Ashafa, Taken from the printable version of a video documentary of the "The Imam and the Pastor: Healing Conflict in Nigeria." Muslim-Christian Dialogue Forum in Nigeria. http://www.peoplebuildingpeace. org/thestories/print.php?id=93&typ=theme (Assessed: September 15, 2008.

4. To enhance interreligious relationships and cooperation within the state;
5. To support and build the capacity of local partners who are involved in peacemaking.[292]

These two leaders, who for several years were nursing the feeling of vengeance and hatching plots to kill each other in the name of religion, are today the best of friends to the extent that one can put his life on the line to save the life of the other. Their families also relate as one. The two are today serving as mediators across the country and beyond in communities torn apart by religious riots.

This campaign for peace and mutual co-existence among the religious faithful brought Ashafa and Wuye to Minna, the Niger State capital for a national summit for Nigerian Youths on Inter-religious Dialogue and Peaceful Co-existence, which was organized by the Nigeria Inter-religious Council. The Executive Secretary of NIREC, Prof. Ishaq Oloyede, presented the clerics to the audience that had 500 Muslim and Christian youths from all states of the federation in attendance. The professor said that the seminar was brought to Minna in appreciation of the efforts of the state governor, who is also the Chairman of the Northern Governors Forum, Dr. Muazu Babangida Aliyu, in promotion of peace and mutual co-existence in the country. He praised Aliyu for abolishing all forms of discriminatory fees in the state; an effort he stated would go a long way in the promotion of peace among the indigenes of the state. He described the North-Central region of the country as the region with the highest level of religious plurality going by the ratio of the Christians to the Muslims, adding that the recent outbreak of religious crisis in Jos called for stakeholders to intensify efforts at creating awareness

---

[292] Ibid.

and enlightening the youths on the need to shun religious violence and practice religious intolerance.

Wuye observed that various passages abound in the Bible and Quran that could be used negatively to foment trouble or instigate violence, but advised on the need for the people, especially religious leaders, to look at those sections that preach mutual co-existence, forgiveness and love. He described the two religions as emphasizing peace, love and forgiveness, while urging Muslims and Christians on the need to imbibe these principles. Wuye, who was a CAN official in 1987 and 1995, spoke on how he became a religious militant. He said, "Nobody recruited us and no Christian leader assembled us for the role. We believed it was enough of turning the second cheek; I just believed and saw the need for me to defend my religion. I brought people of same minds together. We looked at things from the angle that if the Muslims had spared lives, then we too could go and borrow one; but if they were ready to sacrifice their lives in the defense of their religion, then we should be ready to sacrifice our own too."[293] He added, "I discovered that hate begets hate, if I hit you and you hit me back, it becomes a vicious circle. I have learnt that loving the Muslims is the strongest weapon that a Christian can use. If you love and you keep on loving without caring what the other person is doing one day he or she will be compelled to love you in return. We need as Christians and Muslims to inch into one another and get closer to understand one another. We have been programmed to hate each other; we need to de-program ourselves from this and reprogram ourselves positively."[294]

The pastor admitted that it was a nightmare for him the first time he visited Ashafa in his mosque as he was filled

---

[293] Francis Falola, "27 Years After, handshake between Islam and Christianity," *The Punch Newspaper*. February 1, 2009.

[294] Ibid.

with fear that he might not come out of the mosque alive. But he expressed joy that the two of them had attended several conferences and seminars together all over the world and had on several occasions had to sleep on the same bed. "We are now like husband and wife that must not divorce; if we divorce our children will suffer and our children in this context are the Nigerian youths whom we must not allow to suffer, so we have vowed to stay stuck together," he said.

Ashafa stated the need for Nigerians to build a culture where people are judged on the strength of their character, and not based on their religion. "My dream is for a Nigeria where the son of a Muslim and that of a bishop will work together to make Nigeria great. It is regrettable that we are the most religious nation in the world when it comes to going to church and mosque, but when it comes to actions or living by our faith we are the worst. We need to change so that we can have a nation we will all be proud of," the Imam said.[295]

4.3.3. Standing By and With Each Other.

In the spirit of collaboration and friendship, Muslims and Christians in Nigeria have stood side by side, rejoicing with and consoling each other. Cases abound of this fact at the grassroots and in the daily lives of Muslims and Christians in Nigeria that go unnoticed and unpublished by the dailies. Often times what make headlines are the conflicts.

Such examples of collaboration existed between me, my parish community and the Muslim community in Arochukwu, Nigeria. We were always there for each other in good times and in bad. For instance, during the pastoral

---

[295] Ibid.

visit of my bishop to Arochukwu, the Muslim leader had an audience with him right inside the Church. They presented him with gifts as a sign of solidarity. At the dedication of St. Thomas Church, Amuvi Arochukwu and the inauguration of the parish, the Muslim community was there to celebrate with us. When our Church and rectory was burgled, they were there to condole us, and even offered cash support. During their own Sallah celebrations, we were there to rejoice with them. When they lost their leader (Oga Shehu, as we fondly called him, a very good friend of mine) to armed robbers, I as person and the entire community of Saints Theresa and Thomas stood behind them in their mourning and grief.

At the national scene, there are examples of relationships among Christian and Muslim leaders. One such example is contained in news published in the *Daily Trust Newspaper.* It reads:

> It was religious unity exemplified in Abuja at the weekend as the Catholic Archbishop of Abuja, Rt. Rev. John Onaiyekan, delivered a message of goodwill at the third triennial delegates' congress of the Northern States Council of the Ansar-Ud-Deen Society of Nigeria. In the message, the Catholic archbishop enjoined well-meaning Nigerians, of whatever creed, to do everything possible to promote the current climate of peace and freedom in the country and to avoid whatever could disturb or disrupt it. The News Agency of Nigeria (NAN) reports that Rt. Rev. Onaiyekan told the congress that it was "a pity that religion has been turned into a cause of trouble, instead of a major remedy for our self-inflicted problem." He said it was unfortunate that in the last two years, some serious problems have been

fomented between Christians and Muslims in Nigeria by some politicians for reasons other than religious. Rt. Rev. Onaiyekan, who is also the National Vice-President of the Christian Association of Nigeria (now president), said he was convinced, however, that the problems created were within the capacity of religious leaders and their followers to resolve with a minimum of goodwill. He said Nigerians should thank God that there were a great number of citizens who were sincere in their worship and that God had been answering prayers, especially in the country's moments of serious crises. In a message which she sent to the congress, wife of the vice-president, Mrs. Titi Atiku Abubakar, said Muslims must preach the gospel of religious tolerance and harmonious relationship between Muslims and non-Muslims. "Our mode of worship may be different, but we worship the same God," she stressed. Mrs. Abubakar also said Muslims must contribute to efforts to pull Nigeria out of the "decadence and confusion it found itself during the dark ages of military dictatorship." The message, entitled, "let's use religion as an instrument of peace," was delivered to the congress on her behalf by Dr. Garba Idris, Technical Assistant to the Minister of State for Health, Dr. Amina Ndalolo.[296]

---

[296] "Catholic Archbishop Graces Islamic Congress." *Daily Trust*, April 1, 2002. World Wide Religious News. http://www.wwrn.org/article.php?idd=10515&sec=4&con=60 (Assessed: July 27, 2009.)

The same show of solidarity is been expressed by Muslims towards their Christian brothers and sisters in Nigeria. As reported in *This Day Newspaper*:

> The leadership of Jama'atu Nasril Islam (JNI) has taken a bold initiative to bridge the unhealthy and suspicious gap that has pervaded the relationship between Christians and Muslims in Plateau State by visiting the Catholic Arch-Diocese headquarters in Jos.
> Leader of the delegation and Chairman of Jos North Local Government area branch of JNI, Alhaji Inuwa Ali informed the Arch-Bishop of Jos Diocese, Bishop Ignatius Kaigama that the delegation brought "a message of peace and love" in the spirit of Eid-el-Kabir. Ali noted that there was hardly any difference between the two religions even as he noted that there was no reason why adherents of both should not work in unity.
> He recalled that during the September 7, 2001 crisis in the state, the Bishop gave shelter to fleeing Muslims who sought refuge in the church adding that the Muslims who took refuge in the church were adequately taken care of. While expressing hope that the sallah visit will cement the relationship between the two groups and enhance peace in the state, Inuwa noted that the two religions abhor vices like drunkenness, prostitution and inhuman killings. Responding, Bishop Kaigama said he was overwhelmed by the visit but commended the JNI for taking the bold initiative. The Bishop stressed that religious leaders must enlighten their followers not to use religion for political

ends or to settle old scores. "Religion is about piety and good works; it is about showing love to one another no matter your religion or ethnic background. Everybody deserves freedom of religion wherever he/she is," he stated. Kaigama condemned the notion that some states were "Muslim states" whiles some are categorized "Christian states." "This is bad and should be condemned. It does not augur well for the development of the nation. We should be able to worship anywhere and anytime without molestation. We are all the same and worship the same God and should therefore work together in fellowship," Kaigama affirmed.[297]

4.3.4. Morality for Peace and Stability in the Society.

Morality, which is one of the bedrocks for peace and stability in society, is another common ground that brings Muslims and Christians together in Nigeria. Going through their teachings and ethical principles, it is obvious that "both Islam and Christianity exhort men and women to virtuous deeds and pious life."[298] Both religions condemn selfishness, falsehood, dishonesty, greed, hypocrisy, injustice, cruelty malice, vindictiveness, pride, vanity, arrogance and violence. They advocate, promote and enjoin

---

[297] "Religious Crisis: Muslim Leaders Visit Bishop." *This Day.* February 9, 2004. World Wide Religious News. http://www.wwrn.org/article.php?idd=5519&sec=4&con=60(Assessed: July 27, 2009.)

[298] Joseph Stoutzenberger, *The Christian Call to Justice and Peace.* (Minnesota: St Mary's Press, 1994), 62.

upon their followers peace, love, unity, justice, tolerance, forgiveness, mercy, self-control truth, integrity, purity and charity among other virtues. To cite one concept that is essential for the stability of society and harmonious relationships among people, a concept, which is common to the two faiths, let us take the word "peace." In Christianity, peace is valued as a behavior for the followers of the faith: "Blessed are the peacemakers: For they shall be called the children of God." (Matthew 5:9) Identical with this we find that the Holy Quran exhorts the Muslims to be peace-loving people.[299] Surah 23: 63 of the Quran says: "And the servants of the Beneficent God are they who walk on the earth in humility, and when the ignorant address them, they say, "peace."

Quite a good number of Christians and Muslims have understood this message of peace and have worked together in creating an atmosphere that will cultivate and promote this peace in Nigeria. As reported by Hajiya Bilkisu Yusuf,

> From the women's religious leader meeting, interfaith activities moved to Maiduguri, Borno State where the high power Nigeria Inter Religious Council NIREC held its quarterly meeting between May 4-7 2008. Established in 1999 as a non government organization, NIREC's objective is to promote the inculcation of Muslim and Christian morals: ethical and cultural, for the re-birth and rebuilding of a better society. The council has as its Co-chair, the president general of Nigeria Supreme Council for Islamic Affairs NSCIA, His Eminence, the Sultan of Sokoto,

---

[299] Abdelmoneim m. Khattab, "The Muslim-Christian Relationship: A Challenge and Promise," *Muslim-Christian Dialogue: Promise and Problems.* M. Darrol Bryant & S. A. Ali, Eds. (Minnesota: Paragon House, 1998), 61.

Alhaji Muhammad Sa'ad Abubakar III and the president of the Christian Association of Nigeria CAN, His Grace Archbishop John Onayeikan . . . The two major religions in the country, Islam and Christianity, preach the message of peace and accommodation of diversity. NIREC members believe that religious organizations have an important role to play in promoting peace and called for the capacity (*sic*) building for religious organization to enable them embark on peace and confidence building measures through constant inter-faith dialogues that emphasize the common values of our belief and create understanding and respect for our differences. They called on governments to take urgent measures at curbing the proliferation of small arms in our society which tend to create a culture of violence and is a major source of rising violent crimes in our society.[300]

The two Co-Chairmen of NIREC, in a single voice on May 4, 2009, called on Nigerian leaders and citizen to avoid violence and put in place structures that will enable peace to reign in Nigeria. As reported in the *All African News*,

The co-chairman of Nigeria Inter-Religious Council (NIREC), who is also the president of Christian Association of Nigeria (CAN), Rt. Rev. John Onaiyekan has advocated sanctions

---

[300] Bilkisu Yusuf, 'Nigeria: Building an Interfaith Bridge of Peace," in *Leadership Newspaper*. June 5, 2008. All Africa.com http://allafrica.com/stories/printable/200806050166. html (Assessed: December 18, 2008).

for religious leaders who preach inciting messages as a way of curtailing incessant religious crisis in the country. Similarly, the Sultan of Sokoto and co-Chairman of the same council, Alhaji Saad Muhammad Abubakar III, has repeated his call for a constitutional advisory role for traditional rulers to enable them contribute (*sic*) meaningfully to forging peace. The two religious leaders spoke, yesterday, while presenting papers at the National Institute for Policy and Strategic Studies (NIPPS), Kuru, Plateau State.[301]

The basis for peace and understanding already exists in Islam and Christianity. It is part of the very foundational principles of both faiths: love of the One God, and love of neighbor. These principles are found repeatedly in the sacred texts of Islam and Christianity.[302]

---

[301] Taye Obateru, "Nigeria: Onaiyekan, Sultan Preaches Religious Tolerance," *All Africa,* May 5, 2009, Cited in *Religious Diversity News* http://www.pluralism.org/news/view/21518 (Assessed: August 27, 2009)

[302] "A Common Word among Us." (Assessed: August 27, 2009).

CHAPTER FIVE

INTERFAITH RELATIONSHIPS AMONG THE THREE RELIGIONS IN NIGERIA/SOUTH-EAST: AREAS OF CONVERGENCE *(A TRIALOGICAL APPROACH).*

5.1 AFRICAN TRADITIONAL RELIGION (ATR), ISLAM, AND CHRISTIANITY.

In the spirit of this work; a trialogue of the three religions in Nigeria, this chapter examines the trialogical relationships, interactions and convergences that exist among ATR, Islam and Christianity in Nigeria.

It is often thought that relationships exist only between Christians and Muslims in Nigeria. On the contrary, all three religions have influenced and are still influencing each other, and have come together on several issues—religious, social, and cultural. As observed by Parrinder, a pioneer professor of ATR in Nigeria,

> Christianity in Africa affects traditional religion, but is also affected by it. And Islam is touched by both ATR and Christianity . . .

Today some Africanization of music, liturgy and costume is at work in the Churches and Mosques. Doctrines of Christianity and Islam are being reinterpreted into African forms without reverting to ideas that contradict a monotheistic faith. The effect of traditional religion may be seen in the independent Churches, which are often most successful in proselytization by joining Christians and African practices . . . Traditional religion has equally affected Islam. This is seen in many elements that remain or even revive under long established dominance, not only in rites of circumcision, marriage and funerals, but dance and possessions.[303]

There is no doubt that the old traditional African religion is declining in outward manifestation in some towns and villages in Nigeria. Islam and Christianity have enormous advantages in superior organization, education, social prestige and international power. Nevertheless, while the old clay temples and shrines vanish, many traditional beliefs persist and influence and continue to shape the nature of things in the society, including the life of Christians and Muslims. One such influence in the making of the new Nigerian society is Nigeria's hosting and celebration of the Festival of Arts and Culture (FESTAC), in 1977 in Lagos, when all Nigerians (Christians and Muslims), and indeed all Africa gathered in Nigeria to celebrate Nigeria and Africa's religio-cultural heritage. Since then, a Ministry of Culture and Tourism has been established in the Federation and in all the states of Nigeria.

Being a Christian or Muslim or traditional religionist is no longer a matter of importance to many in Nigeria today.

---

[303] Parrinder, *Religion in Africa*, 228-230.

What seems to matter most now is that we are religious people. More so, being a Christian or Muslim does not make people less traditional in Nigeria today. In fact, both Islam and Christianity could not replace traditional in Nigeria, especially among the Yoruba's, thus enabling the Yoruba to moderate the tension and competition between Islam and Christians in constructive ways, thanks to the influence of ATR. According to Samuel Quanoo,

> An examination of the relationship between ATR, Islam and Christianity show some positive results. Relying on Gastils democracy date set, World Fact book and Encyclopedia of the Third world, it may be argued that the influence of Christianity and Islam on Nigeria is superficial. ATR are polytheistic in nature and easily incorporate other religions such as Islam and Christianity. Even though these two Abrahamic religions are monotheistic, most African Christians and Muslims convert to them and still retain some aspects of their traditional religions. In this regard Christians and Muslims have become Africanized, diluting the rigidity of the 'original' doctrine. The tolerant nature of ATR may therefore be responsible for the African derivations of Islam and Christianity.[304]

In Nigeria, a convert to Christianity does not become exactly a Christian like an Italian, or German. He/she becomes an authentic Igbo, Hausa or Yoruba Christian with the values and the categories of thought that are taught by African

---

[304] Samuel Ebow Quanoo, *Transition and Consolidation of Democracy in Africa.* (Ohio: Ohio Central State University Press, 2000), 40,

Traditional Religion and passed down the centuries through customs, proverbs, wise-sayings and traditional religious expressions. A convert to Islam does not become a true copy of an Arabic Muslim from Saudi Arabia. His practice of Islamic religion is colored by the culture of his people. This internalization is possible because "Africans are translators, who by transculturating the incoming religious expressions, refit them for their own experiences and in so doing transform both expressions and experience."[305]

Leaders of the three religions have started coming together to speak of diverse issues affecting the nation and to condemn violence. An example of a such gathering took place after the Jos Crisis of November/December 2008. As reported by Ise-Oluwa Ige,

> Religious leaders across the nation yesterday met in Abuja behind closed doors in search of peace for the crisis-ridden Jos, the capital of Plateau State. The leaders who gathered under the name and style of the Nigeria Inter-Religious Council of Nigeria (NIREC) said the latest Jos mayhem, which claimed hundreds of lives, and property worth several millions of naira was a source of worry to them. The leaders expressed regrets over the unfortunate incident blaming it on poverty, ignorance and political instability in the country. The Council is however urging the Federal Government to convoke a judicial panel of enquiry with the mandate to investigate the remote and immediate causes of the crisis, and fish out its masterminds for

---

[305] Thomas D. Blakely, Ed. *Religion in Africa*. (London: Frank Cass, 1990), 18.

the sole purpose of prosecuting them. NIREC, which spoke on the Jos crisis yesterday in Abuja after a three-hour deliberation, said that the Council is planning to convoke a summit on various issues threatening the oneness of the Nigerian nation including the contentious issue of indigenship. Other issues that would top the agenda of the national dialogue include poverty, electoral reform, Niger Delta, political instability, religious intolerance and good governance. Spokesperson for the Council, Professor Ishyaq Oloyede told reporters after the meeting that the national dialogue has been slated for March 2009.[306]

On a similar note, the Sultan of Sokoto, Alhaji Saad Abubakar III (a Muslim) and the Chairman of Eastern States Council of Traditional Rulers, Eze Cletus Ilomuanya (a Traditionalist) have jointly canvassed religious tolerance as a means of cementing the unity of the country. According to the eminent leaders, religious tolerance and respect for one another will go a long way in strengthening the peace in Nigeria and enhance her unity. They both spoke at the recently concluded 15th Zumunta Annual International Convention held in Los Angeles, United States of America (Zumunta International Convention is a Nigerian-Socio-Cultural organization based in the USA). According to a statement issued in Owerri, Imo State from the palace of Eze Ilomuanya, the convention attracted many dignitaries including the chairman of the Christian Association of Nigeria, Archbishop John Onaiyekan. The sultan emphasized the need for communities to co-exist

---

[306] Ise-Oluwa Ige, "Nigeria: Religious Leaders Meet in Abuja," in *Vanguard,* December 4, 2008.

in peace and condemned the practice whereby innocent people are herded into fighting senseless wars. He was of the view that Nigerian leaders owe it to the citizenry to educate them on how to co-habit peacefully irrespective of their religious belief.[307]

The following are areas where ATR, Islam and Christianity in Nigeria converge, relate and interact with one another.

5.1.1. Beliefs and Rituals.

The most visible point of convergence among the three religions is a belief in a Supreme Being, called Allah by Muslims, God by Christians, and *Chukwu* (and other native names according to tribe) by the Igbos. Nigerians of all faiths are commonly agreed that whether Allah, God, or Chukwu, it is the same GOD. Beliefs in spirits and the spirit world as against the material world, holy men, saints or ancestors, the place and importance of communion with the Divine through prayers and sacrifices, and the role of rituals in religion, are all points of convergence that offer a basis for relationship, interaction and discussion among ATR, Islam and Christianity in Nigeria. Interestingly, many do express their faith in Allah, God, and Chukwu at the same time, while some ritualize their devotion to deities of the three religions.

An example can be found in a report filed in the *Champion's Newspaper*:[308] Oshogbo, Nigeria—Wasiu

---

[307] Anselem Umunnakwe, "Royal Fathers Seek for Religious Harmony," in *This Day,* August 16, 2008.

[308] "Nigerians meld Christianity, Islam with ancient practices" in *World Wide Religious News.* (October 14, 2007) accessed: March 22, 2009. http://www.wwrn.org/article. php?idd=26568&sec=con=60

Olasunkani drops to his knees in the sacred grove, lowers his chin to his chest and turns his palms skyward: a gesture of thanks to a traditional water goddess embodied by the massive stone idol with outstretched arms that sweep over an ancient shrine. Olasunkani, a Muslim whose 1998 pilgrimage to Mecca fulfilled one of the five pillars of Islam, joins tens of thousands of ethnic Yoruba people each year to pray before the idol and offer libations to her mermaid-like spirit, Osun. Last year, Olasunkani beseeched the goddess for a baby. This year he's thanking her for twin boys, Farook and Cordroy. "If you want to get a baby, you come here and pray, and you'll certainly have one," said the 46-year old doctor after finishing his riverside reverie. Speaking of his fellow Yoruba people of southwestern Nigeria—20 million strong and roughly evenly split between Christians and Muslims—he says: "We've been doing this for centuries." He says his prayers to Osun, only one goddess in the Yoruba pantheon, are cultural, and should not be considered in conflict with Islam's monotheism. "I believe that there is God. What I mean is that we should have the fear of God," he says, water still dripping from his face after ablutions in the river also called Osun, near the city of Oshogbo. "In Saudi, they'll tell you that this isn't good. But God is our creator, and he made everything. If God thought this wasn't good, he wouldn't allow it," he concluded.

Across West Africa, churches or mosques can be found in virtually every settlement: evidence of deep Christian and Muslim roots sown by the merchants, missionaries and slave traders who brought the religions hundreds of years ago. Also firmly settled in the red soil are indigenous practices that West Africans integrate with the foreign beliefs.

In Nigeria, shrines with old icons abound, with members of many ethnic groups praying to their old gods. Prayer to multiple gods, or treating animals as deities, continues even among self-avowed Christians and Muslims. While many of the old practices go on in secret, others do not. Annually upwards of 100,000 Yoruba people like Osunleti and Olasunkani travel to the forest in the middle of the southern city of Oshogbo to pray to Osun. Osun, the fable holds, rose from the river to help lead the Yoruba people to the area, and each year hordes of Yoruba people of all ages cram into the riverside glen that has been named a UNESCO world heritage site.

On a recent Friday, throngs of people made their way down into the forest to partake in the festivities, where they give thanks and praises. Beneath the stone idol of Osun, about five meters high with arms flung straight out like the bars of a cross, worshippers cast money into the river and toss in doves, their wings broken so they can't immediately fly away. As cash and birds swirl the bank of the muddy river, droves of Nigerians fill jerry cans from the river, carting home the sacred water. Later, a virgin is presented to the water goddess amid nearly hysterical drumming and dancing. Worshippers touch the stone Osun statue.

The results may sometimes seem to flout the monotheistic holy books, the Bible and Qur'an. But many West African faithful say their interpretations are equally valid—although they don't always tell their pastors or imams.

Tunde Osunleti, a Christian also at a recent festival celebrating Osun, agrees. "Jesus is the one who created this Osun. I just believe we're serving one God,' says the 19-year old artist. "My pastor would say, 'Don't go here.' But my pastor is not my God. I only believe in God, and myself." "We Yoruba people, we have many small deities, but they are all servants of God," says Osunleti, the artist. "All these idols are servants of God: I'm a Christian, I'm a Muslim, I'm an idol worshipper, I'm an artist, I believe in everything" he says. "I just believe in God. We're all servants of God, and we can pray through anything." He concluded.

In the largely Christian areas farther south, many professed Christians have more than one wife, which tallies with pre-Christian practices where men took on many spouses to ensure survival of the bloodline during times of drought or war. Some people practice both Islam and Christianity. One taxi driver tells of travelling with his first wife to mosque on Friday and his second wife to church on Sunday, and goes to the native shrine every other day.[309]

This type of combination exists in every part of Nigeria where followers of the three religions live.

Another area of belief and ritual where ATR, Islam and Christianity in Nigeria converge and interact is the belief in spirits and spiritual powers. In traditional religion, the spirits are considered benevolent, but sometimes mischievous or even evil. Witchcraft is a sellout to the evil power. As noted by David Shenk,

> Traditional religion seeks ways to pacify the spirits and control evil powers. The ritual and social devices used to control and pacify the spirits and other powers are complex and awesome. Both Islam and Christianity have responded to the need not to be overwhelmed by the spirits or powers. These faiths have brought hope for the exorcism of evil spirits and freedom from the curse of witchcraft, because Muslims and Christians believe spirits [have powers but still] are under the authority of the Creator. Islam provides various talismans and Quranic incantations to protect from or cajole these evil powers. The Muslim community brings with it expertise for dealing with spirits. Attempts to exorcise spirits from possessed

---

[309] Ibid.

people have been a Muslim vocation in African societies ... Church ministers, in the confidence that the powers do not have the last word, have various rituals and prayers for exorcising and casting out evil spirits.[310]

Various forms of rituals for exorcising and casting out these evil spirits used by Muslims and Christians are imbedded with African traditional religious practices.

5.1.2. Community Life.

In the Nigerian culture, the community is the basis of existence. The sense of community and humane living are highly cherished values of traditional African life. This statement remains true in spite of the apparent disarray in the experience of modern politics and brutal internecine wars, crises, and conflicts in Nigeria and in many parts of Africa. For Africans, (ATR, Muslims and Christians) the community is basically sacred, rather than secular, and surrounded by several religious forms and symbols. A visitor to Africa is soon struck by the frequent use of the first person plural 'we', and 'ours' in everyday speech.[311]

In Nigeria, the primary community loyalties to one's extended family and village continue to exert their hold over people who live away from the communities of their home-towns. People generally return to their villages from their residence in the cities from time to time to join members of their village community to celebrate important

---

[310] David W. Shenk, *Global Gods: Exploring the Role of Religions in Modern Societies.* (Pennsylvania: Herald Press, 1995), 92-93.

[311] Aylward Shorter, *African Christian Theology.* (London: (Geoffrey Chapman, 1975),123

religious rituals: Christmas, Easter, Sallah, Id El-Kabir, New Yam celebration, and cultural events like initiation, title taking or festivals. From their residence in urban cities, they send substantial financial contributions to their rural home communities to support various development projects like provision of electricity and pipe-borne water, building of educational institutions and scholarship awards, funds to send young men and women on further studies in foreign countries or in one's own country. Primary communities based on clan, or ethnic descent, or religious (ATR, Muslim, Christian) affiliation equally abound in many modern Nigerian cities.

Underscoring the belief and sense of the community among traditional Africans and their religions, John Mbiti writes,

> In traditional Africa, the individual does not and cannot exist alone except corporately. He owes existence to other people, including those of past generations and his contemporaries. Whatever happens to the individual is believed to happen to the whole group, and whatever happens to the whole group happens to the individual . . . The individual can only say: I am because we are, and since we are, therefore I am. This is a cardinal point in the understanding of the African view of man.[312]

A strong sense of community life equally characterizes the Christian religion. Christ and his disciple, were a community, the early Church was a community of believers that transcended cultural barriers to the extent that there

---

[312] John S. Mbiti, *African Religion and Philosophy*. (Ibadan: Heinemann, 1990), 106

was no longer a distinction between Jews and Gentile, slave or free, men and women, as all were one community in Christ (Galatians 3:26-29). The sense of community drives through the patristic period, the middle ages, down to our time. To be a Christian is to belong to a community of those who believe in Christ and it is within this community that one realizes one's true essence in life as a Christian. Recalling the theology of St. Thomas Aquinas on Christianity and community life, John C. Raines writes,

> For Aquinas the political and the social order is part of the created order of nature, not as a result of the fall. To understand the human person is to understand our being as essentially rational. Moreover, to understand humans as reasoning-beings means also to understand them as members of a common and public discourse (the community or society). It is by talking and living together, Thomas held that we actualize our human potentials. By talking together we enter a world of shared meanings, and so come to order and make sense of our life . . . It is therefore natural for man to be a social animal.[313]

In Islam, the belief and reliance upon the community (Umma) is one of the basic essences of the religion. A Muslim can truly be a Muslim to the extent that he/she identifies with the Umma, and takes part in the community prayer, all facing one direction—the Kaaba in Mecca—as

---

[313] John C. Raines, "The Nation State and Social Order: In the Perspective of Christianity", in Faruqi, *Trialogue of the Abrahamic Faiths*, 43.

one community of believers. On this note, Isma'il Faruqi writes,

> A person's membership in the tribe or nation (community) does entitle him to love, honor, assistance, and protection by fellow tribesmen on the basis that charity begins at home or, as Islamic jurisprudence has formulated it, "the nearer is more entitled to your deed (*al ma'ruf*) than the farther." . . . By belonging to the tribe, the tribesman is no more entitled to one's charity than the distant neighbor whose need for that charity is greater; nor for one's protection if the distant neighbor stands in greater need for that protection . . . Being a realistic religion bent upon the promotion of human welfare, Islam does not deny that humans are born into their tribes and/or nations.[314]

The implication of this is that the community offers persons the basic necessities and protection, and gives them their identity. On the other hand, as part of the social group, the individual sacrifices personal interests and gives up selfishness for the well-being of other members of the community for the continued existence of the community.

This shared ideal among the three religions in Nigeria has greatly advanced relationships among them and advanced the peace and stability of the nation. Each follower of these religions sees himself first as belonging to the larger Nigerian, Hausa, Yoruba, or Igbo community before seeing himself as a member of a religious group or community.

---

[314] Isma'il R. al Faruqi, "The Nation State and Social Order in the Perspective of Islam.," in Faruqi, *Trialogue of the Abrahamic Faiths*, 53-54.

As such, he sees it as a binding communal responsibility to contribute to the peace of this community by avoiding violence, and living harmoniously with other members of the larger community, their religious affiliations or minor communities not withstanding. This expresses the view of Parrinder, who stated,

> A general tolerance allows people of different religions to live side by side, to learn from another, and prepare the way for a religious dialogue that was difficult in earlier centuries. The closer understanding of all religions, Christians, Muslims and traditional, can help toward better adjustment of all African life to the many problems of modern times.[315]

5.1.3. Social Justice.

In Nigeria, as in many other African countries, the failure of the nation-state and of secular ideologies has enhanced the relevance of religion. Religion continues to provide many alternatives to social injustices and ills: hope that the future will be bright for millions of people traumatized by the failure and corruption of the government has given rise to a number of Ethnic militia, the emotional strength to handle stress occasioned by these failures, shared identity for the hopeless and the marginalized in the cities and towns, and social support for women, children, and spouses. The three religions in Nigeria have lived up to this responsibility as individual religions, and collaboratively as religions in Nigeria.

The concept of social justice and the need to apply it to all in the society is deeply imbedded in the teachings of ATR,

---

[315] Parrinder, *Religion in Africa*, 237.

Islam and Christianity in Nigeria and world over. In African Traditional Religion and culture, social justice is intended to contribute to social stability, and harmonious relationships within the ethnic group and the lesser groupings of which it is composed. The expectations of the individual are largely dictated by structures, relationship patterns and roles. Social justice, therefore, implies conformity to these things. Each individual is given his due within the scope of his expectations, and in the framework of a hierarchical or highly structured society. Distribution is made to people according to rank, status or function, and although there are no classes in the strict economic sense, there are social strata defined by age and achievement. African traditional society is communitarian, but it is not strictly egalitarian. Egalitarian ideals in modern African socialism, therefore, are developments of traditional concepts under the light of Islamic or Christian egalitarianism.[316]

In Islam, for justice and equilibrium to be realized there must be a strong correlation between the spiritual and the material well-being of the individual and this is the right of all human beings. From this premise, Islam holds two main principles. First, that no individual or group may exploit another; second, that no group insulate and separate itself from the rest of humanity with a view of restricting its economic condition to themselves be it one of misery or affluence.[317]

On the part of Christianity, the Magisterium of the Church and the Encyclicals of various Popes through the centuries have focused on the Christian stand on the social

---

[316] Aylward Shorter, "Concepts of Social Justice in Traditional Africa," *Africa: Journal of the International African Institute.* Vol. XXXIX, n.3, 1996, pp58-84.

[317] Mashuq ibn Ally, "Islam: Global Issues," in *Ethical Issues in Six Religious Traditions*, Peggy Morgan and Clive Lawton, Eds. (Edinburgh: Edinburgh University Press, 1996), 256-257.

teaching of the Church. Amongst them include, *Rerum Novarum* (Of New Things) of Leo XIII (May 15, 1891), *Quadragesimo Anno* (In the fortieth year) of Pius XI (May 15, 1931), *Mater et Magistra* (Mother and Teacher) and *Pacem in Terris* (Peace on Earth) of John XXIII, (May 15, 1961, and April 11, 1963 respectively), *Laborem Exercens* (On human work), *Sollicitudo Rei Socialis* (On Social Concern), and *Centesimus Annus* (Hundredth year) of John Paul II (September 14, 1981, December 30, 1987, and May 1, 1991 respectively), and finally (as of the time of writing this dissertation) *Caritas et Veritas* (Charity in Truth) of Benedict XVI (June 29, 2009). Special emphasis should be made on *Rerum Novarum*, the first of these encyclicals on social justice. *Rerum Novarum* subtitled "On Capital and Labor", was given at St. Peter's in Rome, the fifteenth day of May, 1891, the fourteenth year of the pontificate of Leo XIII. In this document, Pope Leo XIII set out the Church's response to the social instability and labor conflict that had arisen in the wake of industrialization and that had led to the rise of socialism. The Pope taught that the role of the State is to promote social justice through the protection of rights, while the Church must speak out on social issues in order to teach correct social principles and ensure class harmony. He restated the Church's long-standing teaching regarding the crucial importance of private property rights, but recognized, in one of the best-known passages of the encyclical, that the free operation of market forces must be tempered by moral considerations[318]

All three religions have demonstrated common interest and concern on the need of social justice in Nigeria. A clear example is the call on the Federal government by leaders of these religions to address the injustice and underdevelopment in the Niger-Delta region of Nigeria

---

[318] Leo XIII, *Rerum Novarum: On Capital and labor*, (Rome: Vatican Press, 1891).

that has led to much violence, loss of lives, destruction of property, and decrease in the national revenue income.

Among other things that act as a catalyst for social justice among the three religions in Nigeria is the principle of the "The Golden Rule," inscribed in their ethical teachings. People of all faiths lament the injustice, conflict and violence "for God's sake" that has been, and continues to be, practiced. It is the conviction of all Nigerians that we must be moved and at same time, we must move others to act with love, peace and tolerance. While we do not need to be of one belief, nor of one religion, we do need to act on behalf of the behavioral ethic that is common to all faiths. In the true spirit of interfaith relationships, below are quotations taken from the sacred tradition of the three faiths in Nigeria, all extolling the guidance offered in "The Golden Rule." In Christian ethics, the maxim is: "Always treat others as you would like them to treat you." (Matthew 7:12). For Islam, it is: "Not one of you truly believes until you wish for others what you wish for yourselves," (Muhammad's Hadith). In ATR, the maxim is, live and Let Live.[319]

5.1.4. Hospitality and Social Action against Poverty.

Related to the teaching and action on social justice among the three religions, but different from it, is the place of hospitality and social action for the poor and the needy in the society. This is a prominent area where the teachings of these religions manifest visible convergence, and where traditionalists, Muslims and Christians have worked as one to impact Nigerian society. Nigerians are very generous

---

[319] The Golden Rule in Children's Catechism. http://www.pflaum.com/catalog/childcat/mapsposter.htm (Assessed: August 29, 2009).

and giving people. In their various communities, they care for strangers more than they care for themselves. They are willing to go hungry to feed the stranger in their midst or home. They see it as a divine mandate to provide and cater for the needs of less privileged members of the society. In times of crises, political unrest and other natural disaster, all have come together to offer help to all the afflicted irrespective of religion. As expressed by Aguwa,

> A key effect of communal life is the deep sense of hospitality, which permeates Nigerian and African social relationships. The practice requires more than verbal expressions of welcome, since material things are given with an open heart and a readiness for friendly exchange. Members of the kin group consider hospitality an obligation they owe one another.[320]

In the agrarian Yoruba society, "farmers freely give maize, yams, beans and other farm products to those who do not have crops. Women give freely palm oil, sugar-cane, and water."[321] The Igbo people go as far as ritualizing the acts of hospitality during social visits with kola nut presentations, which are usually done with grandiose prayers and expressions of good will, wellness and good faith. As a growing child, I always saw my grandfather and my father presenting and praying with kola nut. In addition, I have witnessed my parents sharing farm produce of various kinds with the less privilege. On one occasion, as a little

---

[320] Aguwa, "Christianity and Nigerian Indigenous Culture," 16.

[321] M.K. Ademilokun, "Moral Values among the Yoruba," in *Socio-Philosophical Perspective of African Traditional Religion*, eds. Emma Ekpunobi and Ifeanyi Ezeaku. (Enugu: New Age Publishers, 1990), 79.

boy, I asked my parents, "Why do you always give, don't you think our food will finish and we will go hungry? Where shall we go to get what we shall eat?" They responded to me: "We shall never go hungry by giving; rather we go hungry by not giving. Whoever gives to those who don't have is giving to God and fulfills his communal obligation and God will always give him more so that he will keep giving." This philosophy of my parents informs my establishing a group called *Social Action for the Poor* in the parishes where I have served. The work of this group is to make appeals for money, food and items of clothing and to identify those mostly in need that we can visit. In one of my parishes, I was feeding breakfast twice a week to the poor irrespective of church or religions. Donors to the fund were from ATR, Islam and Christianity.

Shorter's description of the traditional society long before the advent of Islam and Christianity in Nigeria underscores our point on the place of hospitality toward strangers, minority groups and poor people among Nigerians.

> Stranger is a relative term. There are those who are strangers in a family, others who are strangers in a village or chiefdom, and finally there are ethnic strangers. The stranger who was not an enemy was always welcome in traditional Africa—at least for a limited period. The stranger represented the mysterious and the unknown; he was a link with foreign parts. He brought news and peculiar information. The stranger was the symbol of man's communication with the world of the gods and spirits, and his coming was a blessing. Many chiefs and rulers justified the rule of their dynasty through a myth charter which told how

their ancestor, the first ruler, had come as a stranger from a mystical, faraway place. People are attracted by the stranger, but they also fear not to show him hospitality. In a society where co-operative production and common consumption were the norms, it was virtually impossible for a class of poor to exist. There were even instances when crippled strangers without relatives were taken in and cared for.[322]

ATR strongly believes that there is a sense of the sacred in hospitality and in the coming of a guest, be it a known guest or a stranger. They truly believe that love of neighbor, especially the poor and needy, love of stranger, and the guest, is inseparable from the love of God.[323]

In Islam, the Quran identifies those in need as orphans, the needy and the strangers, and these are entitled to be catered to by the Muslim community. The Quran says, "What Allah has bestowed on His Messenger [and taken away] from the people of town ship, belongs to Allah, the Messenger, the kindred and orphans, the needy, and the wayfarer." (59:7).

The needy extend to the poor, the disadvantaged, handicapped and diseased. It is a concern of the *ummah* to cushion the difficulties experienced by the handicapped. The Muslim is reminded that normality and abnormality in human beings is the result of the divine will, therefore the welfare of the disadvantage is part of the divine responsibility. The wayfarer may be a beggar, a traveler, a

---

[322] Shorter, "Concepts of Social Justice in Traditional Africa," 62.

[323] Schineller, *A Handbook on Inculturation*, 79.

stranger or a person who has lost hope. Muslims have the responsibility to care for such people.[324]

In Christianity, the Gospel of Matthew 25:31-46 lays emphasis on caring and providing for the needy, the sick, stranger, the dejected and the outcast. The letter to the Hebrews (13:2-3), equally admonishes Christian on their duty to strangers and the needy. It says, "Always remember to welcome strangers, for by doing this, some people have entertained angles without knowing it. Keep in mind those who are in prison, as though you were in prison with them."

All three religions are in accord that there is something divine about strangers, and that welcoming them is a communion not only with the stranger, but with some mysteries beyond him/her.

Writing on the Christian sense of hospitality and social action against poverty, Trevor Shannon said,

> The Christian response to the needy in the twentieth century is directed to individuals and to nations through agencies like Christian Aid. There is always a double aim. One is the response to nations, to the immediate problem, perhaps providing as an emergency measure food, warmth, clothing, and medicine and healing (as was the case during the Nigeria-Biafra civil war of 1967-1970). The second is perhaps even more important. It is the attempt to discover the causes of needs and deprivation, so that they can be addressed. Long-term projects to prevent famine, to plan agricultural development, to provide homes, food skills

---

[324] Ally, "Islam: Global Issues," 245-246.

and work for individuals is a vital part of Christian care for those in need.[325]

Nigerians are truly proud to be associated with these three religions for all they have done in assisting the government in alleviating hunger and poverty in the society. I recall with joy and pride and wish to mention that my parish (St. Theresa's Parish, Arochukwu, then including St. Thomas, Amuvi Arochukwu) and I won the prestigious and first Umuahia Diocesan Award for poverty eradication in the society, in 2004.

The religious communities in Nigeria have always gone beyond their ecclesial boundaries in the level of cooperation and collaboration in addressing social problems affecting the needy in the society.

5.1.5. Emphasis on the Family.

There is a common sense among Nigerians, be they traditionalists, Muslims or Christians, that the family is the nucleus of society. In Nigeria, before one thinks himself as member of a religious body, he/she understands himself/herself as belonging to a family. The bond of unity among family members has been a strong factor in the mutual and peaceful coexistence of the three religions in Nigeria. It is not uncommon to have in one Nigeria family a traditionalist, a Muslim and a Christian, or even some who combine two or all three religions, and some who declare themselves irreligious. Yet they live together as parents and children, brothers and sisters, uncles and aunts, nephews and nieces.

---

[325] Trevor Shannon, "Christianity: The Quality and Value of Life," in *Ethical Issues in Six Religious Traditions*, Peggy Morgan and Clive Lawton, Eds. (Edinburgh: Edinburgh University Press, 1996), 197.

For example, when I entered the seminary, my father was not a practicing Christian. He was just a nominal member, but an active member of the *Ekpe* traditional Society. He was in fact the head of this society in my community; a position he inherited from my grandfather. Nevertheless, there was no a misunderstanding between him and my mother who was a practicing Christian, nor between him and myself. There are many more complex examples involving all three religions in one family, but that is more in the South-West of Nigeria.

Writing on the strong sense of family life and solidarity in the Nigerian religio-cultural society, Schineller said,

> The isolated self is an abstraction, it is unreal. One quickly senses and feels the truth of this statement in Nigerian culture. One is identified by one's family, which is the extended family, often including aunts and uncles, cousins, in-laws, nieces, and nephews. Extended also over time, the family is continually linked with those who have gone before. Children too are precious; not to have children is the exception and not a norm, and is often seen as a disgrace. For, it is the children who pass on the family name to future generations. Loyalty and support for one's family are primary. One is one's brother's keeper and sister's keeper. A key image of sin is separation, isolation from family, and breaking familial solidarity.[326]

This very important Nigerian concept and practice that predates Islam and Christianity is much a part of Islam and Christianity in Nigeria. One may be converted from ATR to

---

[326] Schineller, *A Handbook on Inculturation*, 76.

Islam or vice versa, from ATR to Christianity or vice versa, or from Islam to Christianity or vice versa, or even from ATR to Christianity and later to Islam, but one is never converted from his family to another. One remains part of one's family no matter one's change of religion. Hence, whether one is a traditionalist, a Muslim, or a Christian, the maintenance of peace and stability in the family remains one's primary aim. In the family children are taught right behavior and conduct. Wrongs are punished while virtues are rewarded. One such virtue that children are taught is to live in peace, unity and love with family members and with neighbors. Such other family members or neighbors could be followers of another religion.

Islam equally has a strong attachment to family values. As noted by Ally,

> Family plays a very important part in Muslim society. It is a basic institution of the community (ummah) and is organized in such a way that it operates as a society in miniature. The network of rights and obligations that provides the basis of family life aims to produce those virtues that Islam wants to foster in the individual and in the community. Through companionship, it is possible to achieve psychological, spiritual and emotional stability. However, relationships between all the members of a family, and most important of all between the husband and the wife, are important not merely because they are useful. They are spiritual relationships which sustain and generate love, kindness, mercy, compassion, mutual confidence, self-sacrifice, solace, and succor. Muslims claim that it is only in the context of the family that the ethical and

moral potential in human beings becomes real.[327]

Equally, Christianity sees the family as a domestic Church, whose existence and stability is indispensible for the existence, stability and survival of the larger Church and society. Vatican II taught that:

> The family is, in a sense, a school for human enrichment . . . The family is the place where different generations come together and help one another to grow in wisdom and harmonize the rights of individuals with other demands of social life; as such it constitutes the basic society.[328]

Christians maintain that the family is the best environment for raising children and ensuring the stability of society.

It has often been suggested by Nigerians that religious, political, and social unrest in the society are perpetrated through people without family background or family training, popularly called area boys or street boys in Nigeria.

The Nigerian family concept has been an added bonus in fostering and promoting harmonious relationships among the three religions in Nigeria whose memberships cut across family lines and ties.

---

[327] Ally, "Islam: Global Issues," 232
[328] *Gaudium et Spes: The Pastoral Constitution on the Church in the Modern World,* n.52.

5.1.6. Ethical Issues and Concerns.

Another area where the religions in Nigeria work in unison is the area of behavioral ethics. It gives every one serious concern when society turns out immoral. Hence, all the religions have rules and regulations guiding people and behavior in relation to one another and in the society. Among the areas where these religions have come out strongly and strictly are, sexual conduct (adultery and gay relationships), abortion, stealing, lying, irreverence and unkindness to parents and elders.

A closer look at these religions reveals their common concern and stand on ethical and behavioral issues in the Nigerian society.

In ATR, the practical aspect of belief is not only worship but also human conduct. Belief in God and in the other spiritual beings implies a certain type of conduct, conduct that respects the order established by God and watched over by the divinities and the ancestors. Restating the words of Samuel Adewale, what religion forbids or condemns society also forbids and condemns, and similarly society approves those things which religion approves of and sanctions. An offence against God is an offence against man, and in like manner, an offence against man is an offence against God, since man is a creature of God. Either offence is criminal. Traditional African Religion has no written legal documents showing what is legal or illegal, moral or immoral, but traditional Africans have a code of conduct that they all know. This code constrains individuals to live in conformity with the well-being of society. The components of the code have been transmitted conventionally from generation to generation. Forbidden criminal actions include adultery, breach of covenant, burglary, fornication, incest, kidnapping, irreverence and unkindness to parents, lying, murder, rape, seduction, speaking evil of rulers, swearing falsely, theft, sodomy and malice. All prohibited acts or taboos are crimes in African Traditional Religion and any person committing any of them is regarded as a criminal and is punishable. Abnormal behavior, which is not in conformity with the norms of society, is a criminal act.[329]

At the center of traditional African morality is human life. Africans have a sacred reverence for life, for it is believed to be the greatest of God's gifts to humans. To protect and nurture their lives, all human beings are inserted within a given community and it is within this community that one works out one's destiny and every aspect of individual life. The promotion of life is therefore the determinant principle of African traditional morality and this promotion is guaranteed only in the community. Thus, offenses against life such as abortion, suicide and homicide are treated as the highest crime in the land.

Sexual sins—adultery and homosexuality—are seriously forbidden. They are not just treated as criminal but at same time as a taboo. Violators attract the wrath of the gods and ancestors requiring atonement and purification of the land through various forms of sacrifices.

In Islam also, morality and human conducts are held in very high esteem. The Quran and Islamic jurisprudence are vocal on issues of sexual behavior, and protection of life and property. Sexual immorality and destruction of life and stealing are condemned and are punishable with lashes, death and cutting off hand, depending on the seriousness of the crime. In the case of adultery or fornication, the Quran says,

> The woman and the man guilty of adultery
> or fornication, flog each of them with a
> hundred stripes: let not compassion move

---

[329] Samuel A. Adewale, "Crime and African Traditional Religions," in *Orita Journal*, Vol. XXVI, 2, 1994, pp55-66.

you in their case, in a matter prescribed by Allah . . . Let no man guilty of adultery or fornication marry any other but a woman similarly guilty, or an unbeliever: nor let any but such a man or an unbeliever marry such a woman: to the believers such a thing is forbidden. (Surah 24:2-3).

In Nigeria, the Shariah Law now prescribes death by stoning (rajm) to a person guilty of adultery. For example, the following cases have been reported: In October 2001, a Muslim woman named Safiya was sentenced to death by stoning (rajm) by the Islamic Sharia Court at Sokota in North Nigeria. She got a reprieve because the Islamic Appeal Court ruled in March 2002 that the act of adultery was committed before it was made an illegal act. In August 2002, a 30-year-old Muslim widow named Amina Lawal was sentenced to Rajm by the Islamic Shariah Court at Bakori in State of Katsina, also in North Nigeria. Amina had an 8-month-old daughter. The Appeal Court rejected her appeal but stayed the execution of the sentence until the end of the weaning period. Ahmadu Ibrahim and Fatima Usman, convicted of adultery, also stand sentenced to death by stoning. They are also awaiting the Order of the Appellate Court. Muslim jurists think that the Quranic punishment Surah 24:2, applies only to fornication and that in the case of adultery, the Sunnah of the Prophet prescribes stoning to death. The most accepted collection of Hadith Sahih al Bukhari has 4 entries under 3829, 8804, 8805 and 8824 which refer to stoning by death. 8805 says, "A married man from the tribe of Bani Aslam who had committed illegal sexual intercourse and bore witnesses four times against himself was ordered by the Prophet to be stoned to death." The Hadith is very clear but is silent on the question whether the Prophet ordered stoning to death before or after the revelation of the Surah 24:2.[330]

Commenting on Islam's stand on homosexuality, Ally, writes,

> Though love is the basis of all relationships, Islam forbids homosexual and lesbian relations. Islam views such relations as unnatural and deviating from the norm. Specific mention is made of its practice in the Quran (26:165-6): 'What! Of all creatures, do you approach males and leave the spouses whom your Lord had created for you? Indeed, you are people transgressing all limits.' This verse reminds Muslims that the Prophet Lot was sent by God to warn his people against the practice of homosexuality and lesbianism. In addition sodomy is considered to be an act against the natural disposition of human beings.[331]

Islam values human life and is concerned with its preservation; therefore, it does not allow abortion, unless the continuation of the pregnancy will result in the death of the mother. Muslim jurists agree unanimously that after the fetus is completely formed and has been given a soul, aborting it is prohibited provided the mother is in no danger.[332]

---

[330] Syed Shahabuddin, "Should the Islamic Punishment of Adultery be reconsidered?" http://www.guidedones.com/metapage/gems/adultery.htm (Assessed: August 30, 2009)

[331] Ally, "Islam: Global Issues," 229

[332] Ibid, 246

Islam equally forbids stealing. In a case of proven acts of theft, the Quran prescribes the following punishment, which is strictly adhered to in Nigeria by Muslims:

"As to the thief, male of female, cut off his or her hands: a punishment by way of example, from Allah, for their crime: and Allah is Exalted in Power." (5:38).

In Nigeria, especially in the North that is predominantly Muslim, the sight of a person without a hand tells you something about such a person: He or she is a thief. However, the reason for the punishment in Islam for stealing is not to create a lot of handicapped people in the society. Rather, it is to create an environment where the stealing itself will not happen.

Christians in Nigeria equally adhere strictly to biblical morality that condemns ungodly behavior. The most referred to biblical passages by Nigerian Christians besides the famous 10 commandments of Exodus 20, are 1 Cor. 6:9-10 and Galatians 5:19-26. The passage of 1 Cor. 6:9-10 says:

> You know perfectly well that people who do wrong will not inherit the kingdom of God: people of immoral lives, idolaters, adulterers, catamites, homosexuals, thieves, usurers, drunkards, slanderers, and swindlers will never inherit the kingdom of God.

The controversy surrounding abortion and gay relationships that exists among Christians in some countries does not even arise in Nigeria. The Nigerian Anglican Communion, for example has severed relationship with the branch of the Episcopalian Church in United States of America that affirms gay marriage. In addition, the Nigerian government does not interfere in matters of morality; it is left within the confines of religion. One can affirm that the influence of traditional religion and culture on moral issues is behind such stance on morality by the government and the public.

The Christian view of sex is that it is God's gift and is to be used and enjoyed. Like other gifts of God, it ceases to be a joy and blessing when it is abused. Traditional Christian belief has been that it is only within marriage that sexual activity can properly fulfill its role of being unitive and procreative. As such, Nigerian Christians condemn acts of adultery and fornication in strong terms. Sexual immorality is therefore seen as a capital sin. Speaking against adultery and other sins against chastity, the *Catechism of the Catholic Church* stated:

> Adultery is an injustice. He who commits adultery fails in his commitment. He does injury to the sign of the covenant which the marriage bond is, transgresses the rights of the other spouse, and undermines the institution of marriage by breaking the contact on which it is based. He compromises the good of human generation and the welfare of children who need their parents' stable union . . . Among the sins gravely contrary to chastity are masturbation, fornication, pornography, and homosexual practices.[333]

Expressing the Christian stand on Abortion,

> The Roman Catholic Church view is that a unique life is formed at conception and therefore abortion is wrong at any time. The life of the embryo and fetus is, in theory, as important as that of the mother. If a Roman Catholic doctor has to save one life at the

---

[333] CCC, 2381, 2397.

expense of the other, in practice it is usually the life of the mother, which is saved, as this is common medical practice.[334]

From the foregoing, Nigerians turn to religion for guidance in issues of morality and ethical concerns, and the three religions in Nigeria have both individually and collectively offered this service to their adherents and to the nations. They can truly be described as the conscience of the Nigerian nation.

5.2 A SYNOPSIS OF THE AREAS OF INTERACTIONS AND CONVERGENCE AMONG THE THREE RELIGIONS IN NIGERIA.

In summary, the three religions in Nigeria converge, collaborate and relate in the following areas.

IN THE RELIGIOUS SPHERE
- ❖ There is widespread belief in a supreme God, unique and transcendent.
- ❖ ATR, Islam and Christianity have a sense of the sacred and a sense of mystery; there is high reverence for sacred places, persons and objects; sacred times are celebrated.
- ❖ Belief in the afterlife is incorporated in myths and in funeral ceremonies.
- ❖ Religion enfolds the whole of life; there is no dichotomy between life and religion.
- ❖ Belief in the efficacy of intercessory prayer is widespread.
- ❖ Worship requires a fundamental attitude of strict discipline and reverence.

---

[334] Shannon, "Christianity: The Quality and Value of Life", 198.

IN THE RITUAL SPHERE

- ❖ Rites form an essential part of worship and celebration.
- ❖ The seasonal cycles and the stages of life are sanctified by ritual action. Ritual attention is given to crises.
- ❖ The whole person, body and soul, is totally involved in worship.
- ❖ In worship and sacrifice, there is co-responsibility: each person contributes his share in a spirit of participation.
- ❖ Symbols bridge the spheres of the sacred and secular and so make possible a balanced and unified view of reality.
- ❖ Rites of passage, of initiation and of consecration are widespread.
- ❖ Religious sacredness is preserved in ritual, in dress and the arrangements of the places of worship.

IN THE RELIGIO-MORAL SPHERE:

- ❖ There is respect for life: children are treasured, abortion is an abomination.
- ❖ Taboos and rituals guard the sacredness of human life.
- ❖ That life makes moral demands is accepted, and this is shown among other things by the sense of the person and attachment to life itself.
- ❖ Sin is perceived in both its personal and communal dimensions.

IN THE RELIGIO-CULTURAL SPHERE:

- ❖ The community is for the transmission of culture.
- ❖ Attention is given to locating man within his environment and making him feel at home in it.

❖ Tradition is handed down through stories, poems, hymns, proverbs, riddles and art.

❖ The whole community is involved in the training of the young, and education itself has a necessary community and social aspect.

❖ The moral education of youth is taken seriously.

❖ Life has a festive dimension and is celebrated in adequate rites.

❖ Respect for elders. The community regards their wisdom as prophetic, that is, as able to give direction for living in the circumstances of the present day.

❖ Marriage is an alliance between families and persons; cultural provisions are made to uphold its stability.

❖ Blood alliances bind with a bond that is rarely broken irrespective of religious affiliations.

IN THE RELIGIO-SOCIAL SPHERE:

❖ Hospitality is a duty that every body owes the other especially the less privileged and strangers.

❖ Between kith and kin and people of the same clan there is a very strong sense of sharing and of solidarity and belonging.

❖ Efforts are made to secure and promote justice and peace within the community.

❖ The nuclear family and the extended family are the pivots of the social system.

5.3 PRACTICAL EVIDENCE OF IMPROVED RELATIONSHIPS AMONG THE THREE RELIGIONS IN NIGERIA.

The twenty first century has witnessed improved relationships between the three religion and their followers in Nigeria. A number of groups focused on improving and advancing religious interactions, relationships and collaborations have recently emerged in Nigeria. Among these are the Nigerian Inter-religious Council (NIREC), and the Nigerian Interfaith Youth Forum (NIYF).[335] While NIREC is more inclined to improving the relationship between Muslims and Christians, the NIYF is all-embracing. At its first official meeting, followers of the three religions were represented. Reporting on this, the Executive Director of NIYF, Emmanuel Ivogba, said,

> Exactly one year after the initial attempt in April 2005, an inaugural meeting of the Nigeria Interfaith Youth Forum was held in Jos-Nigeria on April 23, 2006 to mark the closing of the April 21—23, 2006 National Days of Interfaith Youth Service Sponsored by the Chicago-based Interfaith Youth Core. The 17 participants at the meeting representing Christian, Muslim and traditional religious groups deliberated on a number of important issues, including membership, programs, leadership, partnerships, peace initiatives, conflict resolution, and funding.[336]

The Foundation for the emergence of the Nigeria Interreligious and Interfaith Youth Council was laid at the International Christian Youth conference on Peace Building, organized by the African Christian Youths Development

---

[335] The African Christian Youth Development Foundation is the coordinating organization for the Nigerian Interfaith Youth Forum.

[336] Emmanuel Andre Ivogba, African *Christian Youth Development Foundation: The Nigerian Interfaith Youth Forum.* http://www.takingitglobal.org/images/resources/tool/docs/783.doc (Assessed: August 31, 2009)

Forum (ACYDF), in collaboration with project Hope-Nigeria from 28th-30th April 2005, at the Zainab Hotel, Jos-Nigeria. The theme of the conference was, "The Role of Christian Youths in Promoting a Culture of Peace in Africa." The 35 participants at the conference included representatives of seven Non-Governmental Organizations within Nigeria and the United States of America (USA). Together they agreed to create a platform for interfaith dialogue and youth service in Nigeria, to enhance awareness and understanding of each other's activities in the context of our diverse, pluralistic faith traditions, and to initiate the process of promoting our cherished "unity in diversity." The mission and essence of the group as revealed in their mission statement is very interesting and encouraging as far as enhancing relationships among the three religions in Nigeria. The effort is towards building a peaceful and harmonious society. This mission reads:

> The Nigeria Interreligious and Interfaith Youth Council is committed to providing peaceful and constructive solutions to difficult situations by giving hope to humanity through nourishment and enrichment of our own faith traditions and the consequent inspiration to actions that support and strengthen those most in need. Our goal is to promote peaceful co-existence in Nigeria, and by extension, Africa through the healing process of repentance, dialogue, forgiveness and reconciliation.
>
> The essence of the Interreligious and Interfaith Youth Council is interfaith dialogue, cooperation, and positive social action. Members will be encouraged to deliberately engage in peaceful dialogue and constructive service with others who may have radically

different and sometimes, opposing religious, cultural and political views. Membership of the council will be made up of liberals and conservatives as well as diverse religious representation from mainline faith traditions in Nigeria to the smallest sects.

We believe that religion and young people are very powerful instruments in promoting global peace, social harmony, friendship and lasting partnership, if properly harnessed. Religion has the capacity of facilitating the attainment of appropriate standards of excellence, motivating and equipping a compassionate response and influencing decision—makers at various strata of society, to become effective and powerful voices for the promotion and sustenance of peace and social justice. The youths are creative agents for social change, transformation and renewal. When properly educated, well informed, mobilized and engaged, the youths can initiate actions that would bring about unprecedented societal growth and development.

The Nigeria Interreligious and Interfaith Youth Council is therefore committed to informing, educating, uniting, equipping and mobilizing Nigerian Youths, regardless of their beliefs, especially within the context of family and community helping them to become responsible and active agents for social transformation and renewal, by the provision of clear service opportunities that honor and appreciate their gifts and abilities.

Without compromising our religious and cultural values, we are committed to developing partnerships with the government, NGO, FBOs, and CSOs in improving the quality of life, by challenging and changing the rules and practices that generate public and social mistrust and conflict of all ramifications.[337]

What I found very interesting while studying this group, besides their compelling and reassuring mission statement and guiding philosophy, is that this initiative was taken by the youths themselves, who are often if not always instruments of religious violence and conflict in Nigeria. This is truly a step in the right direction in improving relationships among the religions in Nigeria.

This shift in direction that has brought about some improvement in the religious environment of Nigeria is better captured in the title of a book published by a Philippine Priest: *From Pagans to Partners*.[338] What is witnessed today is that those followers of African Traditional Religion who were described in derogatory terms as "Pagans and Infidels" and "idol worshippers" by Christians and Muslims, and those Muslims who were addressed as "Mohammedans" and "Gentiles" by Christians, and those Christians who were addressed as "Infidels" and "Shirks," and those Muslims and Christians who were seen by traditionalists as "intruders and destroyers of our sacred traditions," have now become dialogue and trialogue partners, collaborators in projects of common concern and fellow pilgrims on the way to truth. To reach this stage, it

---

[337] Ibid.

[338] Leornardo M. Marcado, *From Pagans to Partners: The Change in Catholic Attitudes towards Traditional Religion.* (Manila: Logos Publications Inc., 2000).

took several years of study and discernment on both sides to accept each other.

It must be emphasized that this effort whose fruits we are now seeing did not originally start with any of the religions in particular. The seed was sown in the late 19th and early 20th centuries after the abolition of the slave trade. There was need for Africans to establish themselves as worthy members of the world community. The devastating impact of slavery and the humiliating conscription of Africans by the Colonial masters to fight in the battlefields of World War I meant that there was need to affirm African identity.

It all began in Paris, France. The year was 1934 when the Negritude Movement was born. The leading figure was Leopold Sédar Senghor (later elected first President of Senegal in 1960), who along with Aimé Cesaire of Martinique and Léon Damas of French Guyana, challenged France's "assimilation" program which professed theoretically the equality of all human beings but which in reality asserted the superiority of European culture and civilization. In a sense, the assimilation policy assumed that Africa had no history or culture. The concept of Negritude affirms that the mystic warmth of African life, gaining strength from its closeness to nature and its constant contact with ancestors, should be continually placed in proper perspective against the soullessness and materialism of Western culture.[339]

The Movement brought about a black Cultural Revolution in literature by black students, and it led to the birth of another important group in Paris: *Société Africaine de Culture* (SAC). Africans in Germany (notably Freiburg) and Italy (Rome) came together and identified themselves with SAC. The impact of the Society was phenomenal.

Interest in black culture began to spread around the world. Two historic Congresses of Black Writers and Artists

---

[339] "Negritude," in *The New Encyclopedia Britannica*, Vol.8, Micropaedia 15th edition, 583.

were organized in Paris (1956) and in Rome (1959). In Paris, the participants agreed that African Traditional Religion held the deposit of African values and Black identity and it was indispensable for the construction of "African theology." During the meeting in Rome, Pope John XXIII granted audience to the participants and addressed them in the following words:

> We follow with the greatest interest your efforts in searching for the basis of a cultural fellowship of African inspiration, and we express the wish that it may repose on the right criteria of truth and action . . . . The Church's worldwide attention to the human resources of all peoples places her at the service of true world peace. She helps the elite that turn to her guidance, in developing the cultural possibilities of their country and their race, and in doing so the Church invites them to collaborate harmoniously and in a spirit of deep understanding, with other currents issuing from authentic civilizations.[340]

The members of SAC expressed their desire to bring African contributions to the Second Vatican Council, which the Pope had just then convoked.

In 1967, Pope Paul VI published his historic document, *Africae Terrarum*, in which he praised the value of African Traditional Religion and culture and encouraged Africans to hold tight to their rich spiritual heritage.[341] This was followed in 1968, by the publication of a booklet entitled

---

[340] S. Palermo, Ed, *Africa Pontificia*, (Rome: Editrice, 1993), n.584.

[341] John Paul II, *Africae Terrarum*, nn.7-11

Meeting the African Religions, by the Vatican Secretariat for Non-Christians (renamed Pontifical Council for Interreligious Dialogue in 1988), as a contribution to the effort to deepen the knowledge of African Traditional Religion.

Pope John Paul II urged all Christians to treat followers of African Traditional Religion with respect. In his own words, "The adherents of African Traditional Religion should . . . be treated with great respect and esteem, and all inaccurate and disrespectful language should be avoided."[342] He matched his words with action by demonstrating that he regarded followers of African Traditional Religion as true dialogue partners.

In 1986, the Pope invited, among several religious leaders, three representatives of followers of African Traditional Religion to the day of prayer in Assisi. The three were: Togbui Assenou of Togoville (Togo), Amegawi Attiwoto Klousse of Bé-Lomé (Togo) and Okomfo Kodwo Akom of Cape Coast (Ghana).

In 1998, the World Council of Churches during their Assembly in Harare rededicated itself to the "African dream and agenda for the 21st century." This was an important step towards realizing the hope of greater understanding between Christians and people of other faiths and opened new avenues for interaction and cooperation between peoples of faith, especially in Africa. Sometimes the seeming hostile approach by some member-Churches to African Traditional Religion makes it difficult for a common stand to be taken on the issue of dialogue with adherents of the traditional religion in Africa.

On January 24, 2002, Pope John Paul II invited leaders of various religions for yet another Day of Prayer for peace in the world. Among those he invited was a Priest of Voodoo from the Benin republic. Again, the Voodoo Priest reflected

---

[342] *L'Osservatore Romano*, English Edition, 11 May 1994, n.7.

on peace from the perspective of his religion. He said inter alia:

> I recognize in the first place that peace is a gift of God to us. However, this gift is left to the responsibility of man, called by the Creator to contribute to the building up of peace in this world.... I am convinced of one thing: peace in the world depends on peace among people. Man's responsibility in the world has its influence not only on society but also on the whole of creation. When there is no peace among people, neither is there peace between the rest of creation and man. But when people work for peace in a nation, its land becomes generous and the herds multiply for man's greater good. This is a key law of nature, which comes from the Creator, who has linked creation's destiny to man's responsibility.[343]

With these movements and awareness, the air of religious equality, freedom, interaction, relationship and collaboration began to blow across Sub-Saharan Africa, of which Nigeria is a central figure. Most importantly, African traditional religious experience and expression, having emerged from the limbo of negation and skepticism to eventual recognition, began taking its rightful place among other religions that have established themselves in Africa and is now considered a legitimate expression of a genuine religious experience of African peoples in their encounter with the divine.

---

[343] *L'Osservatore Romano*, English Edition, 30 January, 2002.

This recognition has ushered in much improved relationships among religions in Nigeria. These improved relationships are manifest in the following areas of life.

5.3.1. Daily Life Experience.

There have been improved relationships between ATR, Christians, and Muslims in their day-to-day living as the people of the nation, state, zone, tribe and village community. Hence, beyond organizations and institutions, far away from symposia and congresses centered on peace talk, there are millions of people from different religious backgrounds in Nigeria who live and meet at the level of the family, school, market place,[344] work place, and the military. They fraternize and collaborate with each other without discussing religion. They live out what their religions have taught them about good neighborliness, about honesty, dedication to duty, justice, service to one another, love, duties in the family, and community development. I have uncles and aunts who are followers of African Traditional Religion, and friends who are Muslim whose way of life inspires me and whom I can describe as holy people. These unsung heroes are promoting ATR, Muslim, and Christian relationships at the grassroots level which is the major theatre of religious violence.

---

[344] For instance, my Muslim friends in Arochukwu sell the best meat in Nkwor Market, and every body in town (including ATR and Christians) love patronizing them because of their honesty and good business approach.

5.3.2. Goodwill Messages and Visits:

It has become almost customary for the followers of ATR, Islam and Christianity to exchange goodwill messages on the occasions of the traditional festivals of Id el-Fitr, Sallah, Id el Mallud, Christmas and Easter. These messages are not just courteous words; they touch on areas and elements, which both religions share together, with real perspectives of co-operation. While congratulating each other, they also remind one another of the need of building a crisis-free society, by promoting the culture of peace and tolerance. On these messages, J.O. Kayode remarked:

> During the Islamic festivals of greater Biaram of Eid-il-fitri, gifts are exchanged among the adherents of the three faiths: Islam, Christianity, and African Traditional Religion. At Christmas or Easter, Christians send and receive gifts from their Muslim counterparts, and cultural festivals are considered vital by both Christians and Muslims. Gifts are sent and exchanged with traditionalists.[345]

Beyond messages, visits are made on such and other occasions. On coming to Arochukwu (my then Parish) for a pastoral visit, the Most Rev. Dr. Lucius Iwejuru Ugorji, the Catholic Bishop of Umuahia Diocese, paid a courtesy call to the traditional ruler of Arochukwu Kingdom, His Royal Majesty, Mazi Vincent Ogbonnaya Okoro, The EZE ARO VIII. Issues affecting traditional practices, and Christianity were discussed. Gifts also exchanged hands.

---

[345] J.O.Kayode, "Living in Peace in a Multi-Religious Community," in *The State of Christian Theology in Nigeria.* (Ibadan: Heinemann, 1986), 85

During the same pastoral visit, which lasted four days, the representatives of the Muslim community in Arochukwu paid a courtesy visit to the Bishop in the Church (St. Theresa's Parish). They discussed issues on religious tolerance and peaceful co-existence. The leader of the delegation requested the Bishop to thank the pastor of the parish for all his commitment to good and friendly relationships that he exhibits towards different religions in Arochukwu.

5.3.3. Interfaith Prayer for Peace:

Peace is not an abstract poetic idea, but rather a down-to-earth and practical concept. Religiously, peace is conceived not in relation to conflict and war, but in relation to order, harmony and equilibrium.[346] It is a religious value in that the order, harmony and equilibrium in the universe and society is believed to be divinely established and the obligation to maintain them is religious. It is also a moral value since good conduct is required of human beings if the order, harmony and equilibrium are to be maintained.

Realizing peace as the fullness of life, as the result of harmonious living, as a precondition for progress, above all as a gift from God, followers of the three religions have often come together at the national, state and local/ community level to pray for peace. One such effort at the local level is the gatherings of the Anioha women in Afikpo (the first community in Igboland where Islam entered). These women, drawn from the three religions, devoted a day after their recently concluded August (2009) meeting to pray for peace in Nigeria, Ebonyi State, Afikpo land and

---

[346] Robert Rweyemamu, "Religion and Peace (An Experience with African Traditions)," in *Studia Missionalia,* 38, n. 15, 1989. p. 381.

in particular for Anioha. This prayer exercise is mandatory for all women in the community; religious faith and differences of belief not with standing.

On the State level, prayers aimed at peace and mutual existence have been organized in various states of Nigeria. One such example was the one organized in one of the communities Abia State in 2003, after religious violence that claimed many lives in Nigeria. During the gathering a Muslim, a Christian and a traditionalist were asked to pray. It is interesting and revealing the words chosen by each of these.

The Christian prayed:
Eternal God:
Save us from weak resignation to violence; teach us that restraint is the highest expression of power; that thoughtfulness and tenderness are marks of the strong.
Help us to love our enemies; not by countenancing their sins, but by remembering our own. And may we never for a moment forget that they are fed by the same food; hurt by the same weapons; have children for whom they have the same high hopes as we do.
Grant us the ability to find joy and strength not in the strident call to arms; but to grasp our fellow creatures in the striving for peace, justice and truth. Amen.

The Muslim prayed:
In the name of Allah, the beneficent, the merciful.
Praise be to the Lord of the Universe who has created us and made us into tribes, but one nation and one people; that we may know each other, not that we may despise each other.
Look with compassion on us; take away the controversial teachings of arrogance, divisions and hatreds which have badly infected our hearts; break down the walls that separate us; reunite us in bonds of love; and work through our struggle and confusion to accomplish Your purposes on earth; that, in

Your good time, all nations and races may jointly serve You in justice, peace and harmony. (Amen)

The Traditionalist prayed:
Almighty God, the Great Thumb we cannot evade to tie any knot; the Roaring Thunder that splits mighty trees: the all-seeing Lord up on high who sees even the footprints of an antelope on a rock mass here on Earth.
You are the one who does not hesitate to respond to our call. You are the cornerstone of peace.
Oh Great Spirit of our Ancestors, I raise my pipe to you; to your messengers the four winds, and to Mother Earth who provides for your children.
Give us the wisdom to teach our children to love, to respect, and to be kind to each other so that they may grow with peace of mind.
Let us learn to share all good things that you provide for us on this Earth. Amen.[347]

5.3.4. Communal Celebrations and Festivities.

It is very common to see people of different religions coming together to worship or attending ceremonies of other religions; something that was unheard off some years ago. In my parishes, I have had Traditionalists and Muslims attend religious services in my Church. One such occasion was the dedication of St. Thomas Catholic Church, Amuvi Arochukwu on January 2, 2005.

---

[347] The wordings of these prayers were chosen and modeled after the prayers prayed by people from various religions at the 2002 Day of Prayer for World Peace in Assisi convoked by Pope John Paul II on January 24, 2002. For more on the Day of Prayer for Peace in the World see: http://www.vatican.va/special/assisi_20020124_en.html

Again, during the course of this research I have had the privileges of taking part in Islamic and Traditional ceremonies, in Mosques and Groves/Shrines, and outside these sacred grounds. In my visits to these places, I was never treated with suspicion. The members were glad to see me, welcomed me in their ceremonies, opened up to my questions, had discussions, and in many cases treated me with good food. Some years back when I was growing up, as a kid, such to visits and participation in even a Protestant Church, worst still in a non-Christian faith community, would merit me suspension if not excommunication from the Catholic Church. We were then taught in our Catechism that one of the grave sins was attending a Church or reading a book that is not Catholic, or taking part in traditional or "pagan" ceremonies. Thanks to interfaith perspectives and better understanding today among the three religions, I was able to visit these places without sanctions. Back then also, Muslims would never allow me in their Mosque because I was an infidel, nor would the Traditionalists allow me because I was a non-initiate. Now things have changed for the better.

A major aspect worth mentioning here is the communal celebration of traditional festivals across various communities in Nigeria. These festivals have attracted and still attract the active participation of ATR, Muslims and Christians alike. As observed by Awolanu,

> Traditional festivals which hitherto were secretly observed or were becoming neglected [have] come to be given wide publicity in the news media; and Nigerian men and women, whether Christians or Muslims, show no inhibition or remorse in

going to watch or even to participate actively in such traditional festivals.[348]

This was not the case as late as 1980. I could recall that during my grandfather's traditional funeral ceremonies that lasted between 1979 and 1980,[349] my mother and I were not permitted by our parish priest to take part in the various stages of the ceremony. Eventually, we did, and were suspended from the sacrament for a couple of months. We were also punished in the form of having to cut grass on the church premises before we were re-admitted into the sacraments. This would not have occurred if my grandfather were to be buried today.

Below are some popular traditional festivals among various tribes and zones in Nigeria that exercise overwhelming influences and attract participation from followers of the various religions in Nigeria, even from foreigners.

5.3.4.1. The Osun Festival: South-West (Oshogbo)

---

[348] Awolanu, "The Encounter between African Traditional Religion and Other Religions in Nigeria," 116.

[349] Various stages are involved in the traditional burial. There is the first burial and then the second and final burial. The first burial is a farewell to the land of the spirits; the second burial gives the person the final resting place—a home with the ancestors. Unless the second burial is done, the spirit of the dead is never at rest. However, this second burial is not meant for everybody, it is specifically reserved for elders who will sooner or later be revered as ancestors pending the rites of the second burial.

Yorubaland:

Many festivals abound in the Yoruba tradition. A good number of them honor the most important divinities of the Yoruba, such as Obatala, Orunmila, Sango, Esu, Osun, and Oya. These festivals are always rallying points for people of different religions in the community. During such celebrations, Wande Abimbola states,

> The devotees of these divinities, as well as the Christians and Muslims, trade in some items needed for the celebrations irrespective of religious leanings. What matters here is not the issue of religious differences, but how to effect sales of commodities and make profits. Here it is to be noted, in consequence of these festivals and other items, the issue of religious solidarity has become a phenomenon to be reckoned with in Yoruba religious history.[350]

One such festival that deserves special mention and treatment in this work is the Osun Festival. Osun is one of the divinities in the Yoruba pantheon, whom the Osun State of Nigeria is named after. She is a River goddess and the goddess of love and beauty. Ulli Beir, a European who lived in Oshogbo, the capital of Osun state, in his assessment of the attitude of the present generation of indigenous worshippers of Osun observed that:

---

[350] Wande Abimbola, "The Place of African Traditional Religion in Contemporary Africa: The Yoruba Example," in Jacob Olupona, Ed, *African Traditional Religions in Contemporary Society*. (New York: Paragon House Publishers, 1991), 55.

After the first wild abandonment of traditional values, a certain re-adjustment is now taking place. The largest attendance of the annual Osun festival testifies to this. Few people attending the festival would classify themselves as *Olorisa* (devotees of Osun). Yet every person in Oshogbo, even fanatical Muslims and Christians, knows that they are children of Osun.[351]

The Osun Festival is associated with offering of sacrifices at the Osun shrine, drumming, and dancing, feasting and other merry-making as the main features. The worshipping of Osun goddess at the Osun Shrine is the climax of the festival where the 'Arugba'—the virgin girl, will carry the calabash to the shrine and *Kabiyesi* (the King) will host the visitors from near and far at a big feast.[352] Apart from serving as a birthday of Oshogbo and the remembrance day of the Ataoja's ancestors, it is a time when sons and daughters of Oshogbo (ATR, Muslims and Christians), near and far, come home, where series of meetings are held about the development of Oshogbo. The festival, which is the mother of the festivals in Oshogboland, succeeds other mini festivals like Egungun, Oro Sango, Ifa Obatala, and Ogun, which have significance like Osun.

5.3.4.2. The Eyo Festival: South-West (Lagos)

---

[351] Ulli Beir, *The Return of the Gods.* (London: Oxford University Press, 1975), 57.

[352] Akitunde Adegboye, "Osun Festival Commences,," *Post Express Newspaper*, (Lagos: 2 August, 2002).

Yorubaland:

The Eyo Festival is unique to the Lagos area, and it is widely believed that Eyo is the forerunner of the modern day carnival in Brazil. Eyo also refers to the masquerades that come out during the festival. On Eyo Day, the main highway in the heart of the city (from the end of Carter Bridge to Tinubu Square) is closed to traffic, allowing for a procession from Idumota to Iga Idunganran. Here, the participants, irrespective of religious affiliations, pay homage to the Oba of Lagos. The Eyo festival takes place whenever occasion and tradition demand, but it is usually held as the final burial rites for a highly regarded chief. The Eyo festival is staged specifically in honor of an illustrious diseased person—irrespective of religious faith.

The most recently celebrated Eyo festival was on April 25, 2009 in honor of the late Otunba Tos Benson. Otunba Tos Benson (a Christian) was until his death a remarkable judge and one of the foremost citizens of Lagos. Bisi Silva recalled her experience of the Eyo festival in honor of Otunba Benson, a ceremony that brought together people of all religions in and around Lagos. As Bisi recalled, the Eyo from the different ruling houses came out, drumming, dancing and performing acrobatics. The teeming crowd welcomed them with songs, clapping and dance. It was one of the most spectacular and joyful sights Bisi had witnessed in a longtime. There were murmurs of how beautiful, how fantastic the Eyo looked from everyone. It seemed as if all of Lagos was there and all sat, stood, clapped and sang proudly as they watched the unparallel display of culture unfold before their eyes.[353]

Although it is said that the Eyo festival dates back to ancient times, the earliest recorded performance is known

---

[353] Bisi Silva, "Spectacular Eyo Festival," in *ARTSPEAKAFRICA*. (Sunday 26 April 2009)

to have been held in the 19th century. Apparently, the early masquerades wore print Ankara cloth but today 3 piece white garments and colored caps identifying the Eyo with a particular ruling family have replaced that.[354]

5.3.4.3. The New Yam Festival: Southwest (Igboland):

In Igboland, the occasion of Iri-ji (new-yam eating) is the most prestigious cultural festival, and it is well attended by all in the community, ATR Christians and Muslims. The individual communities, as agrarian people, have their days for this august occasion during which assortments of festivities mark the eating of new yam. To the Igbos, therefore, the day is symbolic of enjoyment after the cultivation season. The new yam festival, traditionally, is the culmination of a work cycle and the beginning of another.

In Igbo communities, the oldest man in the community or the king performs the solemn role of eating the first yam, as the case may be. The belief is that their position bestows on them the privilege of being intermediaries between their communities and the gods of the land, and the ancestors. The rituals that attend the new yam eating are meant to express the community's appreciation to the gods for making the harvest of farm yields possible. The influence of Christianity and Islam in some places notwithstanding, many traditionalists and titleholders in some Igbo communities never taste the new yam until the day traditionally set aside for it.

The importance of this festival among the Igbos is expressed by the fact that the Igbo people living outside their home communities gather together to celebrate the New Yam wherever they are. Such celebrations are held

---

[354] Interview in Lagos, April 12, 2008

annually in New York and London by the Igbos (irrespective of religious faith) who cannot go home because of the distance. Onyema Omenuwa gave an example of this celebration, even in the Diaspora,, as reported in *This Week* Newspaper:

> The pomp and pageantry that attended the recent Igbo Day/new yam festival spoke eloquentlyofthepeople'srichculturalheritage. The occasion held at the main exhibition hall of the National Theater, Lagos, was packaged jointly by the Igbo Council of Chiefs, Lagos chapter, and the All Igbo Speaking States in Lagos. The latter is a nascent umbrella body for all Igbo indigenes, both east and west of the river Niger, resident in Lagos. According to Raph Uwazuruike, the chairman of Igbo Council of Chiefs, Lagos, it aims 'to strengthen the bond of relationship that existed between (the Igbos) before the civil war.'

The ceremony at the National Theatre apparently sought to replicate the new yam festival in its indigenous setting. Interestingly, it was advertised as the first time all the seven Igbo states of Imo, Abia, Enugu, Anambra, Delta, Ebonyi and Rivers were uniformly celebrating the new yam festival. The attempt was not in futility (sic), judging by the carnival nature of the event.[355]

5.3.4.4. The Argungu Fishing Festival: (Kebbi) North-West.

The Argungu International Fishing and Cultural Festival (the most widely attended in Nigeria and perhaps the

---

[355] Onyema Omenuwa, *This Week,* November 24, 1997.

oldest known festival of its kind) predates the "Conquests" of Kanta of Kebbi in the early 16th Century. The festival started initially in the form of religious rites prior to the time of Surame Gungu of the Kebbi Kingdom. In other words, it began as an informal family and communal affair. Since that time, the festival has undergone several changes and modifications.

The Deputy Governor of Kebbi at the International Press Briefing given on the Argungu International Fishing Festival (AIFF) 2008, explained the origin, the essence and the communal nature of this festival that brings all citizens of Kebbi State, Nigerians from all works of life (Muslims, Christians, and ATR, including those who profess no religion at all), and foreigners together for a joyful and memorable celebration. Below is the summary of the briefing.

The Argungu festival began as far back as the 16th century and has become more elaborate and stylish than it was in the past. At the same time it has, since the jihad period, been being progressively enriched with the fielding of more events for the general entertainment of the attending public. The festival at Argungu had already assumed a fairly non-religious or non-animistic tone, devoid largely of the usual Bori and Tsafi exhibitions. However even though Islam had by this time become very widely adopted in the area, with a minority of Christians, the presence of these religions appears to have merely served to neutralize the base for Bori and Iskoki rites so well associated with the festival. This suggest that with the wide spread acceptance of Islam and Christianity among the Kabawa, most individual families in the area have increasingly given up animist practices but continue to look to the festival occasion for periodic displays of the traditional cult. At the same time, attendance at this festival appears to have increased considerably with community representatives taking some conspicuous positions at the festival venue. Dignitaries from the neighboring riverine areas also feature regularly as guests during the festival. The Argungu festival today features the following events: Water sports, Farmer of the year, Traditional wrestling, Goat skinning competition, Camel and Donkey races, a Catapulting competition, a Motor rally, Agricultural show, Cultural dances, and an Archery competition.[356]

5.3.4.5. The Igue Festival: (Bini Kingdom) South-South.

The Igue festival is a period for the Binis to offer thanks to the gods for sparing their lives and to ask for blessings. During this festival, ancestral gods are worshipped for protection, and propitiations are done at various shrines in the community. The shrines are considered holy and therefore traditionally deified. The Oba pays homage at the shrines in and around his palace and some of his chiefs accompany him. Indeed, it is a period of merriment, rituals and dancing.

During this period, chieftaincy titleholders display their Eben emblem in the Ugie dance as they appear in their traditional attire, according to the type of dress the Oba bestowed on individual chiefs during the conferment of title, while the Oba sits majestically in the royal chamber (Ogiukpo).

Narrating the import and influence of Igue Festival on all the citizenry of the Benin Kingdom (Edo People), Ademola Iyi-Eweka writes:

> The Christians have CHRISTMAS, the Muslims have the FEAST OF RAMADAN, the Jews have

---

[356] Ibrahim K. Aliyu. International Press Briefing for AIFF (2008). Sheraton Hotel, Ikeja, Lagos on Tuesday 26, 2008, at 11.00 AM.

the HANUKKAH, the African-Americans have the KWANZAA and the Edos have the IGUE FESTIVAL. If the African-American can invent and contrive a festival called Kwanzaa, it will be sad day were the Edos to desert Igue Festival. Inspite of all out Christian onslaught on IGUE FESTIVAL, it has waxed stronger and stronger over the years. But what is most astonishing and confusing to some Christians and non-Edo speaking people is the fact that no matter how an Edo man preaches and embraces Islam and Christianity, he does not play with the Igue Festival.[357]

During the seven days of elaborate traditional and cultural activities, Bini chiefs are seen in their traditional regalia, including the Iloi (Queens) in their Okuku (hairdo). It is a rare occasion of their public appearance, where the Oba's stalwarts (Ifietes) are seen in active service. In this festival, the chiefs display traditional dances like Esakpaide, Ohogho, and above all, the Eben. As they dance, they pay homage to the Oba who is seen as the physical representation of the gods and ancestors.

The Igue festival has however endured and continues to retain its main features despite modernization in all aspects of political, economic, sociological and technological development. The Bini Kingdom still pays much attention to traditional matters because, according to the Iyase of Benin, Chief Sam Igbe, tradition is supreme. Before this year's event, the Iyase had appealed to all Bini chiefs, Enigie Edionwere, Igiohen and all elders and leaders to encourage

---

[357] Ademola Iyi-Eweka, "Igue Festival," in EDOFOLKS.com http://www.edofolks.com (mhtml:file://K:\Edofolks - IGUE FESTIVAL.mht) (Assessed; September 1, 2009)

and organize youths to enable them take more interest in the Ugie-Ewere celebration. He also appealed to motorists to respect the celebrants on the roads, stressing that, "this festival is a way of expressing our love, joy and goodwill to our people."[358]

5.3.4.6. Unity in Festivals.

All these festivals described above have played very important roles in bringing people of different religions in Nigeria together in an atmosphere of brotherhood, mutual love and friendships. They have greatly contributed to communal developmental projects usually launched during the occasion of these festivals. Peoples of all religions—ATR, Muslims and Christians—joyfully look forward to their celebrations annually.

5.3.5. Usage of Facilities.

Another visible area of improved relationships among the three religions in Nigeria is the common usage of facilities belonging to or controlled by one religion or other religions. For example, in most communities in the South-West, Christian facilities (Church Halls or School grounds) have hosted meetings and gatherings of Traditionalists and Muslims. Muslims grounds and traditional community squares have hosted members of other religions. In my community, the Village Square has on at least seven occasions, to the best of my knowledge,

---

[358] Nowa Omoigue, "History of Igue Festival in Benin City: Oba, Bini mark the end of Year Igue Festival" http://www. edofolks.com (mhtml:file:// K:\Edofolks - History of Igue Festival in Benin-City.mht) (Assessed; September 1, 2009)

housed Muslim nomads from the North, as their camping ground while they graze their cattle. The same square has hosted uncountable numbers of Christian gospel revivals and evangelism. The good thing about this square is that it also houses one of the traditional deities in my community called *Asoka*. Traditional wrestling competitions, cultural dances, and traditional weddings are done in this same square.

In my community, the village hall is also open to different religions, which at times hold their meetings, prayers and worships there. In two of my former parishes, I used to celebrate morning mass in the community hall and square. Traditionalists had their indoor rituals and rites in this same hall. I believe that if there had been Muslims in those communities, they would have had equal access to the facilities as they have in Afikpo and Nsukka

These interactions and sharing of facilities would not have been possible some years back. Each religion would have seen it as an act of desecration to allow followers of other religions to use their facilities for meetings, prayer or worship.

CONCLUSION

As we draw the curtain in this second volume of our discussion on Interfaith Series in Nigeria, it should be re-emphasized that when Islam and Christianity immigrated into Nigeria, the indigenes they encountered already knew God and had their own religious belief system. The belief systems and teachings of Islam and Christianity are well documented and preserved in the Holy Quran and the Bible, which are said to come from or inspired by God. In contrast, ATR is an oral religion, without a scripture. Thus, the belief systems in ATR are transmitted orally and in rituals from one generation to another. The three religions in Nigeria are not simply dogmas, but are ways of life, which are expressed and practiced by believers through worship, prescribed duties, and actions. Although ATR has been long marginalized in Nigeria, one would be naive to think that it has not influenced the worldviews of Islam and Christianity.

The tenets and beliefs of these religions examined in this work offered us a clearer picture of the thought patterns and actions of their followers. These tenets and beliefs are the bases of convergence, divergence, mutual co-existence and conflicts that are experienced in the relationships among the three religions in Nigeria.

Obviously, the relationships between the three religions in Nigeria have not been as pleasant as all Nigerians would have expected it be. Nevertheless, it has not always been bad; Nigeria has witnessed areas of improved relationships among these three religions. Muslims and Christians, ATR and Christians as well as ATR and Muslims in Nigeria dialogically share a lot in common in their daily lives and relationships. Some of these go unnoticed in the eyes of scholars and reporters, but they have contributed immensely in promoting peace and harmony among the religions in Nigeria.

Trialogically, much improvements have been witnessed in the relationships among these religions. One thing very interesting is that these trialogical relationships are coming from the grassroots. Furthermore, it has been observed that wherever this trialogue is practiced in the various parts of Nigeria, interreligious cooperation and understanding seem to have grown stronger. The trialogical relationships also indicate that what unites Traditionalists, Muslims and Christians in Nigeria, is far deeper than what separates them. This is why trialogue is the answer to religious violence in Nigeria as well as a solid ground towards better and improved relationships among the religions in Nigeria.

However, this progress and improved relations should not blind us. A lot has gone wrong in the past and is still going wrong in many parts of Nigeria in the name of religion. In the next volume, we shall discuss ways of better improving and consolidating these positive relationships and interactions among the three religions in Nigeria through practical interfaith relationships and activities.

SELECTED BIBLIOGRAPHY

1. Abimbola, Wande. "The Place of African Traditional Religion in Contemporary Africa: The Yoruba Example" in *African Traditional Religions in Contemporary Society*, edited by Jacob K. Olupona. New York: Paragon House, 1991.
2. Achebe, Chinua. *Things Fall Apart*. New York: Anchor Books, 1994.
3. Adegboye, Akitunde. "Osun Festival Commences," *Post Express Newspaper*. Lagos: 2 August, 2002.
4. Ademilokun, M. K. "Moral Values among the Yoruba," in *Socio-Philosophical Perspective of African Traditional Religion,* eds. Emma Ekpunobi and Ifeanyi Ezeaku. Enugu: New Age Publishers, 1990.
5. Adewale, Samuel A. "Crime and African Traditional Religions," in *Orita Journal*, Vol. XXVI, 2, 1994.
6. Adogame, Afe. "Politicization of Religion and Religionization of Politics in Nigeria", in *Religion, History, and Politics in Nigeria: Essays in Honor of Ogbu U. Kalu*. Edited by Chima J. Korieh & Ugo G. Nwokeji. New York: University of America Press, 2005.
7. Aguwa, Jude C. "Christianity and Nigeria Indigenous Culture" in Chima J Korieh and Ugo Nwekeji

ed, *Religion, History, and Politics in Nigeria: Essays in Honor of Ogbu U. Kalu.* New York: University Press of America, 2005.

8. Ahmed, Akbar S. *Islam Today: A Short Introduction to the Muslim World.* New York: I.B. Tauris Publishers, 1999.

9. Ali, S. A. "Christian-Muslim Relations: Ushering in a New Era," in *Muslim-Christian Dialogue: Promise and Problems.* M. Darrol Bryant and S. A. Ali, eds. Minnesota: Paragon House, 1998.

10 Aliyu, Ibrahim K. *International Press Briefing for AIFF (2008)* at Sheraton Hotel, Ikeja, Lagos on Tuesday 26, 2008.

11. Allen, John L. "Tough love with Islam—Church in Nigeria may be model of dialogue," in *Catholic Online.* March 30, 2007. http://www.catholic.org/international/international_story.php?id=23597

12. Ally, ibn Mashuq. "Islam: Global Issues," in *Ethical Issues in Six Religious Traditions.* Peggy Morgan and Clive Lawton, (eds). Edinburgh: Edinburgh University Press, 1996.

13. Aniagolu, Anthony N. *The Making of the 1989 Constitution of Nigeria.* Ibadan: Spectrum, 1993.

14. Anyanwu, Donatus. *The Imo Cultural Heritage.* Owerri: Assumpta Press, 1989.

15. Aquinas, Thomas. *Summa Contra Gentiles,* Book 1, Chpt. 16, Art.4. Trasn. Anton C. Pegis. Indiania: University of Notre Dame Press, 1991.

16. Arinze, Francis. *Sacrifice in Igbo Religion.* Ibadan: university Press, 1970.

17. Arinze, Francis. "Pontificum Consilium Pro Dialogo Inter-Religiones," *Bulletin, 1996/2: Pro Dialogo, Plenary Assembly,* 20-24 Nov. 1995, Rome, 1996.

18. Armstrong, Karen. *A History of God: The 4,000-Year Quest of Judaism, Christianity and Islam.* New York: Ballantine Books, 1993.
19. Asadi, Mohammed A. *Islam & Christianity: Conflict or Conciliation?* San Jose: Writers Club Press, 2001.
20. Aslan, Reza. *No god But God.* New York: Random House, Inc., 2006.
21. Awolalu, Joseph Omosade. "The Yoruba Philosophy of Life," in *Presence Africaine*, Vol.3, no. 2, 1970.
22. Awolalu, Joseph Omosade. "The Encounter between African Traditional Religion and Other Religions in Nigeria" in *African Traditional Religions in Contemporary Society,* edited by Jacob K. Olupona. New York: Paragon House, 1991.
23. Bakoji, Sukuji. "Religious Crisis Looms in Zaria over Church Building. Enough is Enough, CAN Warns," in *Sunday Independence.* September 21, 2008.
24. Barker, Jason. "The Key to effective religious dialogue." *The Watchman Expositor.* 1998, Vol. 15, No 4.
25. Barth, Karl. *The Doctrine of the Word of God.* New York: T. & T. Clark Publishers, 1956.
26. Baudin, Pere Noel. *Fetishism and Fetish Worshippers.* Paris: L'Harmattan, 1885.
27. Beir, Ulli. *The Return of the Gods.* London: Oxford University Press, 1975.
28. Benzow, Greg. "Interfaith Dialogue in Nigeria: The need for reconciliation" *Qantara News.* December 8, 2005.
29. Bettenson, Henry. *The Early Christian Fathers.* New York: Oxford University Press, 1982.

30. Bettenson, Henry. *The later Christian Fathers.* New York: Oxford University Press, 1982.
31. Blakely, Thomas D. Ed. *Religion in Africa.* London: Frank Cass, 1990.
32. Boer, Jan H. *Nigeria's Decade of Blood, 1980-2002.* Ontario Canada: Essence Publishing, 2003.
33. Braybrooke, Marcus. *Pilgrim of Hope: One Hundred Years of Global Interfaith.* New York: SCM, 1992.
34. Broderick, Robert. *The Catholic Encyclopedia.* New York: Thomas Nelson Publishers, 1976.
35. Bumstead, Robert. "Christianity" in *The Religious World: Communities of Faith.* Robert F. Weir, Ed. New York: Macmillan, 1982.
36. *Catechism of the Catholic Church (CCC).* Vatican: Libreria Editrice Vaticana, 1994.
37. "Catholic Archbishop Graces Islamic Congress." *Daily Trust.* April 1, 2002.
38. Christensen, Thomas G. *An African Tree of Life.* New York: Orbis Books, 1990.
39. "Christianity vs. the old gods of Nigeria." *Associated Press.* September 4, 2007. http://wwrn.org/sparse.php?idd=26135.
40. Clarke, Peter B. *West Africa and Islam.* London: Eduard Arnold Pub., 1982.
41. Clarke, Peter B. & I. Linden. *Islam in Modern Nigeria: A Study of a Muslim Community in a Post Independence State, 1960-1983.* Mainz and Munich: Entwicklung und Frieden, 1984.
42. Curran, Charles. *A New Perspective in Moral Theology.* Notre Dame Fides Publications, 1976.
43. Dan-Fulani, Habila U. "Factors contributing to the survival of the Bori Cult in Northern Nigeria," in *Numen.* Vol. 46, n. 4, 1999.
44. Denny, Frederick Mathewson. *An Introduction to Islam,* 3rd Ed. New Jersey: Prentice Hall, 2006.

45. Eck, Diana. *Inter-religious dialogue as a Christian Ecumenical Concern.* New York: Columbia University Press, 1998.
46. Edike, Tony. "Tension in Enugu as Youth Destroy Shrines." *Vanguard.* January 5, 2005.
47. Ejizu, Christopher. "The Influence of African Indigenous Religions on Roman Catholicism, the Igbo Example", in *African Theological Journal* 17, 1988.
48. El Fadl, Khaled Abou. *The Great Theft: Wrestling Islam from the Extremists.* New York: HarperCollins Publishers, 2007.
49. Esposito, John L. *Islam: The Straight Path, 3rd ed.* Oxford University Press, 2005.
50. Falola, Francis. "27 Years After, handshake between Islam and Christianity." *The Punch Newspaper.* February 1, 2009.
51. Falola, Toyin. *Violence in Nigeria: The Crisis of Religious Politics and Secular Ideologies.* New York: University of Rochester press, 1998.
52. Fārūqī, Ismāil Rājī al. *Trialogue of the Abrahamic Faiths.* Maryland: amana publications, 1995.
53. Fisher, Mary Pat. *Living Religions, 6th ed.* New Jersey: Prentice Hall, 2005.
54. Flynn, Eileen and Gloria Thomas. *Living Faith: An Introduction to Theology, 2nd Ed.* Kansas City: Sheed and Ward, 1995.
55. Gilles, Anthony E. *The People of the Creed: The Story Behind the Early Church.* New York: St Anthony Messenger Press, 1985.
56. Hakim, Salman. *Basic Beliefs of Islam.* Nashville: Thomas Nelson Publishers, 2008.
57. Haneef, Suzanne. *Islam: The Path of God.* Chicago: Kazi Publications, Inc., 1996.

58. Hastings, Adrian. "Geoffrey Parinder," *Journal of Religion in Africa* XXXI, 3, 2001.

59. Hick, John "Interfaith Studies: John Hick's descriptions of types of interfaith activities." http://www. interfaithstudies.org/interfaith/hicktypes. html.

60. Hopfe, Lewis M. & Mark R. Woodward. *Religions of the World, 8th Ed.* New Jersey: Prentice Hall, 2001.

61. Hunt, Arnold D. & Robert B. Crotty. *Ethics of World Religions.* Minnesota: Greenhaven Press, Inc. 1978.

62. Hunter-Hindrew, Vivian. *Mami Wata: Africa's Ancient God/dess Unveiled.* *(Reclaiming the Ancient Mami Wata Vodoun history and Heritage of the Diaspora).Vol.I.* Martinez: Mami Wata Healers Society of North America Inc., 2007.

63. Ibrahim, Bako. "Tension between Christians and Muslims increase in Bornu State," in *Daily Independence.* December 13, 1998.

64. Ibrahim, Hassan. "Terrorists Killed 6 Pastors in Jos Crisis—CAN," in *Nigerian Tribune.* December 18, 2008.

65. Ibrahim, Izz al-din. "Islamic-Christian Dialogue: A Muslim View," in *Muslim-Christian Dialogue: Promise and Problems.* M. Darrol Bryant & S. A. Ali, Eds. Minnesota: Paragon House, 1998.

66. Idowu, Bolaji E. *African Traditional Religion: A Definition.* New York: Orbis Books, 1975.

67. Ige, Ise-Oluwa. "Nigeria: Religious Leaders Meet in Abuja," in *Vanguard.* December 4, 2008.

68. Ihenacho, David Asonye. *African Christianity Rises: A Critical Study of the Catholicism of the Igbo*

People of Nigeria, Vol. I. New York: iUniverse, Inc., 2004.

69. Ikenga-Metuh, Emefie. *God and man in African Religion.* London: Geoffrey Chapman, 1981.

70. Ikenga-Metuh, Emefie. *Comparative Studies of African Traditional Religion.* Onitsha: Imico, 1987.

71. Ikenga-Metuh Emefie & Christopher Ejizu. *Hundred Years of Catholicism in Eastern Nigeria: The Nnewi Story.* Nimo: Asele Publishers, 1985.

72. Isichei, Elizabeth. *A History of Christianity in Africa: From Antiquity to the Present.* New Jersey: African World Press, 1995.

73. Isizoh, Chidi Denis. "A Critical Review of the Lineamenta," *The African Synod Documents, Reflections and Perspective.* Maura Brown, Ed. New York: Orbis, 1996.

74. Ivogba, Emmanuel Andre. African Christian Youth Development Foundation: *The Nigerian Interfaith Youth Forum.* http://www.takingitglobal.org/images/resources/tool/docs/783.doc.

75. Iyi-Eweka, Ademola. "Igue Festival," in *EDOFOLKS.* http://www.edofolks.com

76. Janin, Hunt & Andre Kahlmeyer. Islamic Law: *The Sharia from Muhammad's Time to the Present.* Jefferson: McFarland & Company, Inc., 2007.

77. John Paul II. *Colloquium on Holiness in Christianity and Islam.* May 9, 1985.

78. John Paul II. *The Church in Africa: Post Synodal Apostolic Exhortation, "Ecclesia in Africa."* Rome: Vatican Press, 1995.

79. Joseph, Wilhelm. "The Nicene Creed," in *The New Advent Catholic Encyclopedia. Vol. 11.* New York: Robert Appleton Company, 1911.

80. Kalu, Ogbu U. "The Dilemma of Grassroot Inculturation of the Gospel: The Case Study of a Modern Controversy in Igboland, 1983-1989." *Journal of Religion in African.* Vol. 25, Fasc. 1. Feb., 1995.

81. Kamal, Ahmad. *The Sacred Journey, Being a Pilgrimage to Mecca.* New York: Duell, Sloan and Pearce, 1961.

82. Kayode, J. O. "Living in Peace in a Multi-Religious Community," in *The State of Christian Theology in Nigeria.* Ibadan: Heinemann, 1986.

83. Kaufman, Gordon. *The Theological Imagination: Constructing the Concept of God.* Philadelphia: Westminster Press, 1981.

84. Kenny, Joseph. "Shariah and Christianity in Nigeria: Islam and a 'Secular' State." *Journal of Religion in Africa.* Vol. 26, Fasc. 4, Nov., 1996.

85. Khattab, Abdelmoneim M. "The Muslim-Christian Relationship: A Challenge and Promise," *Muslim-Christian Dialogue: Promise and Problems.* M. Darrol Bryant & S. A. Ali, Eds. Minnesota: Paragon House, 1998.

86. Knitter, Paul F. *No Other Name? A Critical Survey of Christian Attitude towards the World Religions.* New York: Orbis Book, 1986.

87. Knitter, Paul F. *Jesus and the Other Names.* Maryknoll, NY: Orbis, 1996.

88. Knitter, Paul F. *One Earth Many Religion: Multifaith Dialogue and Global responsibility.* Maryknoll, NY Orbis Books, 1995.

89. Küng, Hans. Islam: *Past, Present, and Future.* Oxford: One World Publications, 2007.

90. Lenowitz, Harris. *The Jewish Messiahs: From the Galilee to Crown Heights.* New York: Oxford University Press, 1998.
91. Leo XIII, *Rerum Novarum: On Capital and labor.* Rome: Vatican Press, 1891.
92. Leon-Dufour, Xavier. *Dictionary of Biblical Theology, 2nd ed.* Boston: St. Paul Books and Media, 1995.
93. Levtzion, Nehemiah & Abdin Chande. "Islam: Islam in Sub-Saharan Africa" in *Encyclopedia of Religion.* Ed, Lindsay Jones, Vol. 7, 2nd ed. Detroit: Macmillan Reference USA, 2005.
94. Lewis, James R. *Encyclopedia of Death and the Afterlife.* Detroit: Visible Ink Press, 1995.
95. Lewis, M. *Islam in Tropical Africa.* London: Oxford Press, 1966.
96. Lewis, Peter & Michael Bratton. *Attitudes toward Democracy and Market in Nigeria: Report of a National Opinion Survey.* January—February, 2000.
97. L'Osservatore Romano. English Edition, 11 May 1994.
98. Ludwig, Frieder. "Christian-Muslim Relations in Northern Nigeria since the Introduction of Shariah in 1999," in *Journal of the American Academy of Religion.* September 2008, Vol. 76, No.3.
99. Mangematin, Bernard. "Oriki: Yoruba Prayer and the Future of Catechesis in Nigeria," in *Catechesis for the Future: Theology in the Age of Renewal.* Adios Muller, ed. New York: Herder and Herder, 1970.
100. Marcado, Leornardo M. *From Pagans to Partners: The Change in Catholic Attitudes towards Traditional Religion.* Manila: Logos Publications Inc., 2000.
101. Masquelier, Adeline. "Lightening, Death and the Avenging Spirits: Bori Values in a Muslim

World," in *Journal of Religion in Africa*, Vol. 24, n.1, Feb., 1994.

102. Mbachu, Dulue. "Christianity vs. the gods of Nigeria." *Associated Press.* September 4, 2007. http://www.wwrn.org/sparse.php?idd=26135.

103. Mbiti, John S. *African Religions and Philosophy, 2nd ed.* London: Heinemann, 1989.

104. Mbiti, John S. *Introduction to African Religion, 2nd ed.* Ibadan: Heinemann, 1991.

105. McBrien, Richard P. *Catholicism.* New York: HaperCollins Publishers, 1994.

106. Menezes, J. L. *The Life and Religion of Mohammad the Prophet of Arabia.* New York: Roman Catholic Books, 2004.

107. Mukairu, Lawani. "Another 43 Islamic Fanatics Killed in Yobe." *Vanguard.* July 30, 2009

108. Mulago, Vincent. "Traditional African Religion and Christianity," in Jacob Olupona, ed., *African Traditional Religions in Contemporary Society.* New York: Paragon House, 1991.

109. Nasr, Seyyed Hosseein. *Ideals and Realities of Islam.* Pakistan: Suhail Academy, 1993.

110. Nanji, Azim. "African Religions" in *The Religious World: Communities of Faith.* Robert F. Weir, Ed. New York: Macmillan Publishing Co. Inc., 1982.

111. Ndiokwere, Nathaniel I. *The African Church, Today and Tomorrow, vol. I.* Onitsha: Effective Key Publisher, 1994.

112. Ndiokwere, Nathaniel I. *The African Church, Today and Tomorrow, Vol. II.* Enugu: Snaap Press, 1994.

113. "Negritude," in *The New Encyclopedia Britannica, Vol.8,* Micropaedia 15th edition.

114. Neimark, Philip J. *The Way of Orisha: Empowering your Life through the Ancient African Religion of*

Ifa. New York: HarperCollins Publishers, 1993.

115. Nessan, Craig L. "Sex, Aggression, and Pain: Sociological Implications for Theological Anthropology," *Zygon, 33.* 1998.

116. "Nigeria: Continuing Dialogues for Nation Building," in *International Institute for Democracy and Electoral Assistance.* Stockholm, 2000.

117. "Nigerians meld Christianity, Islam with ancient practices" in *World Wide Religious News.* October 14, 2007. http://www.wwrn.org/article.php?idd=26568&sec=con=60

118. Nwachukwu, Mcphilips. "At CBAAC, Olupona Canvasses Inter-Faith Dialogue as Panacea to Religious Crises." *Vanguard News.* April 3, 2008.

119. Nwedo, Anthony G. ed. *Katikisim Nke Okwukwe Nzuko Katolik n'asusu Igbo.* Onitsha: Imico Press, 1964.

120. Nwosu, Nereus I. "Religion and the Crisis of National Unity in Nigeria," in *African Study Monograph* 17(3), October 1996.

121. Nura, Alkali & Adamu Adamu. *Islam in Africa: Proceedings of Islam in African Conference.* Ibadan: Spectrum, 1993.

122. Obateru, Taye. "Jos Riots Escalates." *Vanguard.* November 30, 2008.

123. Obateru, Taye. "Nigeria: Onaiyekan, Sultan Preaches Religious Tolerance," All Africa, May 5, 2009, *Religious Diversity News* http://www.pluralism.org/news/view/21518

124. Obiego, Cosmas O. *African Image of the Ultimate Reality: Analysis of Igbo Ideas of Life and Death in Relation to Chukwu.* Berlin: Peter Lang, 1984.

125. O'Connell, Timothy E. *Principles for a Catholic Morality.* San Francisco: Harper & Row Publishers, 1990.

126. Ogbodo, Patience. "Bauchi Riot Victims' Tales of Horror." *Vanguard.* March 1, 2009.

127. Okere, Theophilus. "The Kite may perch, the Eagle may perch: Egbe bere Ugo bere: An African Concept of Peace and Justice." *International Philosophers of Peace.* New York: Boston University, 1998.

128. Okoro, Azubuike. "Eze Ogo Ugwuavor's New Found Belief as Affront on Aro Culture and Tradition." *AroNews.* July 17, 2009.

129. Olupona, Jacob K. ed. *African Traditional Religion in Contemporary Society.* New York: Paragon House, 1999.

130. Omotunde, Dele. "Tyranny of the Fanatical." *Tell Magazine.* October 28, 1991.

131. Omenka, N. "The Role of the Catholic Mission in the Development of Vernacular Literature in Eastern Nigeria," in *Journal of Religion in Africa*, XVI, 7, 1986.

132. Omenuwa, Onyema. *This Week.* November 24, 1997.

133. Omoigue, Nowa. "History of Igue Festival in Benin City: Oba, Bini mark the end of Year Igue Festival" in *EDOFOLKS.* http://www.edofolks.com (mhtml:file:// K:\Edofolks—History of Igue Festival in Benin-City.mht).

134. Onwubiko Oliver. *African Though, Religion and Culture: Christian Mission and Culture in Africa, vol. I.* Enugu: Snaap Press, 1991.

135. Onwubiko, Oliver. *Echoes from the African Synod.* Enugu: Snaap Press, 1994.

136. Ord, David Robert, & Robert B. Coote. *Is the Bible True? Understanding the Bible Today.* New York: Orbis Books, 1994.

137. Osaghe, Eghosa E., & Rotimi Suberu, *A History of Identities, Violence, and Stability in Nigeria: CRISE Working paper, n.6, 2005*. Center for Research on Inequality, Human Security and Ethnicity: CRISE Queen Elizabeth House, University of London.

138. Osborne, Mary Pope. *One World Many Religions: The Ways We Worship*. New York: Alfred A. Knopf, 1996.

139. Palermo, S. (ed). *Africa Pontificia*. Rome: Editrice, 1993.

140. Parrinder, Geoffrey. *Religion in Africa*. London: Pengium Books, 1969.

141. Parrinder, Geoffrey. *World Religions: From Ancient History to the Present*. New York: Facts On File, Inc., 1985.

142. Pat, William & Toyin Falola. *Religious Impact on the Nation State: The Nigerian Predicament*. London: Avebury, 1995.

143. Peires, Jeffrey B. *The House of Phalo*. Johannesburg: Jonathan Ball Publishers, 2003.

144. Peires, Jeffrey B. *The House of Phalo*. Johannesburg: Jonathan Ball Publishers, 2003.

145. Quanoo, Samuel Ebow. *Transition and Consolidation of Democracy in Africa*. Ohio: Ohio Central State University Press, 2000.

145. *Quran, The Holy*. Ali, Abdullah Yusuf, (Trans.). New Delhi: Goodword Books Pvt. Ltd., 2006.

146. Rahman, Fazlur. *Prophecy in Islam: Philosophy and Orthodoxy*. Chicago: University of Chicago Press, 1979.

147. Raines, John C. "The Nation State and Social Order: In the Perspective of Christianity", in Faruqi, Isma'il. *Trialogue of the Abrahamic Faiths*. Maryland: Amana Publications, 1995.

148. Raji al Faruqi, Isma'il. "The Nation State and Social Order in the Perspective of Islam.," in Faruqi, Isma'il. *Trialogue of the Abrahamic Faiths.* Maryland: Amana Publications, 1995.

149. Raji al Faruqi, Isma'il. *Trialogue of the Abrahamic Faiths.* Maryland: Amana Publications, 1995.

150. Ray, Benjamin C. *African Religions: Symbol, Ritual, and Community, 2nd ed.* New Jersey: Prentice Hall, 2000.

151. "Religious Crisis: Muslim Leaders Visit Bishop." *This Day.* February 9, 2004. http://www.wwrn. org/article.php?idd=5519&sec=4&con=60

152. Riley, Jennifer. "Survey: Interfaith activities increase significantly." *The Christian Post.* Fri, May 12, 2006.

153. Rippin, Andrew. Muslims: *Their Religious Beliefs and Practices, 3rd ed.* New York: Routedge, 2005.

154. Rippin, Andrew & Jan Knappert. *Textual Sources for the Study of Islam.* Chicago: University of Chicago Press, 1986.

156. Ripley, Francis. *This is the Faith.* Rockford: Tan Books and Publishers, Inc., 2002.

157. Robinson, Stephen E. *How Wide the Divide?* Downers Grove, Ill: InterVarsity, 1997.

158. Rushdie, Salman. *The Satanic Verses.* New York: Penguin Group, 1989.

159. Rweyemamu, Robert "Religion and Peace: An Experience in with African Traditions," in *Studia Missionalia.* Vol., 5, no. 38, 1989.

160. Sali, Muhammad. "Islam and Western Education in Nigeria." *Champions Newspaper.* May 15, 1990.

161. Sarpong, Peter. "African Traditional Religion and Peace," in *Studia Missionalia.* Vol., 5, no. 38, 1989.

162. Schineller, Peter. *A Handbook on Inculturation.* New York: Paulist Press, 1990.
163. Scholem, Gershom. *The Messianic Idea in Judaism and Other Essays on Jewish Spirituality.* New York: Schocken Books, 1995.
164. Shahabuddin, Syed. "Should the Islamic Punishment of Adultery be reconsidered?" http://www.guidedones.com/metapage/gems/adultery.htm.
165. Shannon, Trevor. "Christianity: The Quality and Value of Life," in *Ethical Issues in Six Religious Traditions,* Peggy Morgan and Clive Lawton, Eds. Edinburgh: Edinburgh University Press, 1996.
166. Shenk, David W. *Global Gods: Exploring the Role of Religions in Modern Societies.* Pennsylvania: Herald Press, 1995.
167. Shorter, Aylward. *African Christian Theology.* London: Geoffrey Chapman, 1975.
168. Shorter, Aylward. "Concepts of Social Justice in Traditional Africa," *Africa: Journal of the International African Institute.* Vol. XXXIX, n.3, 1996.
169. Shorter, Aylward. *Towards a Theology of Inculturation.* New York: Orbis Books, 1997.
170. Shuaibu, Adamu. *Bori Cult in Bauchi and Jos towns.* MA Thesis, Department of Religious Studies, University of Jos, Nigeria in 1990.
171. Shuaibu, Muhammed Lawal. "50 Leaders Met in Abuja," in *Daily Trust.* October 18, 2007.
172. Silva, Bisi. "Spectacular Eyo Festival," in *ARTSPEAKAFRICA.* Sunday 26 April 2009.
173. Skarsaune, Oskar. *In the Shadow of the Temple: Jewish Influences on Early Christianity.* Illinois: InterVasity Press, 2002.

174. Stamer, Josef P. *Islam in Sub-Saharan Africa.* Estella, Spain: Editorial Verbo Divino, 1995.

178. Steed, Christopher & David Westurland. "Nigeria," in *Islam Outside the Arab World.* David Westurland and Ingvar Svanberg, eds. London: Palgrave Macmillan, 1999.

179. Stoutzenberger, Joseph. *The Christian Call to Justice and Peace.* Minnesota: St Mary's Press, 1994.

180. Swidler, Leonard. "The Dialogue Decalogue: Ground Rules for Interreligious Dialogue." *Journal of Ecumenical Studies* 20, 1, 1983.

181. Tahir, Ibrahim. *The last Imam.* London: Routledge & Kegan Paul, 1984.

182. *The 1999 Constitution of the Federal Republic of Nigeria.*

183. *The Basic Documents Vatican II: Constitutions, Decrees and Declarations,* Edited by Austin Flanery, New York: Costello, Publishing Co., 1996

184. The Golden Rule," in *Children's Catechism.* http://www.pflaum.com/catalog/childcat/mapsposter.htm.

185. *The Jerusalem Bible.* London: Darton, Longman & Todd Ltd., 1966.

186. *The Official Website of the Common Word.* http://www.acommonword.com/index.php?lang=en&page=option1.

187. Trimingham, J. S. *Islam in the Sudan.* London: Oxford Press, 1949.

189. Udeani, Chibueze. *Inculturation as Dialogue: Igbo Culture and the Message of Christ.* Amsterdam: Rodopi, 2007.

190. Ujumadu, Vincent. "5 Killed, 15 Injured in Anambra Communal Crisis." *Vanguard.* September 4, 2009. http://www.vanguardngr.com/2009/09/04/5-killed-15-injured-in-anambra-communal-crisis/.

191. Umudu, Michael. "Slaughter of the gods," in *The Nations.* September 21, 2008.
192. Umunnakwe, Anselem "Royal Fathers Seek for Religious Harmony," in *This Day.* August 16, 2008.
193. Waheed, Adebayo. "Nigerians are too far from God," in *Nigerian Tribune.* Monday, August 20, 2007.
194. Waines, David. *An Introduction to Islam, 2nd ed.* Cambridge: Cambridge Press, 2003.
195. Water, Mark. *Encyclopedia of World Religions, Cults and the Occult.* London: John Hunt Publishing Ltd, 2006.
196. Weir, Richard F. ed., *The Religious World: Communities of Faith.* New York: Macmillan Publishers, 1982.
197. Westley, Dick. *Morality and its Beyond.* Connecticut: Twenty-Third Publications, 1984.
198. Wuye James & Muhammad Ashafa. "The Imam and the Pastor: Healing Conflict in Nigeria." *Muslim-Christian Dialogue Forum in Nigeria.* http://www.peoplebuildingpeace.org/ thestories/print.php?id=93&typ=theme
199. Yusuf, Bilkisu. "Nigeria: Building an Interfaith Bridge of Peace," in *Leadership. June 5, 2008.*